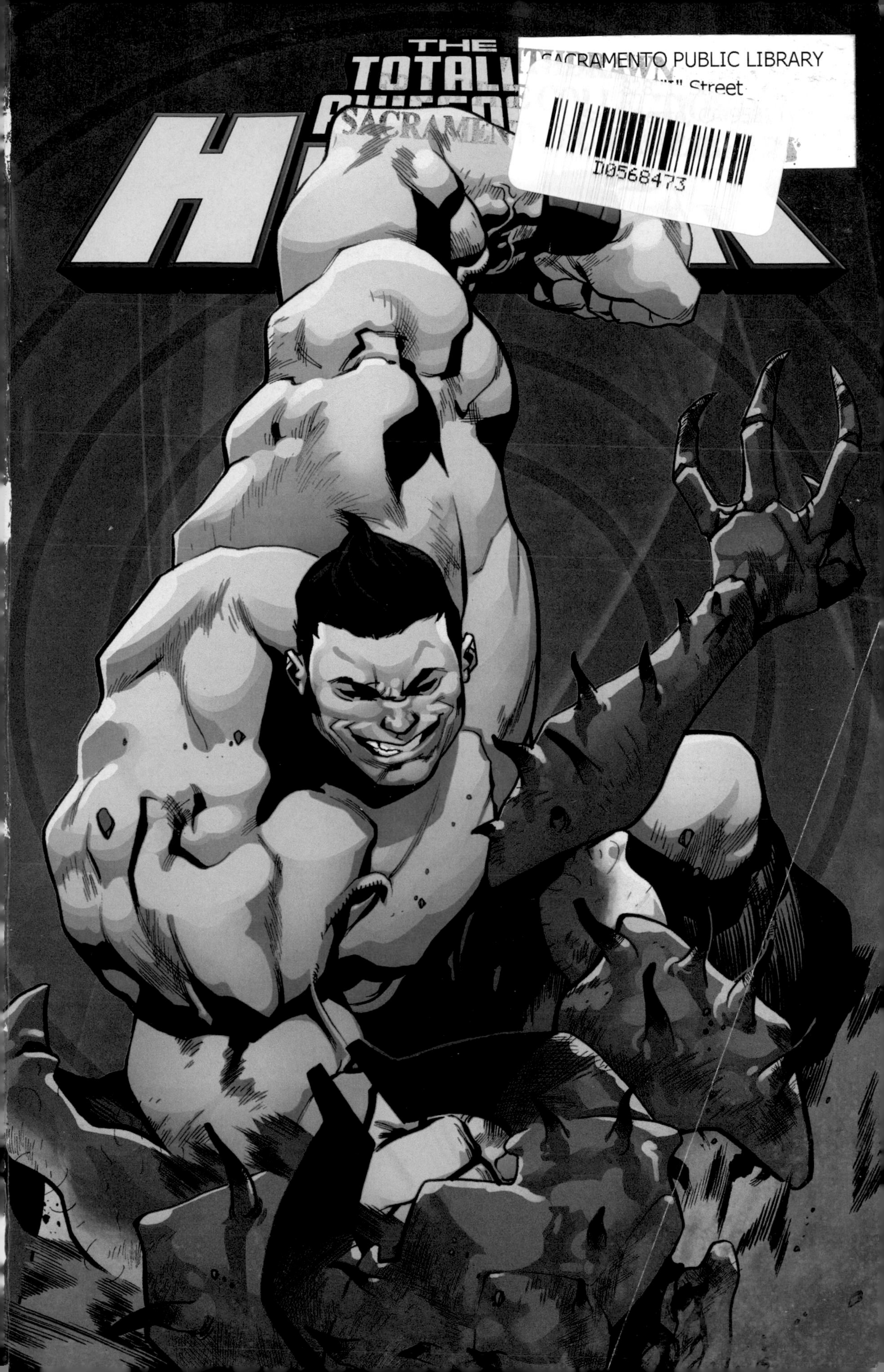
THE

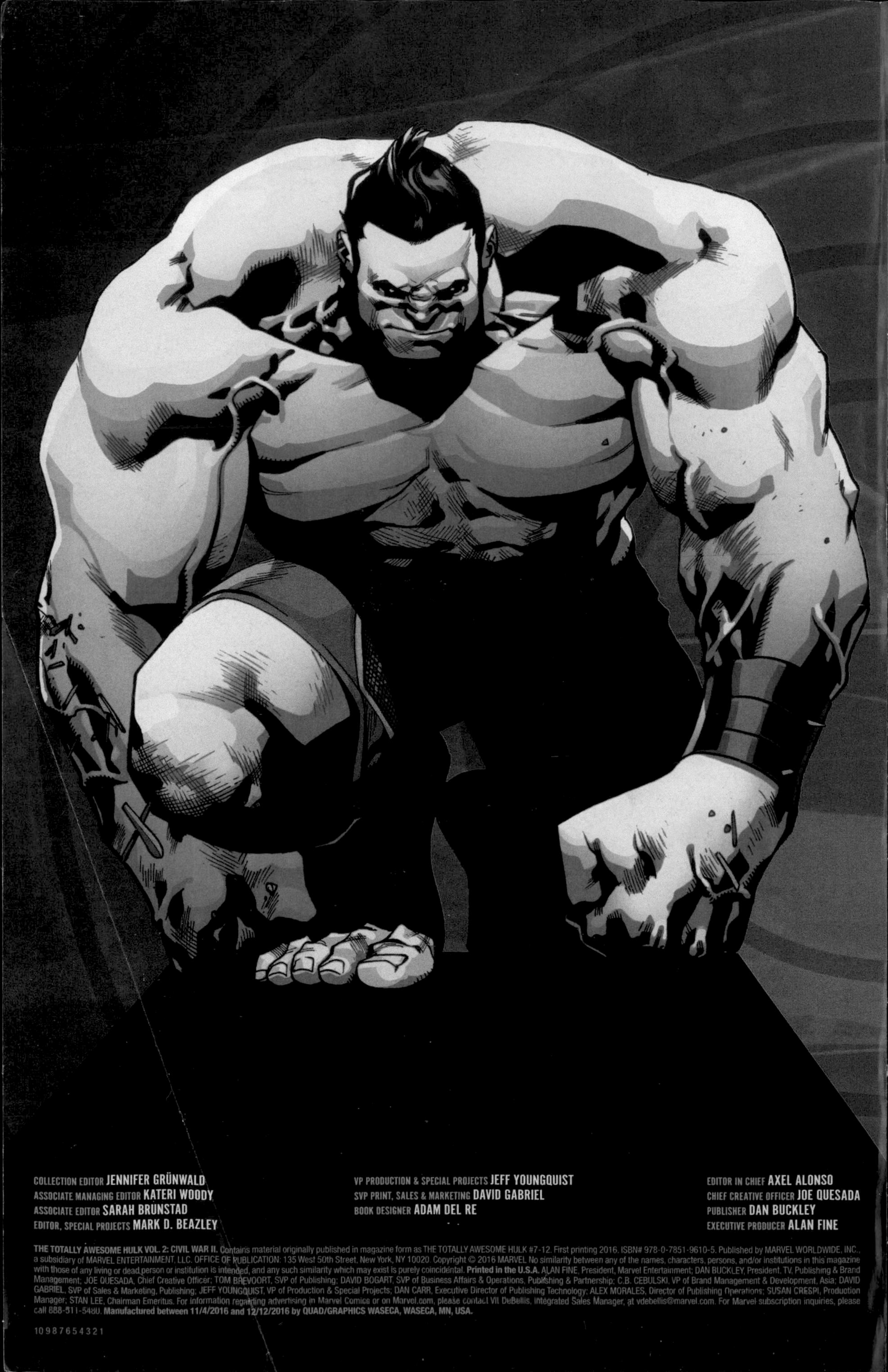

COLLECTION EDITOR **JENNIFER GRÜNWALD**
ASSOCIATE MANAGING EDITOR **KATERI WOODY**
ASSOCIATE EDITOR **SARAH BRUNSTAD**
EDITOR, SPECIAL PROJECTS **MARK D. BEAZLEY**

VP PRODUCTION & SPECIAL PROJECTS **JEFF YOUNGQUIST**
SVP PRINT, SALES & MARKETING **DAVID GABRIEL**
BOOK DESIGNER **ADAM DEL RE**

EDITOR IN CHIEF **AXEL ALONSO**
CHIEF CREATIVE OFFICER **JOE QUESADA**
PUBLISHER **DAN BUCKLEY**
EXECUTIVE PRODUCER **ALAN FINE**

THE TOTALLY AWESOME HULK VOL. 2: CIVIL WAR II. Contains material originally published in magazine form as THE TOTALLY AWESOME HULK #7-12. First printing 2016. ISBN# 978-0-7851-9610-5. Published by MARVEL WORLDWIDE, INC., a subsidiary of MARVEL ENTERTAINMENT, LLC. OFFICE OF PUBLICATION: 135 West 50th Street, New York, NY 10020. **Printed in the U.S.A.** ALAN FINE, President, Marvel Entertainment; DAN BUCKLEY, President, TV, Publishing & Brand Management; JOE QUESADA, Chief Creative Officer; TOM BREVOORT, SVP of Publishing; DAVID BOGART, SVP of Business Affairs & Operations, Publishing & Partnership; C.B. CEBULSKI, VP of Brand Management & Development, Asia; DAVID GABRIEL, SVP of Sales & Marketing, Publishing; JEFF YOUNGQUIST, VP of Production & Special Projects; DAN CARR, Executive Director of Publishing Technology; ALEX MORALES, Director of Publishing Operations; SUSAN CRESPI, Production Manager; STAN LEE, Chairman Emeritus. For information regarding advertising in Marvel Comics or on Marvel.com, please contact Vit DeBellis, Integrated Sales Manager, at vdebellis@marvel.com. For Marvel subscription inquiries, please call 888-511-5480. **Manufactured between 11/4/2016 and 12/12/2016 by QUAD/GRAPHICS WASECA, WASECA, MN, USA.**

10 9 8 7 6 5 4 3 2 1

THE TOTALLY AWESOME HULK

CIVIL WAR II

GREG PAK
WRITER

ISSUE NOS. 7-8

ALAN DAVIS
PENCILER

MARK FARMER
INKER

CHRIS SOTOMAYOR
COLORIST

**ALAN DAVIS,
MARK FARMER
& MATT HOLLINGSWORTH**
COVER ART

ISSUE NO. 9

MIKE DEL MUNDO
ARTIST

MARCO D'ALFONSO
CO-COLORIST

**TERRY DODSON
& RACHEL DODSON**
COVER ART

ISSUE NOS. 10-12

MAHMUD ASRAR
ARTIST

NOLAN WOODARD
COLORIST

**TERRY DODSON
& RACHEL DODSON**
COVER ART

VC's CORY PETIT
LETTERER

CHRIS ROBINSON
ASSISTANT EDITOR

DARREN SHAN
ASSOCIATE EDITOR

MARK PANICCIA
EDITOR

HULK CREATED BY STAN LEE & JACK KIRBY

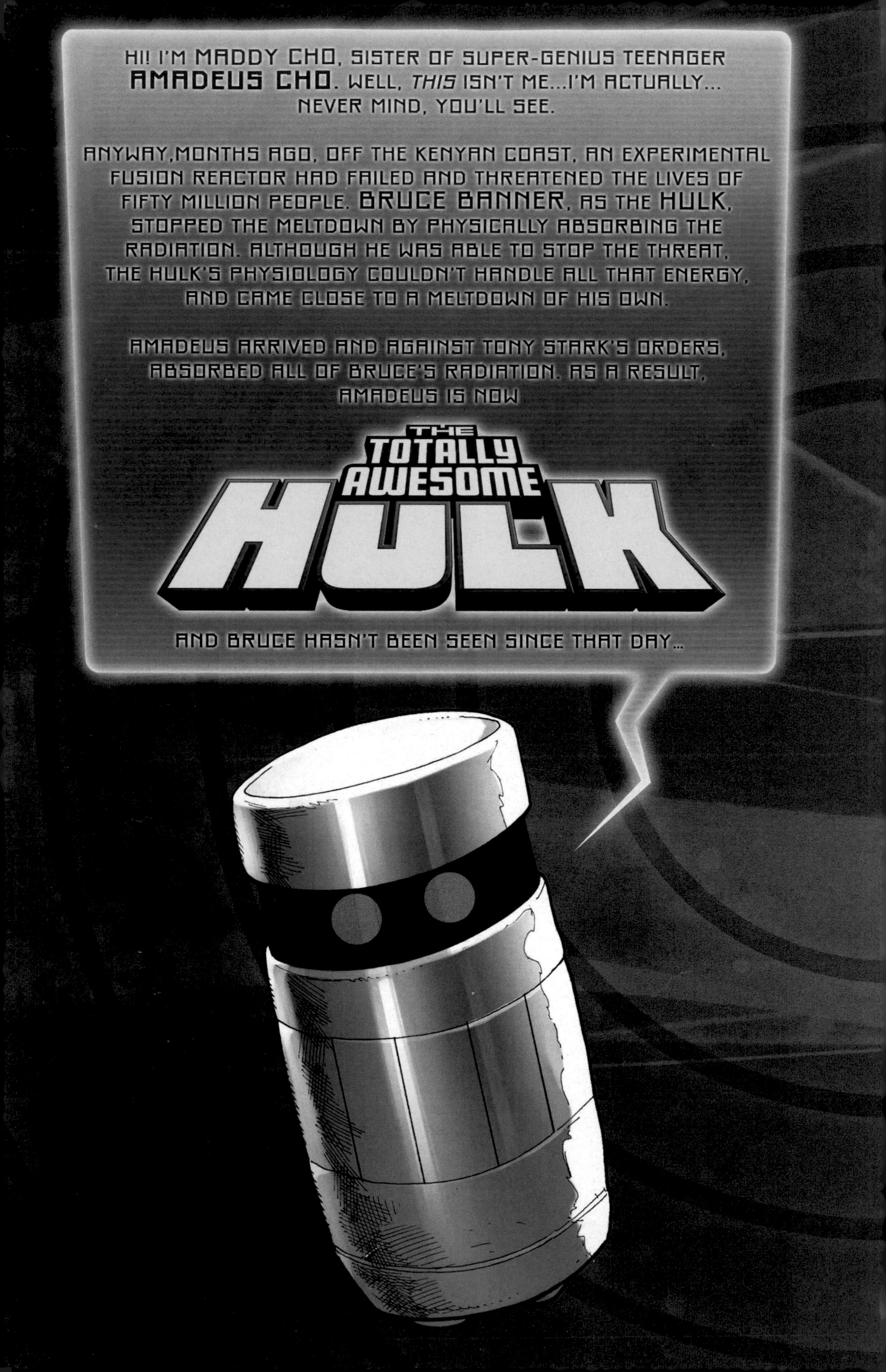

HI! I'M MADDY CHO, SISTER OF SUPER-GENIUS TEENAGER AMADEUS CHO. WELL, THIS ISN'T ME...I'M ACTUALLY... NEVER MIND, YOU'LL SEE.
ANYWAY, MONTHS AGO, OFF THE KENYAN COAST, AN EXPERIMENTAL FUSION REACTOR HAD FAILED AND THREATENED THE LIVES OF FIFTY MILLION PEOPLE. BRUCE BANNER, AS THE HULK, STOPPED THE MELTDOWN BY PHYSICALLY ABSORBING THE RADIATION. ALTHOUGH HE WAS ABLE TO STOP THE THREAT, THE HULK'S PHYSIOLOGY COULDN'T HANDLE ALL THAT ENERGY, AND CAME CLOSE TO A MELTDOWN OF HIS OWN.
AMADEUS ARRIVED AND AGAINST TONY STARK'S ORDERS, ABSORBED ALL OF BRUCE'S RADIATION. AS A RESULT, AMADEUS IS NOW
THE TOTALLY AWESOME HULK
AND BRUCE HASN'T BEEN SEEN SINCE THAT DAY...

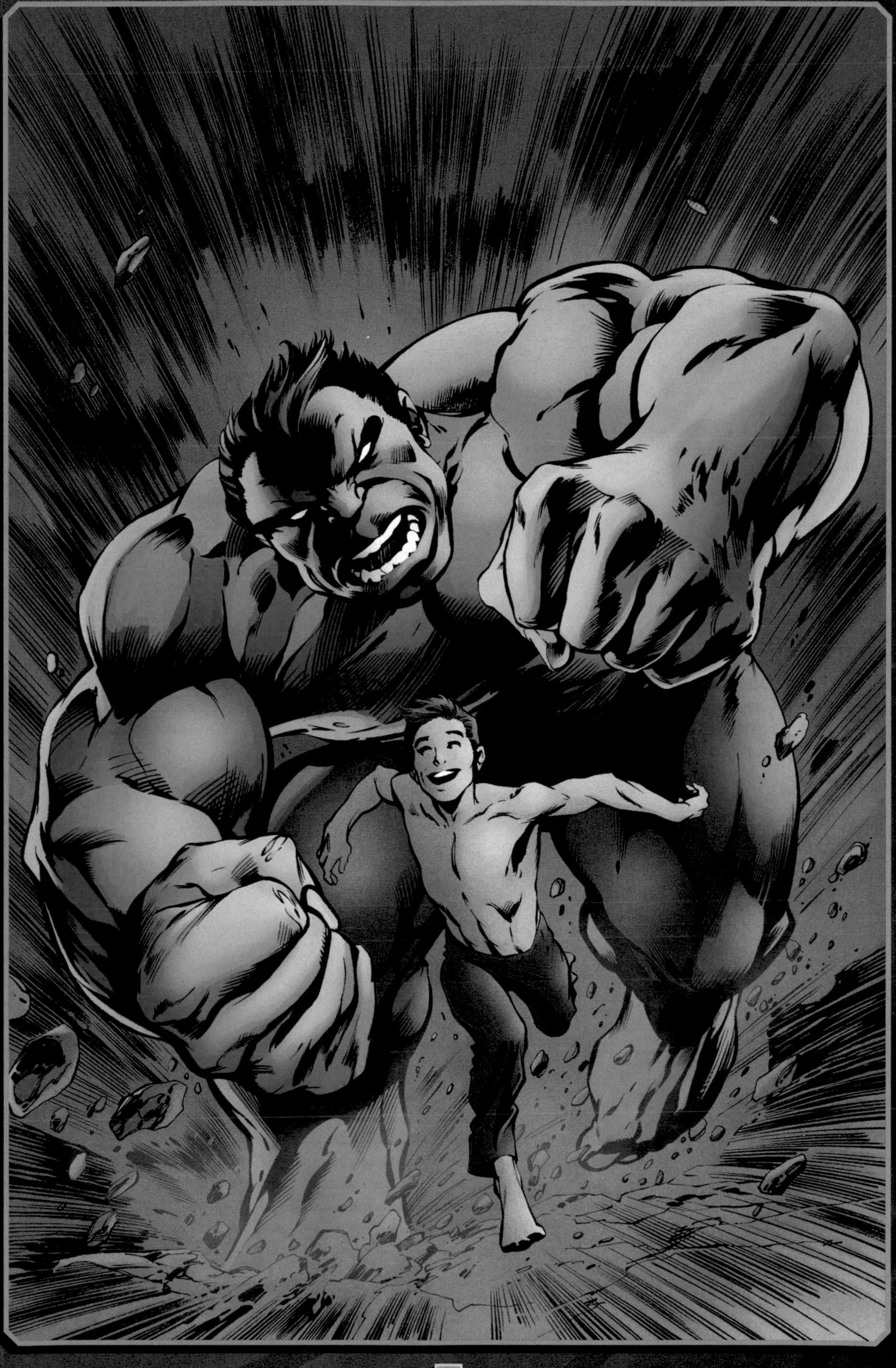

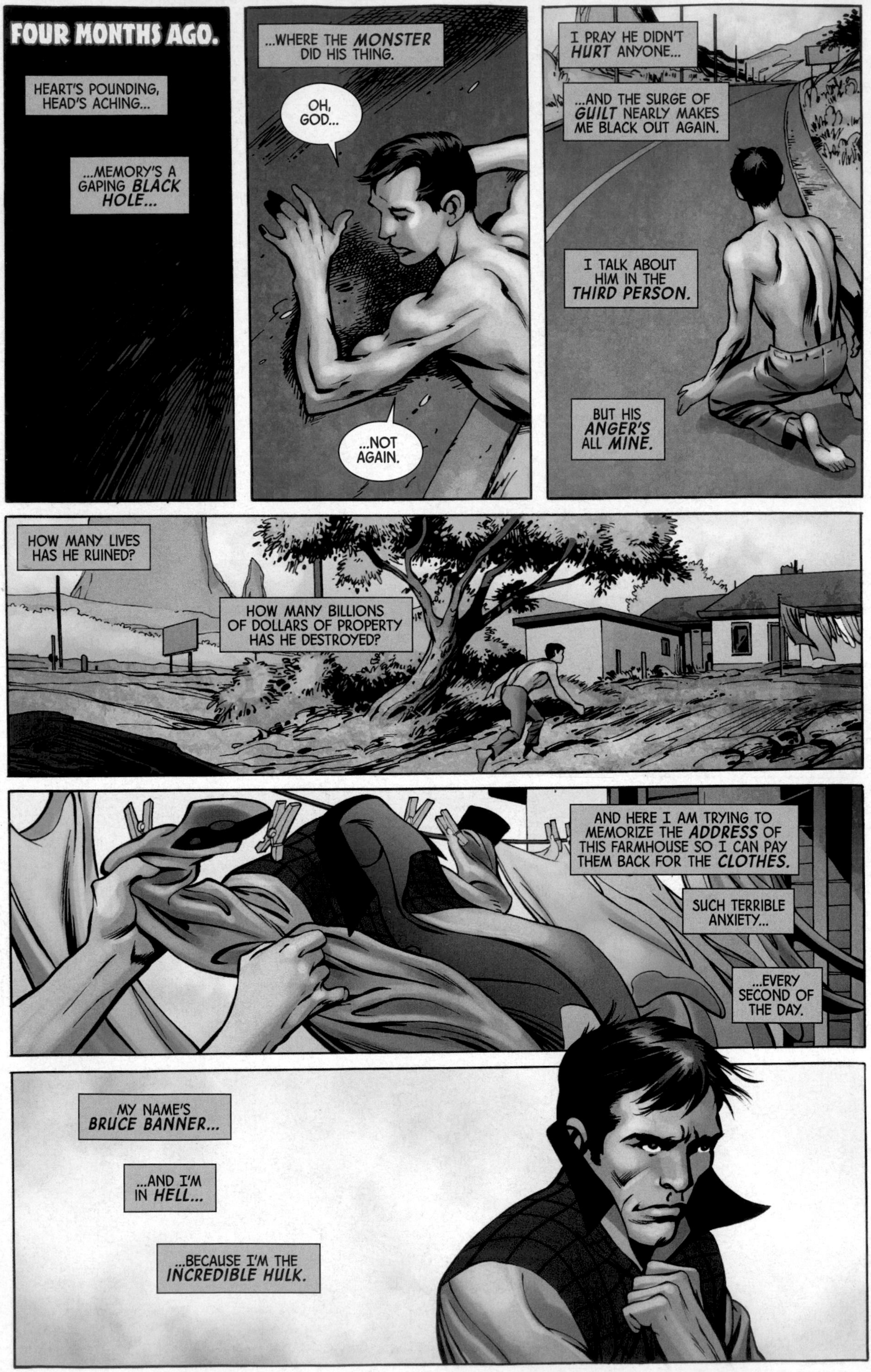
FOUR MONTHS AGO.
HEART'S POUNDING, HEAD'S ACHING...
...MEMORY'S A GAPING BLACK HOLE...
...WHERE THE MONSTER DID HIS THING.
OH, GOD...
...NOT AGAIN.
I PRAY HE DIDN'T HURT ANYONE...
...AND THE SURGE OF GUILT NEARLY MAKES ME BLACK OUT AGAIN.
I TALK ABOUT HIM IN THE THIRD PERSON.
BUT HIS ANGER'S ALL MINE.
HOW MANY LIVES HAS HE RUINED?
HOW MANY BILLIONS OF DOLLARS OF PROPERTY HAS HE DESTROYED?
AND HERE I AM TRYING TO MEMORIZE THE ADDRESS OF THIS FARMHOUSE SO I CAN PAY THEM BACK FOR THE CLOTHES.
SUCH TERRIBLE ANXIETY...
...EVERY SECOND OF THE DAY.
MY NAME'S BRUCE BANNER...
...AND I'M IN HELL...
...BECAUSE I'M THE INCREDIBLE HULK.

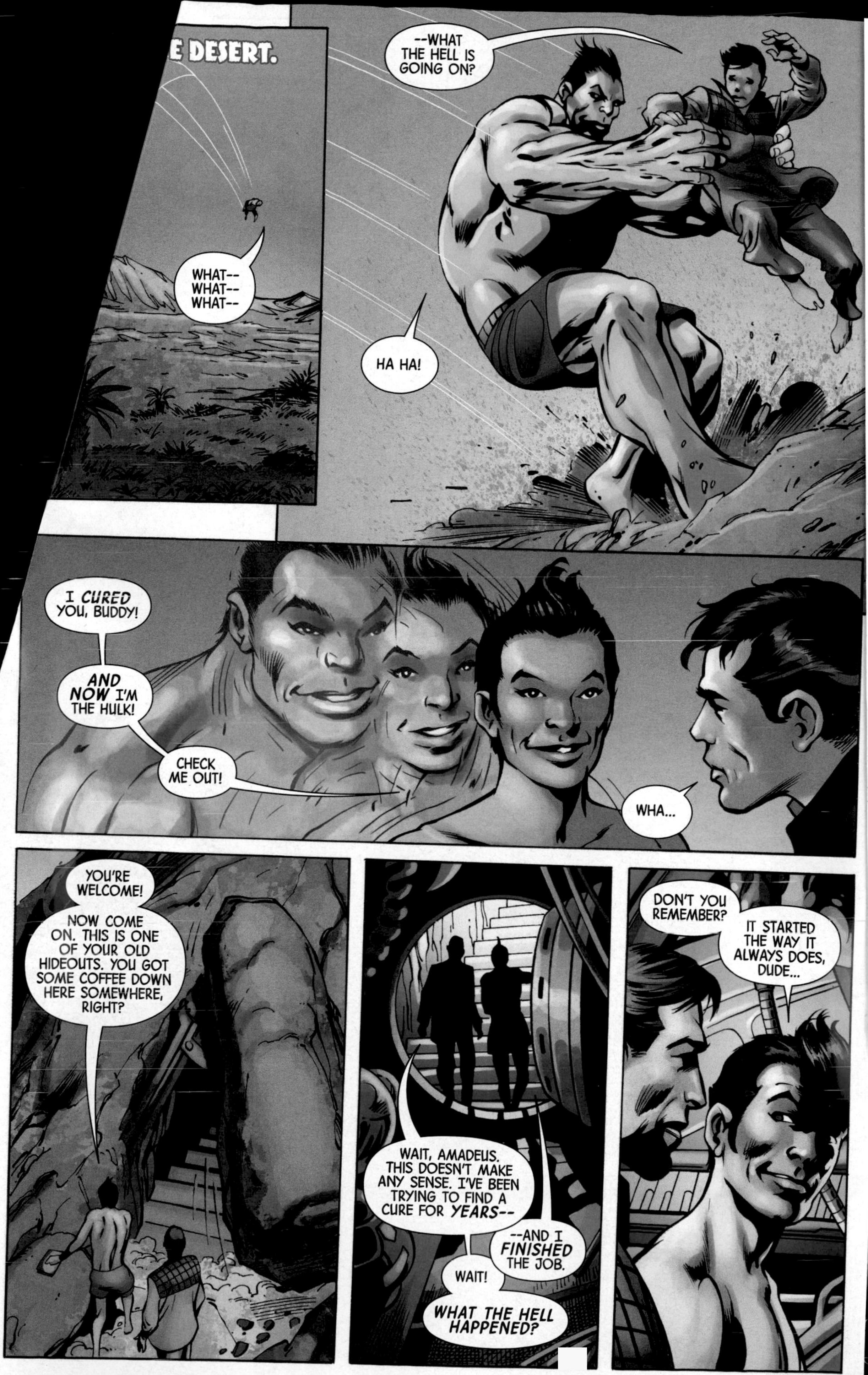
E DESERT.
WHAT-- WHAT-- WHAT--
--WHAT THE HELL IS GOING ON?
HA HA!
I CURED YOU, BUDDY!
AND NOW I'M THE HULK!
CHECK ME OUT!
WHA...
YOU'RE WELCOME!
NOW COME ON. THIS IS ONE OF YOUR OLD HIDEOUTS. YOU GOT SOME COFFEE DOWN HERE SOMEWHERE, RIGHT?
WAIT, AMADEUS. THIS DOESN'T MAKE ANY SENSE. I'VE BEEN TRYING TO FIND A CURE FOR YEARS--
--AND I FINISHED THE JOB.
WAIT!
WHAT THE HELL HAPPENED?
DON'T YOU REMEMBER?
IT STARTED THE WAY IT ALWAYS DOES, DUDE...

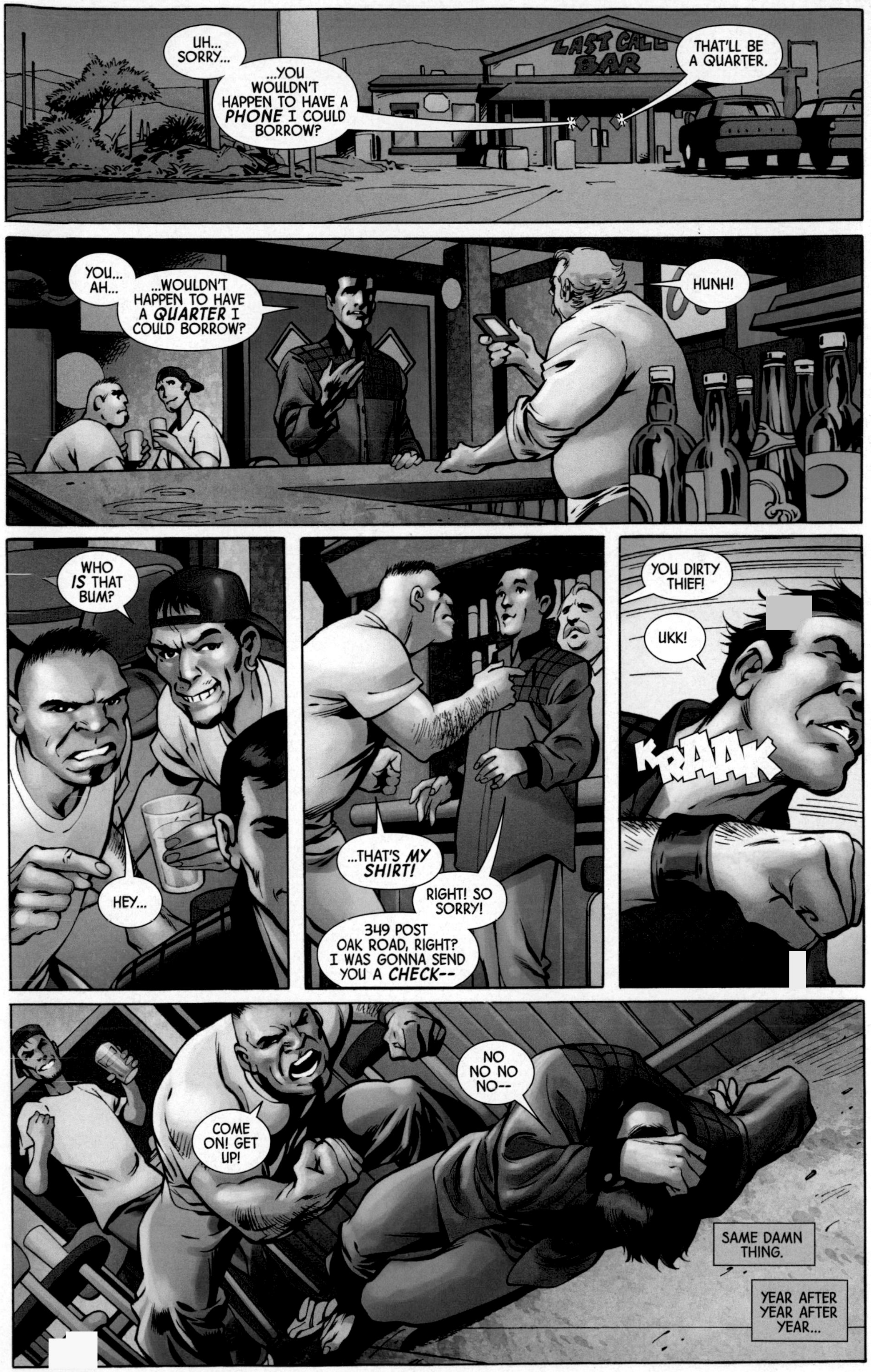
LAST CALL BAR
UH... SORRY...
...YOU WOULDN'T HAPPEN TO HAVE A PHONE I COULD BORROW?
THAT'LL BE A QUARTER.
YOU... AH...
...WOULDN'T HAPPEN TO HAVE A QUARTER I COULD BORROW?
HUNH!
WHO IS THAT BUM?
HEY...
...THAT'S MY SHIRT!
RIGHT! SO SORRY!
349 POST OAK ROAD, RIGHT? I WAS GONNA SEND YOU A CHECK--
YOU DIRTY THIEF!
UKK!
KRAAK
NO NO NO NO--
COME ON! GET UP!
SAME DAMN THING.
YEAR AFTER YEAR AFTER YEAR...

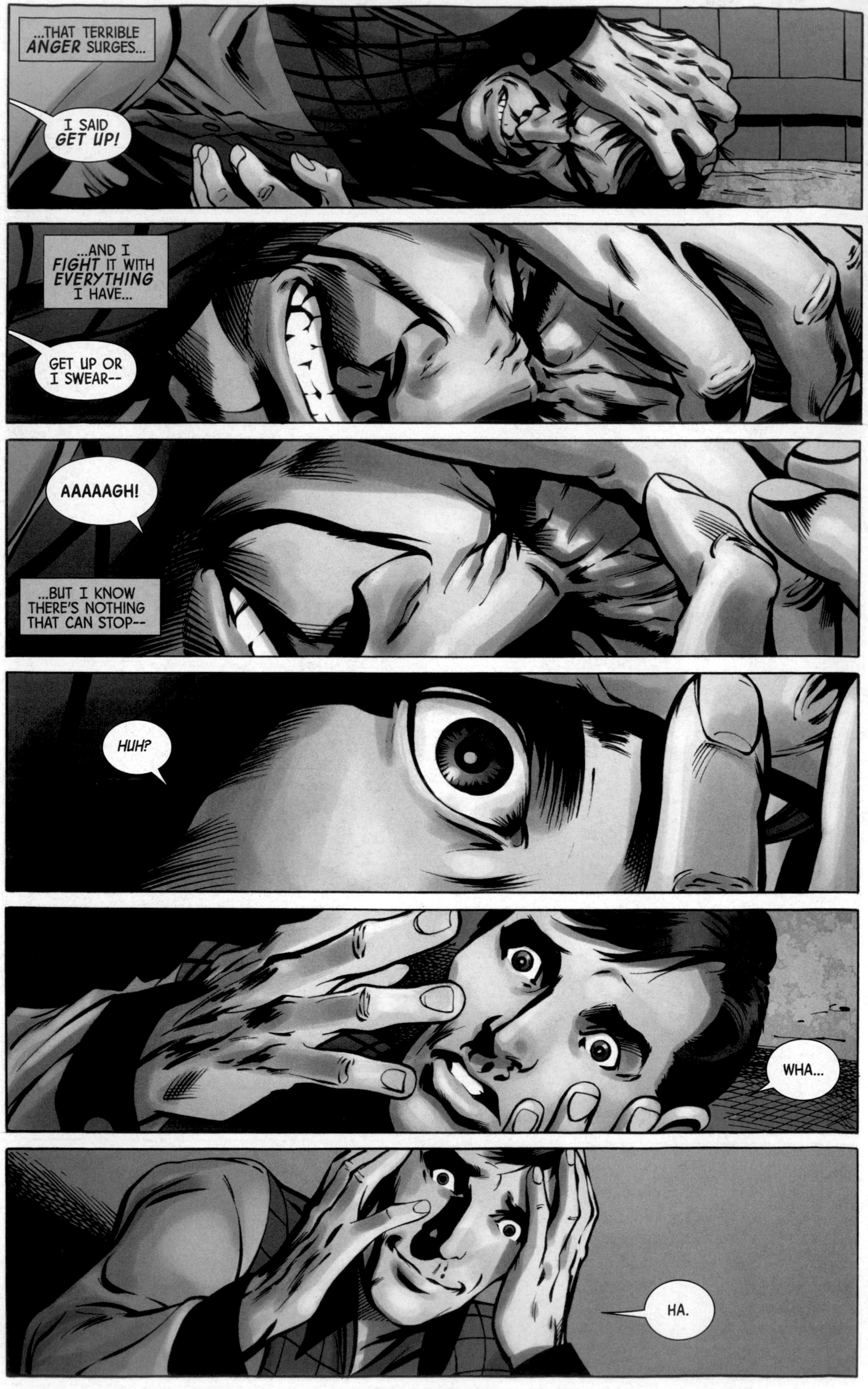
...THAT TERRIBLE ANGER SURGES...
I SAID GET UP!
...AND I FIGHT IT WITH EVERYTHING I HAVE...
GET UP OR I SWEAR--
AAAAAGH!
...BUT I KNOW THERE'S NOTHING THAT CAN STOP--
HUH?
WHA...
HA.

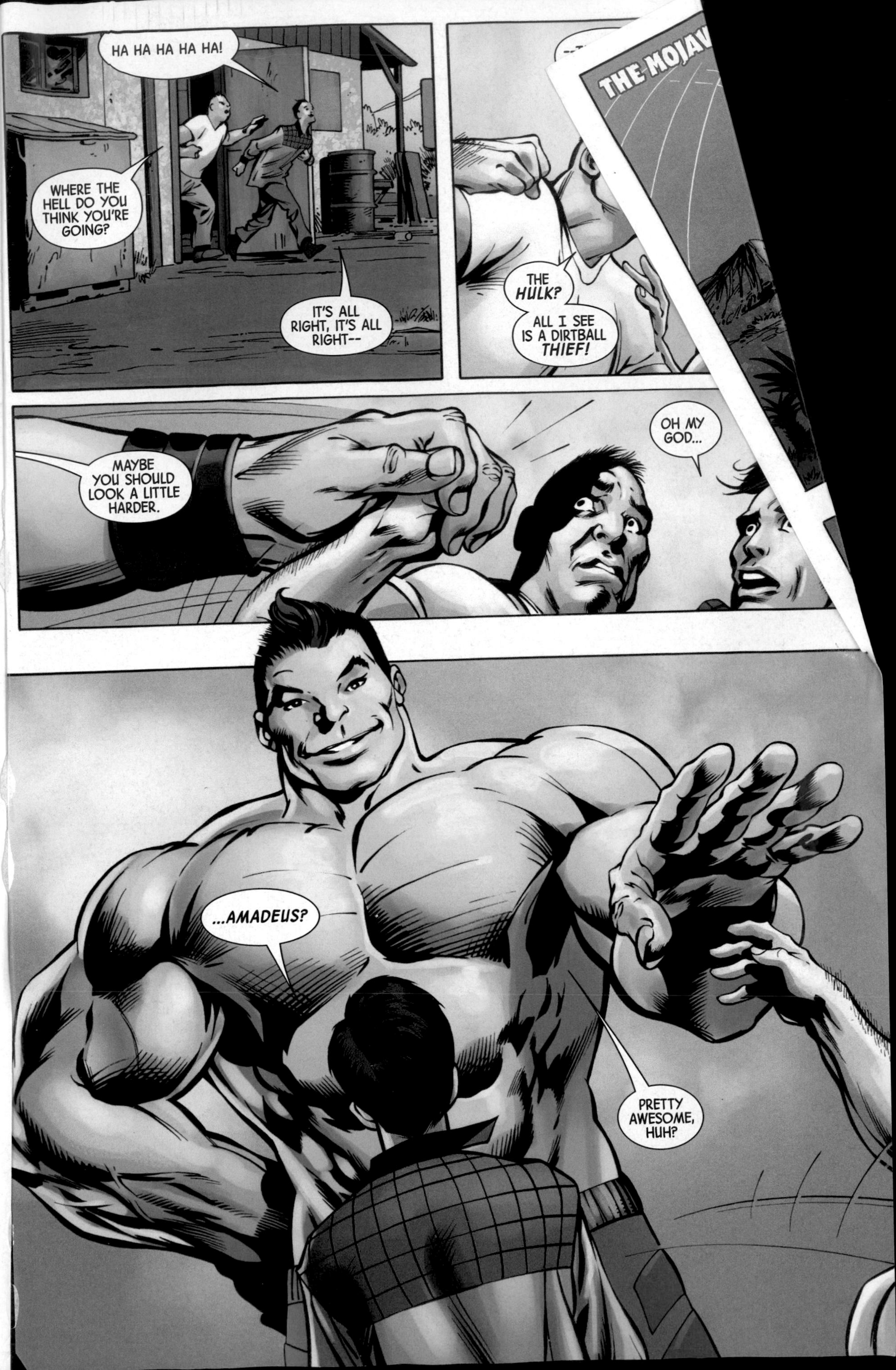
HA HA HA HA HA!
WHERE THE HELL DO YOU THINK YOU'RE GOING?
IT'S ALL RIGHT, IT'S ALL RIGHT--
THE HULK?
ALL I SEE IS A DIRTBALL THIEF!
MAYBE YOU SHOULD LOOK A LITTLE HARDER.
OH MY GOD...
...AMADEUS?
PRETTY AWESOME, HUH?

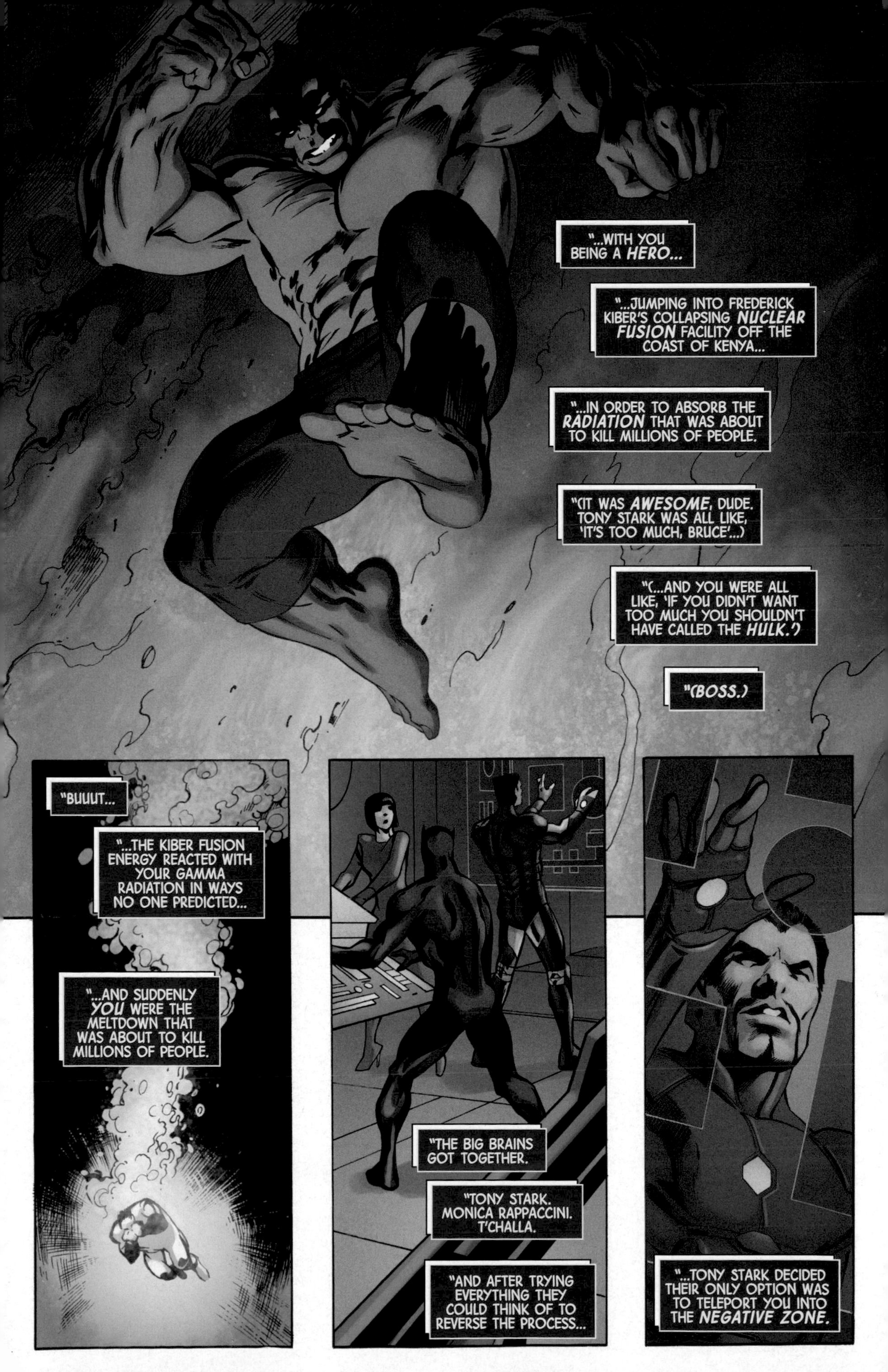
"...WITH YOU BEING A HERO...
"...JUMPING INTO FREDERICK KIBER'S COLLAPSING NUCLEAR FUSION FACILITY OFF THE COAST OF KENYA...
"...IN ORDER TO ABSORB THE RADIATION THAT WAS ABOUT TO KILL MILLIONS OF PEOPLE.
"(IT WAS AWESOME, DUDE. TONY STARK WAS ALL LIKE, 'IT'S TOO MUCH, BRUCE'...)
"(...AND YOU WERE ALL LIKE, 'IF YOU DIDN'T WANT TOO MUCH YOU SHOULDN'T HAVE CALLED THE HULK.')
"(BOSS.)
"BUUUT...
"...THE KIBER FUSION ENERGY REACTED WITH YOUR GAMMA RADIATION IN WAYS NO ONE PREDICTED...
"...AND SUDDENLY YOU WERE THE MELTDOWN THAT WAS ABOUT TO KILL MILLIONS OF PEOPLE.
"THE BIG BRAINS GOT TOGETHER.
"TONY STARK. MONICA RAPPACCINI. T'CHALLA.
"AND AFTER TRYING EVERYTHING THEY COULD THINK OF TO REVERSE THE PROCESS...
"...TONY STARK DECIDED THEIR ONLY OPTION WAS TO TELEPORT YOU INTO THE NEGATIVE ZONE.

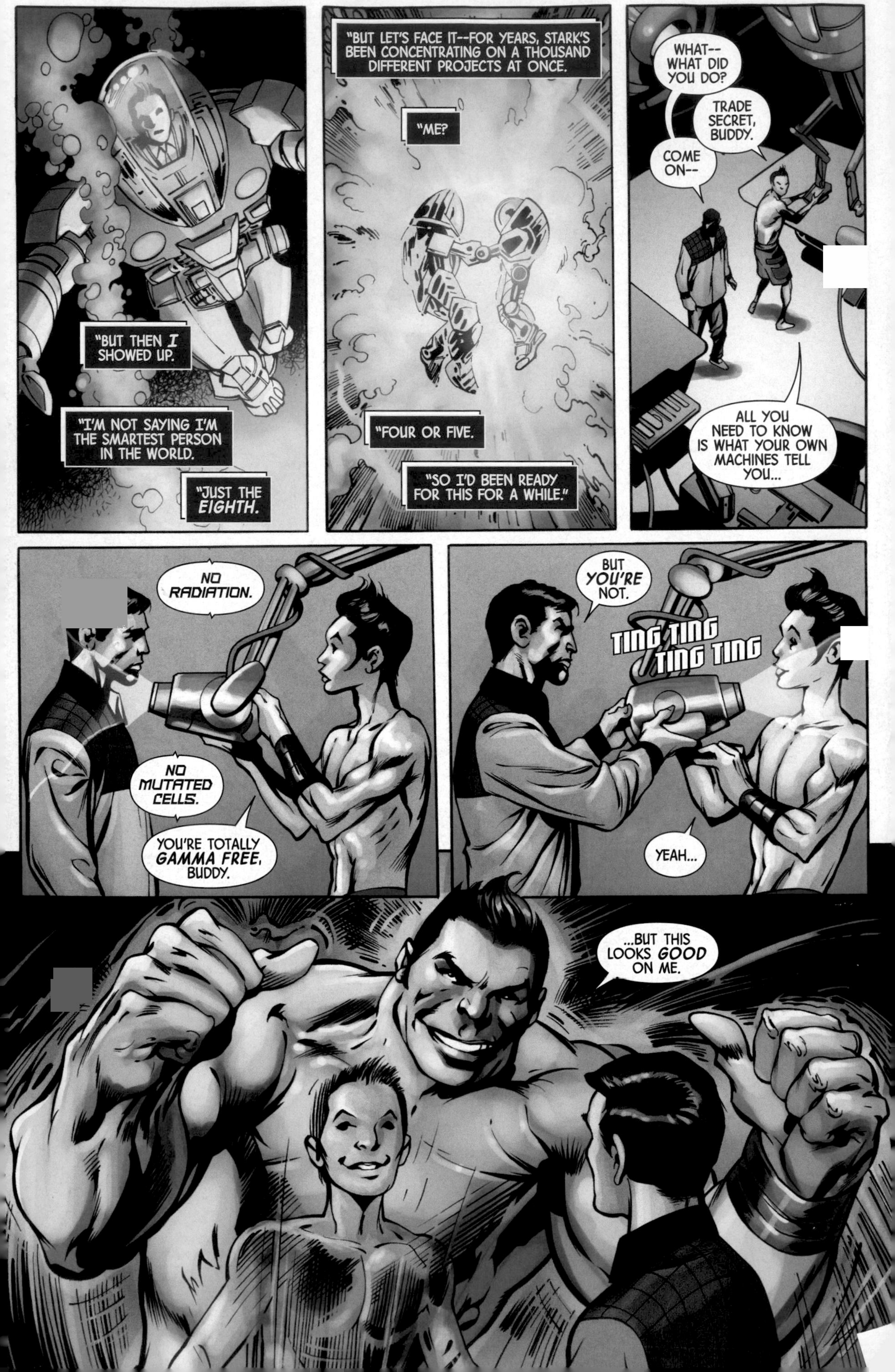
"BUT THEN *I* SHOWED UP.
"I'M NOT SAYING I'M THE SMARTEST PERSON IN THE WORLD.
"JUST THE *EIGHTH*.
"BUT LET'S FACE IT--FOR YEARS, STARK'S BEEN CONCENTRATING ON A THOUSAND DIFFERENT PROJECTS AT ONCE.
"ME?
"FOUR OR FIVE.
"SO I'D BEEN READY FOR THIS FOR A WHILE."
WHAT--WHAT DID YOU DO?
TRADE SECRET, BUDDY.
COME ON--
ALL YOU NEED TO KNOW IS WHAT YOUR OWN MACHINES TELL YOU...
NO *RADIATION*.
NO *MUTATED CELLS*.
YOU'RE TOTALLY *GAMMA FREE*, BUDDY.
BUT *YOU'RE* NOT.
TING TING TING TING
YEAH...
...BUT THIS LOOKS *GOOD* ON ME.

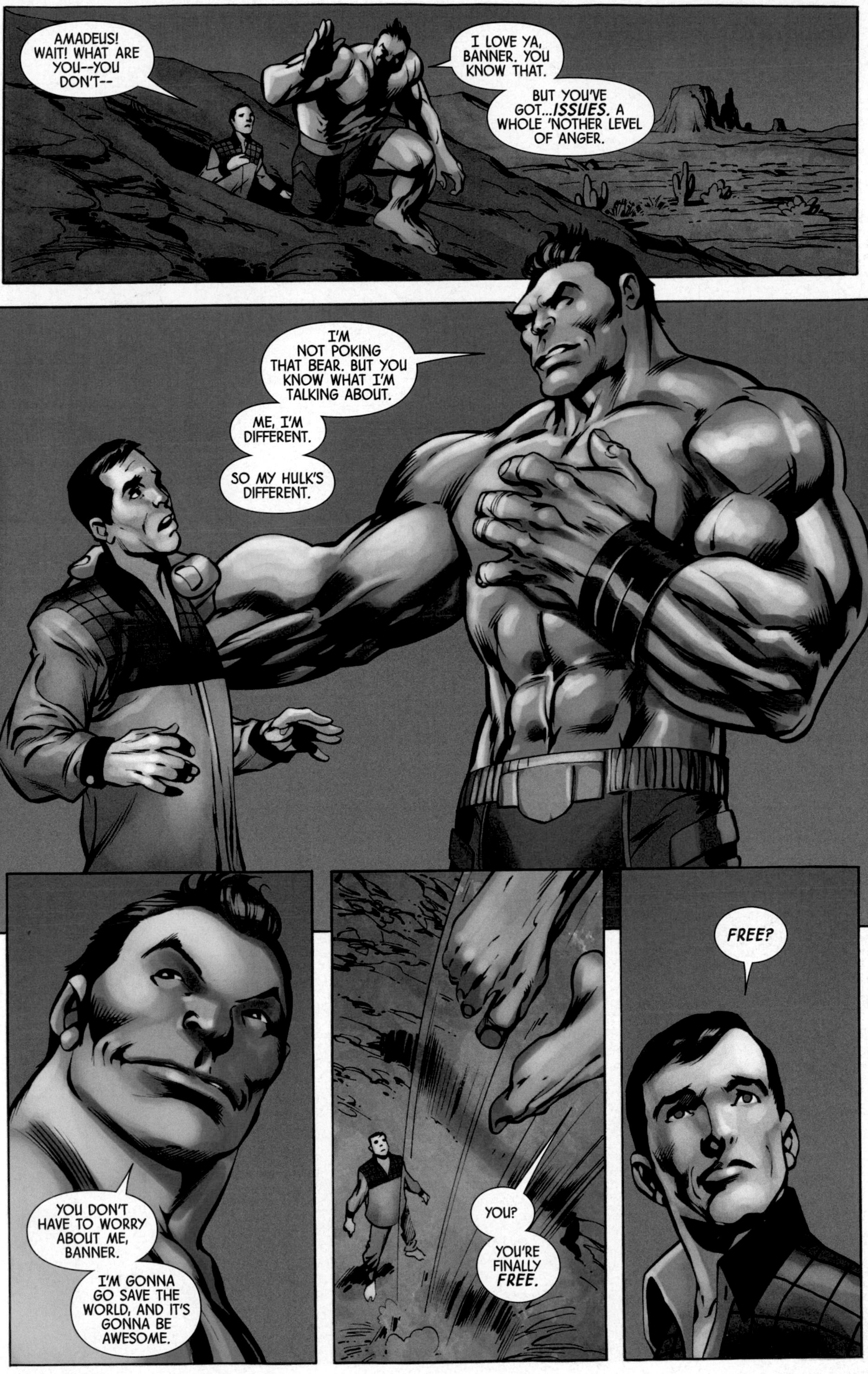
AMADEUS! WAIT! WHAT ARE YOU--YOU DON'T--
I LOVE YA, BANNER. YOU KNOW THAT.
BUT YOU'VE GOT...ISSUES. A WHOLE 'NOTHER LEVEL OF ANGER.
I'M NOT POKING THAT BEAR. BUT YOU KNOW WHAT I'M TALKING ABOUT.
ME, I'M DIFFERENT.
SO MY HULK'S DIFFERENT.
YOU DON'T HAVE TO WORRY ABOUT ME, BANNER.
I'M GONNA GO SAVE THE WORLD, AND IT'S GONNA BE AWESOME.
YOU?
YOU'RE FINALLY FREE.
FREE?

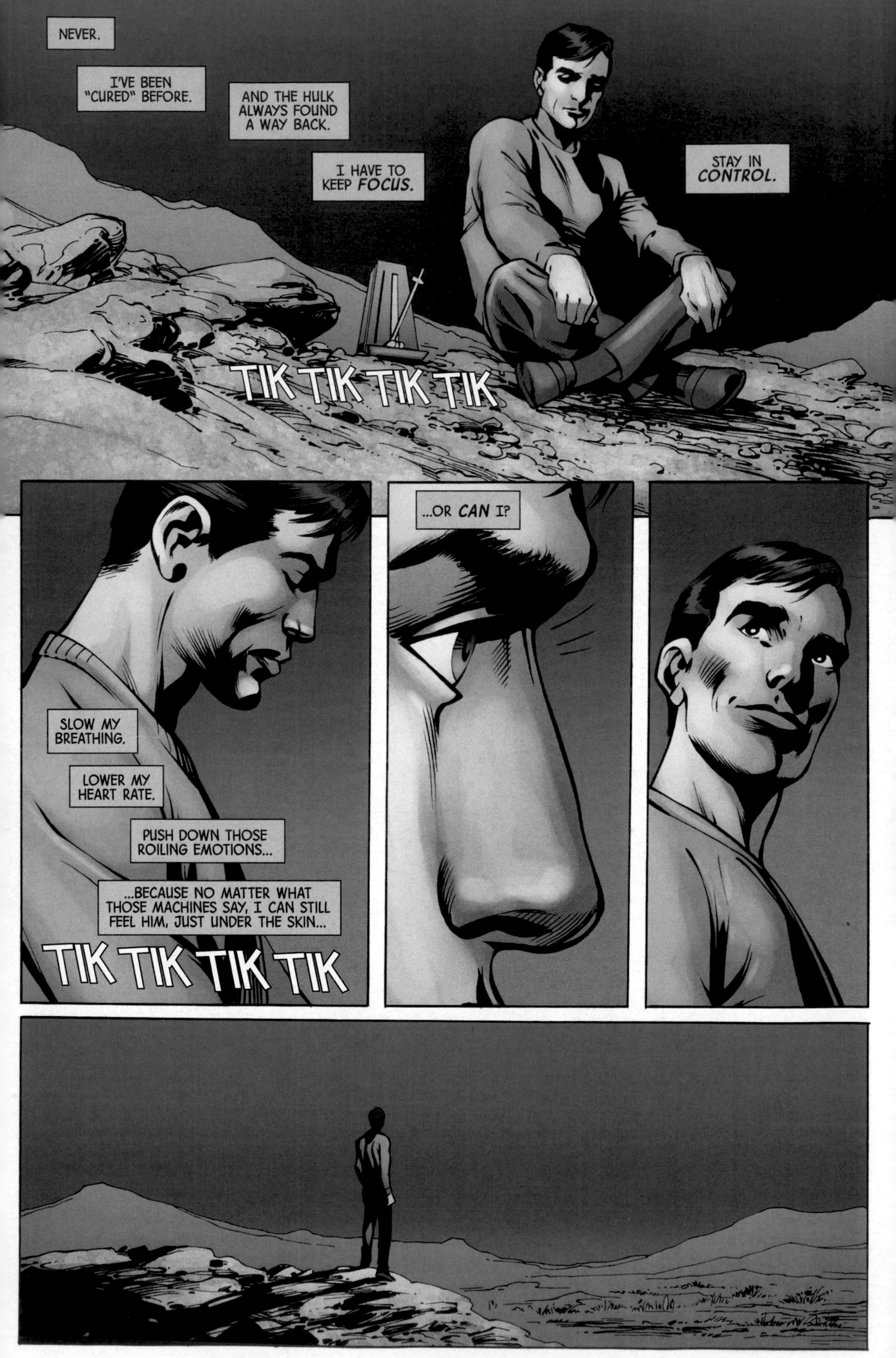
NEVER.
I'VE BEEN "CURED" BEFORE.
AND THE HULK ALWAYS FOUND A WAY BACK.
I HAVE TO KEEP FOCUS.
STAY IN CONTROL.
TIK TIK TIK TIK
SLOW MY BREATHING.
LOWER MY HEART RATE.
PUSH DOWN THOSE ROILING EMOTIONS...
...BECAUSE NO MATTER WHAT THOSE MACHINES SAY, I CAN STILL FEEL HIM, JUST UNDER THE SKIN...
TIK TIK TIK TIK
...OR CAN I?

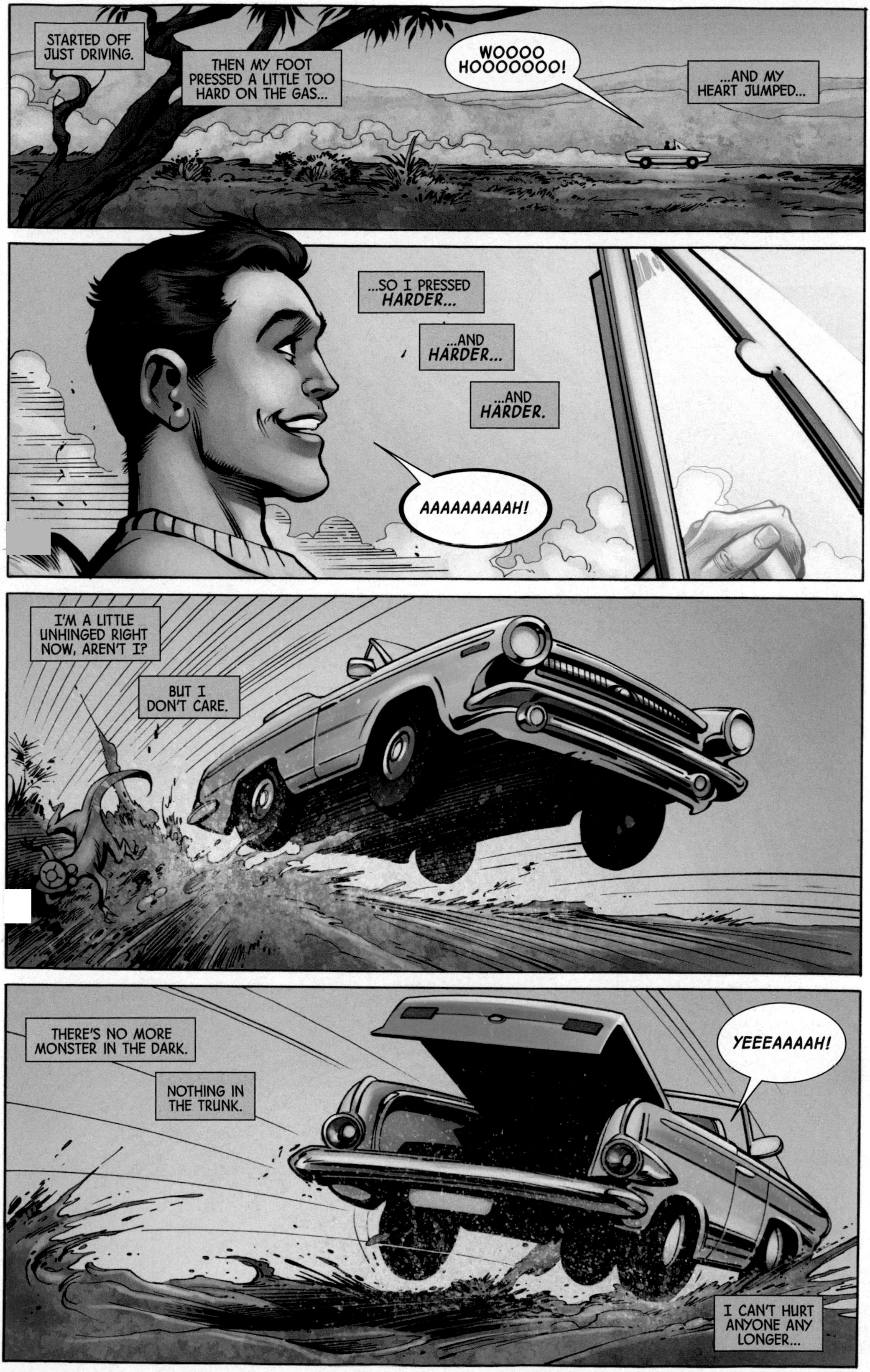
STARTED OFF JUST DRIVING.
THEN MY FOOT PRESSED A LITTLE TOO HARD ON THE GAS...
WOOOO HOOOOOOO!
...AND MY HEART JUMPED...
...SO I PRESSED HARDER...
...AND HARDER...
...AND HARDER.
AAAAAAAAAH!
I'M A LITTLE UNHINGED RIGHT NOW, AREN'T I?
BUT I DON'T CARE.
THERE'S NO MORE MONSTER IN THE DARK.
NOTHING IN THE TRUNK.
YEEEAAAAH!
I CAN'T HURT ANYONE ANY LONGER...

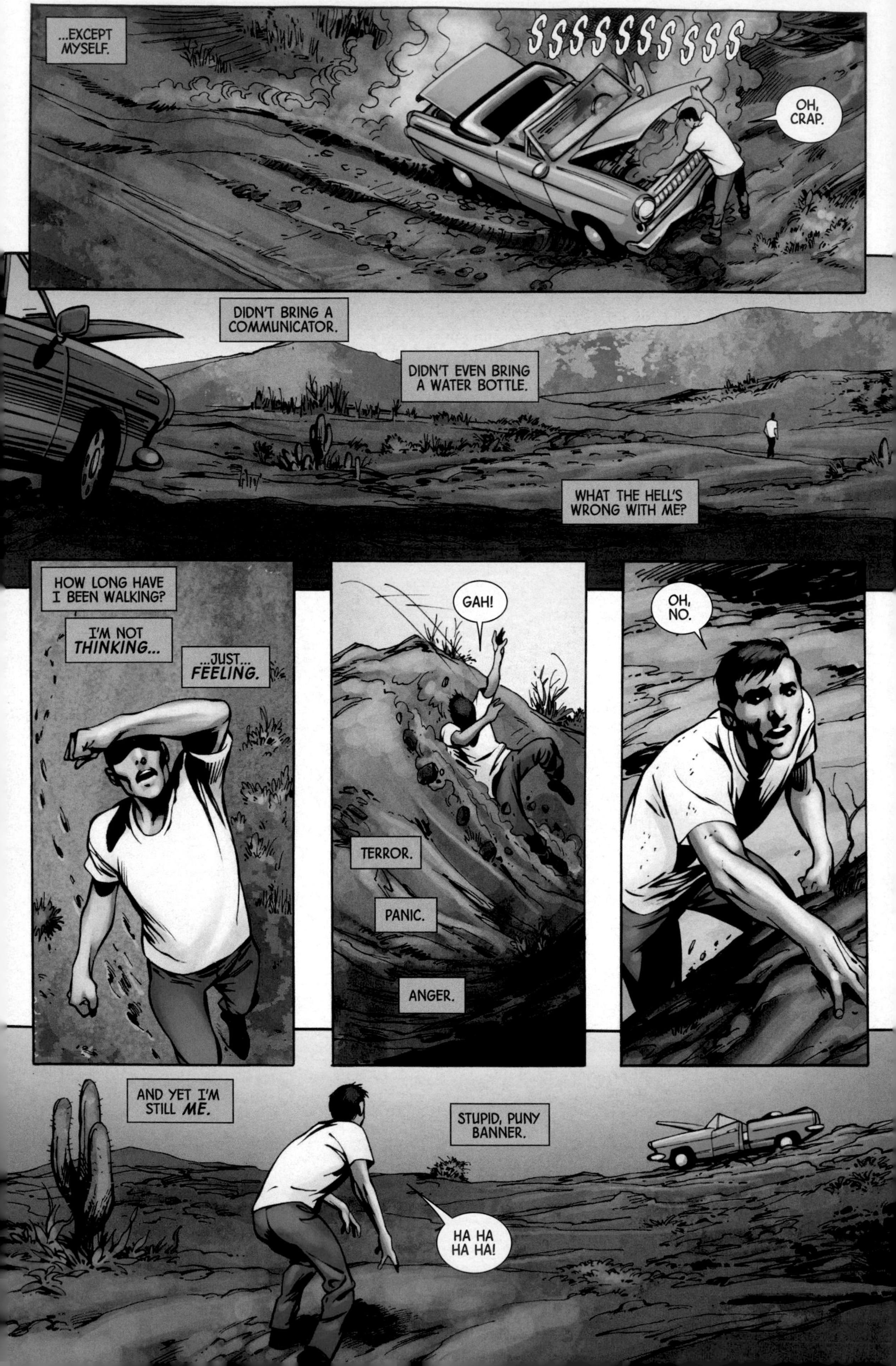
...EXCEPT MYSELF.
SSSSSSSSSS
OH, CRAP.
DIDN'T BRING A COMMUNICATOR.
DIDN'T EVEN BRING A WATER BOTTLE.
WHAT THE HELL'S WRONG WITH ME?
HOW LONG HAVE I BEEN WALKING?
I'M NOT THINKING...
...JUST... FEELING.
GAH!
TERROR.
PANIC.
ANGER.
OH, NO.
AND YET I'M STILL ME.
STUPID, PUNY BANNER.
HA HA HA HA!

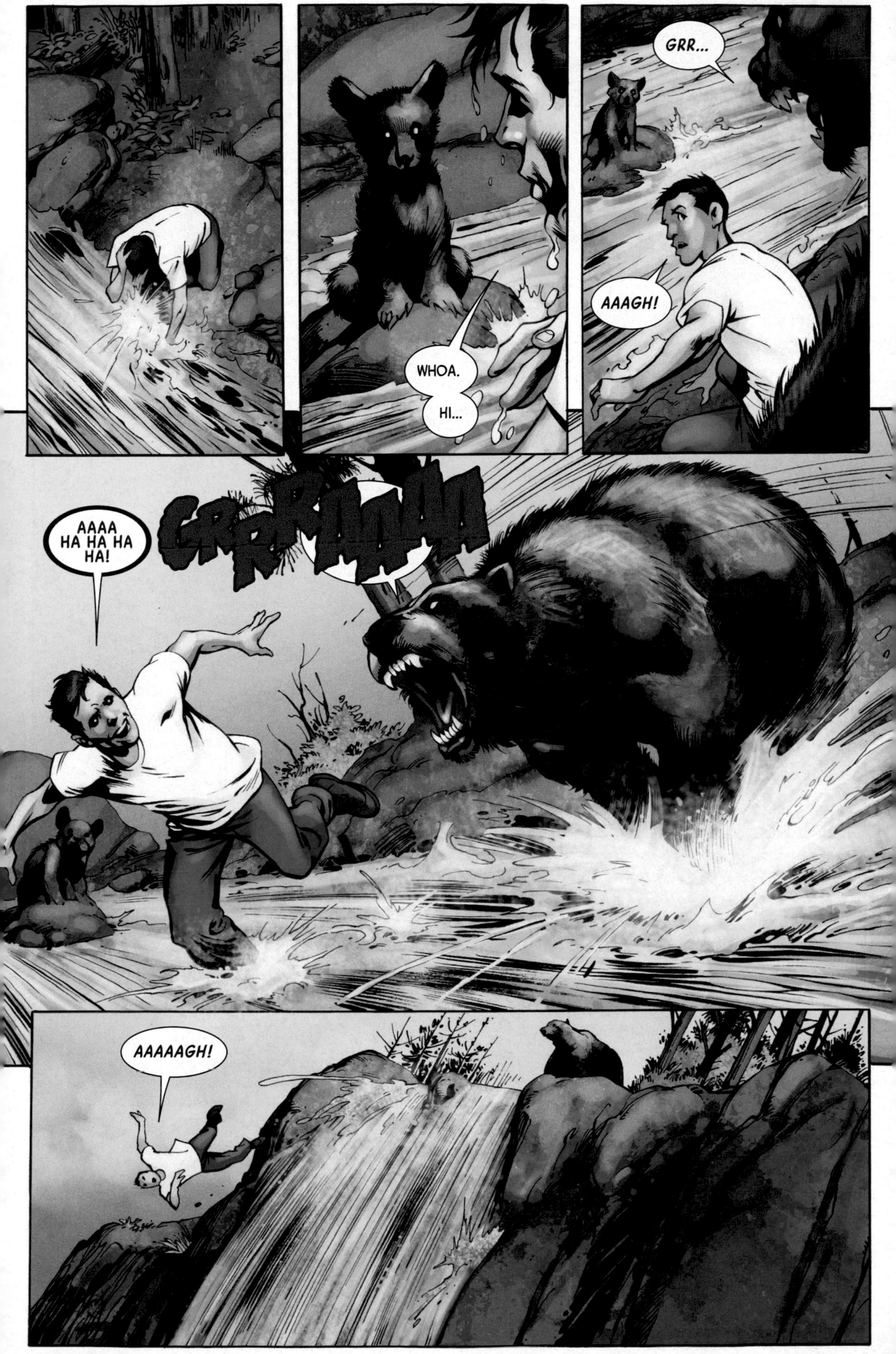
WHOA.
HI...
GRR...
AAAGH!
AAAA HA HA HA HA!
AAAAAGH!

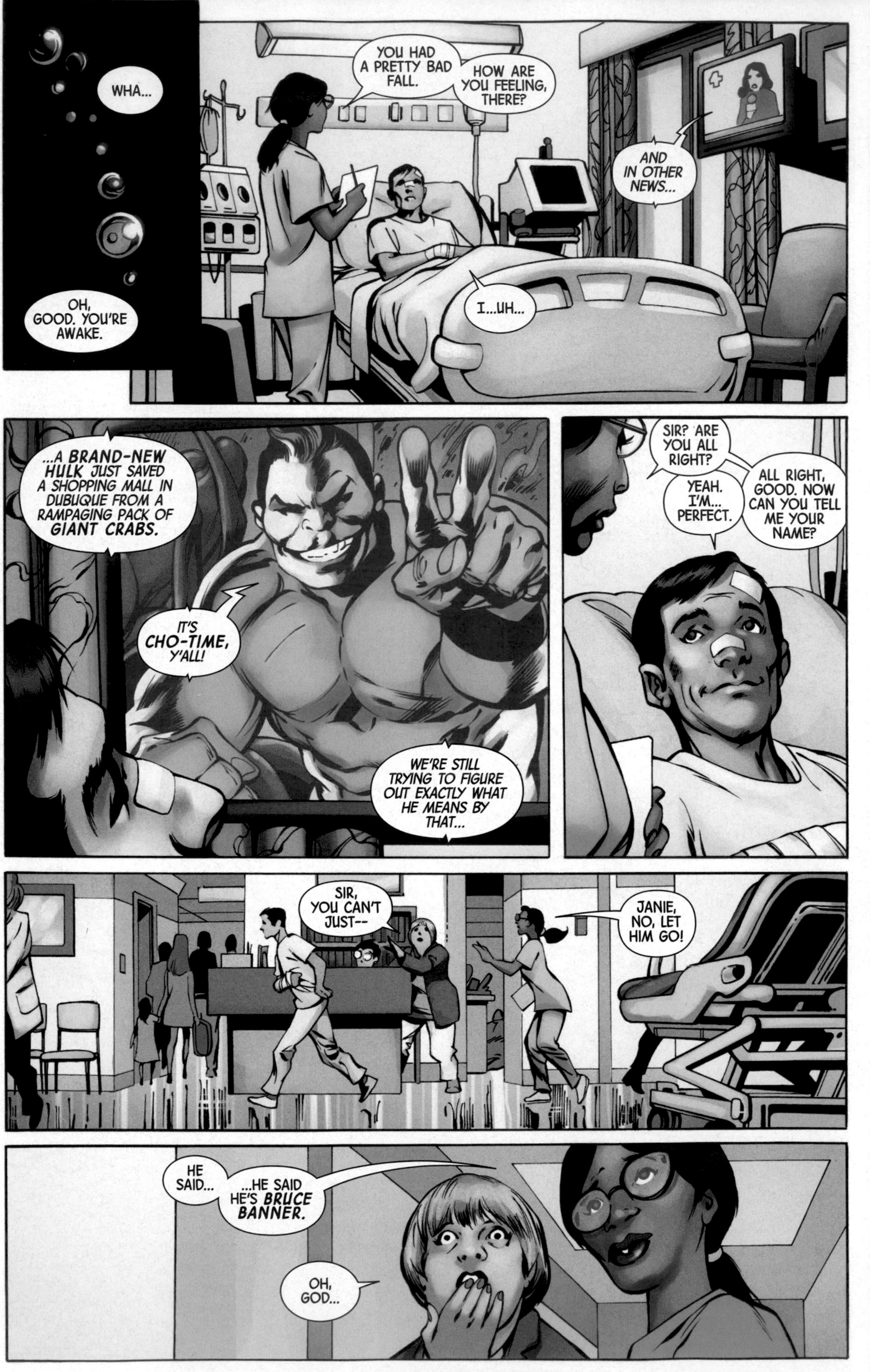
WHA...
OH, GOOD. YOU'RE AWAKE.
YOU HAD A PRETTY BAD FALL.
HOW ARE YOU FEELING, THERE?
I...UH...
AND IN OTHER NEWS...
...A BRAND-NEW HULK JUST SAVED A SHOPPING MALL IN DUBUQUE FROM A RAMPAGING PACK OF GIANT CRABS.
IT'S CHO-TIME, Y'ALL!
WE'RE STILL TRYING TO FIGURE OUT EXACTLY WHAT HE MEANS BY THAT...
SIR? ARE YOU ALL RIGHT?
YEAH. I'M... PERFECT.
ALL RIGHT, GOOD. NOW CAN YOU TELL ME YOUR NAME?
SIR, YOU CAN'T JUST--
JANIE, NO, LET HIM GO!
HE SAID...
...HE SAID HE'S BRUCE BANNER.
OH, GOD...

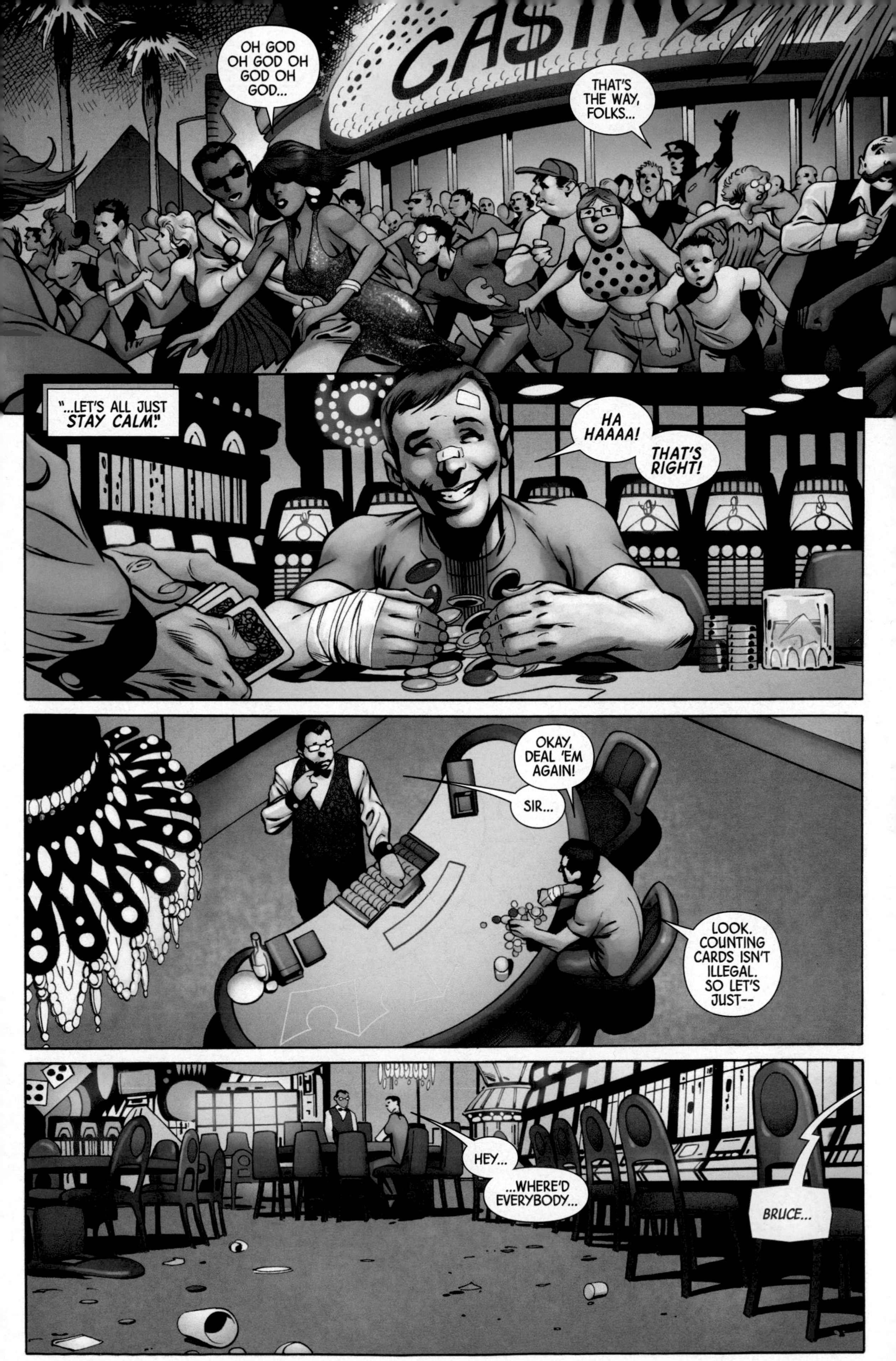
OH GOD OH GOD OH GOD OH GOD...
CASINO
THAT'S THE WAY, FOLKS...
"...LET'S ALL JUST STAY CALM."
HA HAAAA!
THAT'S RIGHT!
OKAY, DEAL 'EM AGAIN!
SIR...
LOOK. COUNTING CARDS ISN'T ILLEGAL. SO LET'S JUST--
HEY...
...WHERE'D EVERYBODY...
BRUCE...

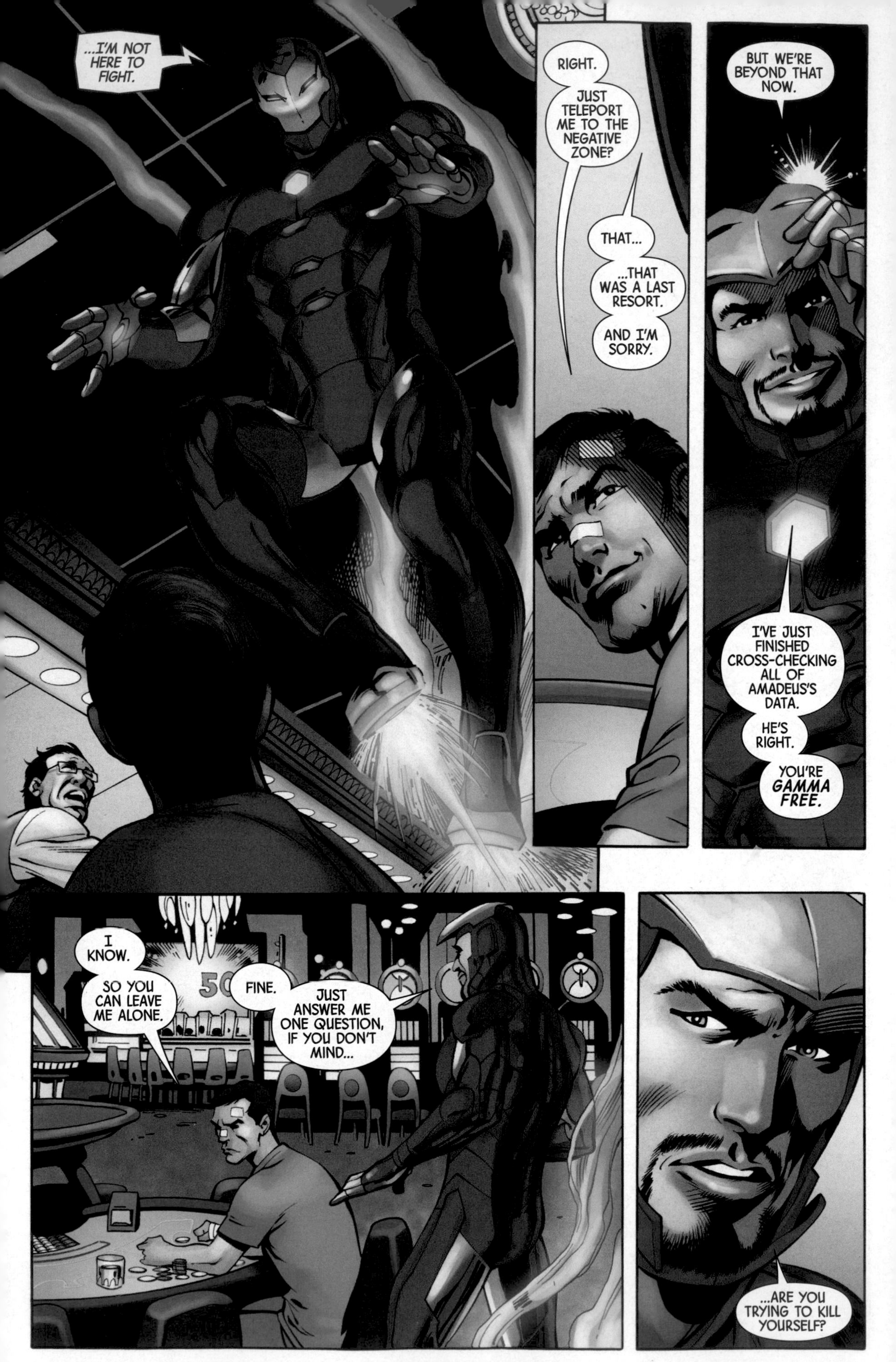
...I'M NOT HERE TO FIGHT.
RIGHT.
JUST TELEPORT ME TO THE NEGATIVE ZONE?
THAT...
...THAT WAS A LAST RESORT.
AND I'M SORRY.
BUT WE'RE BEYOND THAT NOW.
I'VE JUST FINISHED CROSS-CHECKING ALL OF AMADEUS'S DATA.
HE'S RIGHT.
YOU'RE *GAMMA FREE.*
I KNOW.
SO YOU CAN LEAVE ME ALONE.
FINE.
JUST ANSWER ME ONE QUESTION, IF YOU DON'T MIND...
...ARE YOU TRYING TO KILL YOURSELF?

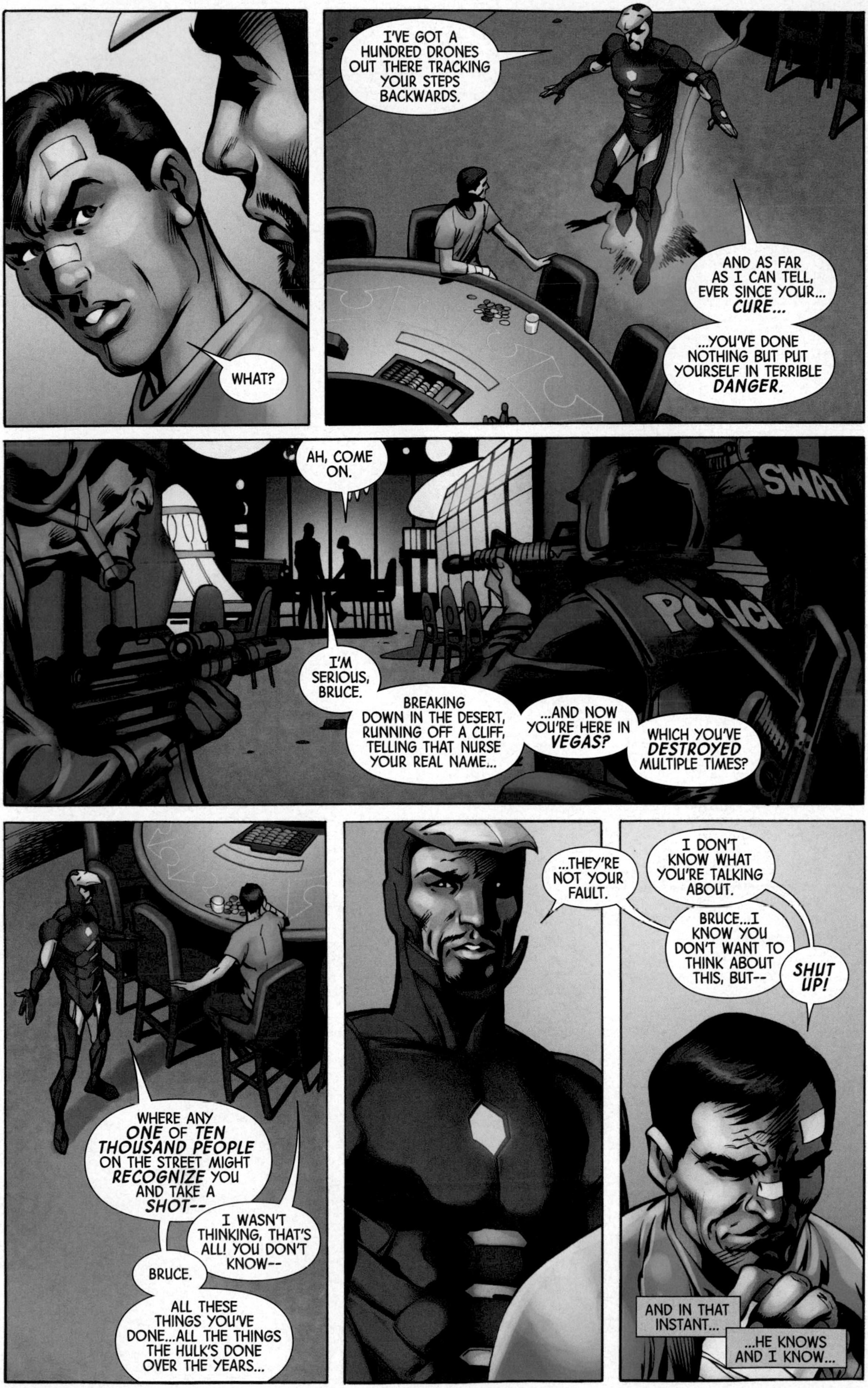
WHAT?
I'VE GOT A HUNDRED DRONES OUT THERE TRACKING YOUR STEPS BACKWARDS.
AND AS FAR AS I CAN TELL, EVER SINCE YOUR... CURE...
...YOU'VE DONE NOTHING BUT PUT YOURSELF IN TERRIBLE DANGER.
AH, COME ON.
SWAT
POLICE
I'M SERIOUS, BRUCE.
BREAKING DOWN IN THE DESERT, RUNNING OFF A CLIFF, TELLING THAT NURSE YOUR REAL NAME...
...AND NOW YOU'RE HERE IN VEGAS?
WHICH YOU'VE DESTROYED MULTIPLE TIMES?
WHERE ANY ONE OF TEN THOUSAND PEOPLE ON THE STREET MIGHT RECOGNIZE YOU AND TAKE A SHOT--
I WASN'T THINKING, THAT'S ALL! YOU DON'T KNOW--
BRUCE.
ALL THESE THINGS YOU'VE DONE...ALL THE THINGS THE HULK'S DONE OVER THE YEARS...
...THEY'RE NOT YOUR FAULT.
I DON'T KNOW WHAT YOU'RE TALKING ABOUT.
BRUCE...I KNOW YOU DON'T WANT TO THINK ABOUT THIS, BUT--
SHUT UP!
AND IN THAT INSTANT...
...HE KNOWS AND I KNOW...

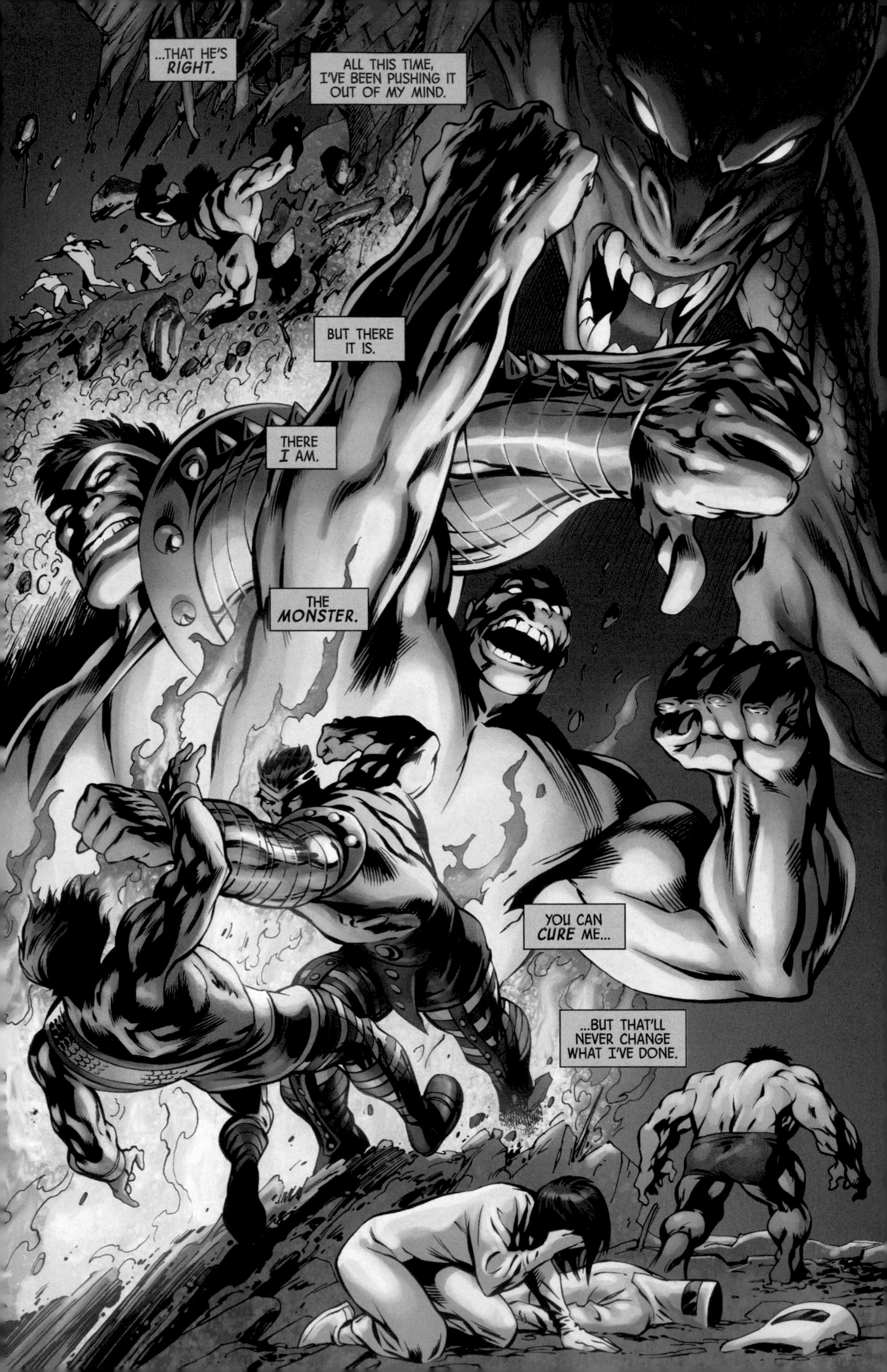
...THAT HE'S RIGHT.
ALL THIS TIME, I'VE BEEN PUSHING IT OUT OF MY MIND.
BUT THERE IT IS.
THERE I AM.
THE MONSTER.
YOU CAN CURE ME...
...BUT THAT'LL NEVER CHANGE WHAT I'VE DONE.

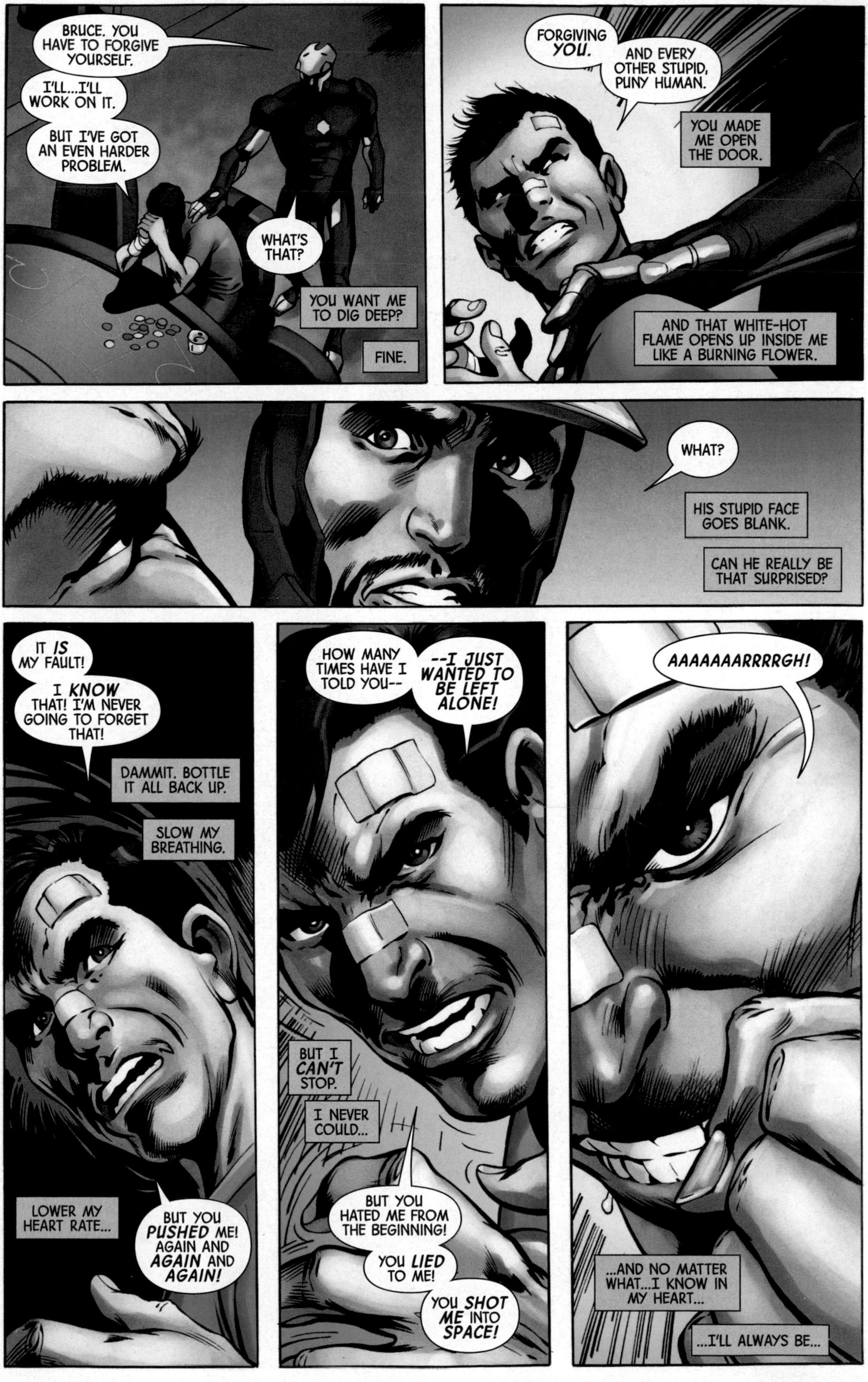
BRUCE. YOU HAVE TO FORGIVE YOURSELF.
I'LL...I'LL WORK ON IT.
BUT I'VE GOT AN EVEN HARDER PROBLEM.
WHAT'S THAT?
YOU WANT ME TO DIG DEEP?
FINE.
FORGIVING YOU.
AND EVERY OTHER STUPID, PUNY HUMAN.
YOU MADE ME OPEN THE DOOR.
AND THAT WHITE-HOT FLAME OPENS UP INSIDE ME LIKE A BURNING FLOWER.
WHAT?
HIS STUPID FACE GOES BLANK.
CAN HE REALLY BE THAT SURPRISED?
IT IS MY FAULT!
I KNOW THAT! I'M NEVER GOING TO FORGET THAT!
DAMMIT. BOTTLE IT ALL BACK UP.
SLOW MY BREATHING.
LOWER MY HEART RATE...
BUT YOU PUSHED ME! AGAIN AND AGAIN AND AGAIN!
HOW MANY TIMES HAVE I TOLD YOU--
--I JUST WANTED TO BE LEFT ALONE!
BUT I CAN'T STOP.
I NEVER COULD...
BUT YOU HATED ME FROM THE BEGINNING!
YOU LIED TO ME!
YOU SHOT ME INTO SPACE!
AAAAAAARRRRGH!
...AND NO MATTER WHAT...I KNOW IN MY HEART...
...I'LL ALWAYS BE...

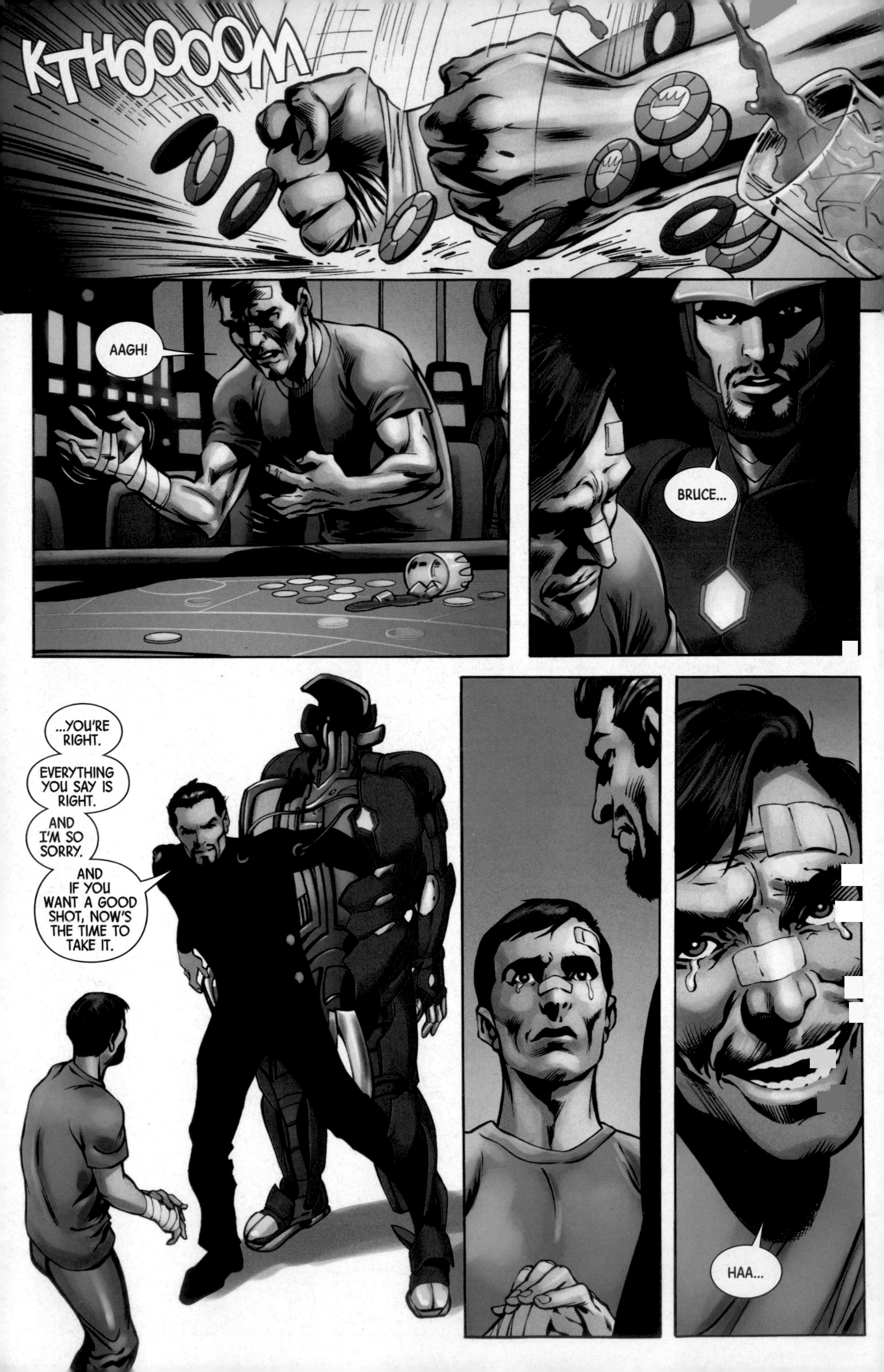
KTHOOOOM
AAGH!
BRUCE...
...YOU'RE RIGHT.
EVERYTHING YOU SAY IS RIGHT.
AND I'M SO SORRY.
AND IF YOU WANT A GOOD SHOT, NOW'S THE TIME TO TAKE IT.
HAA...

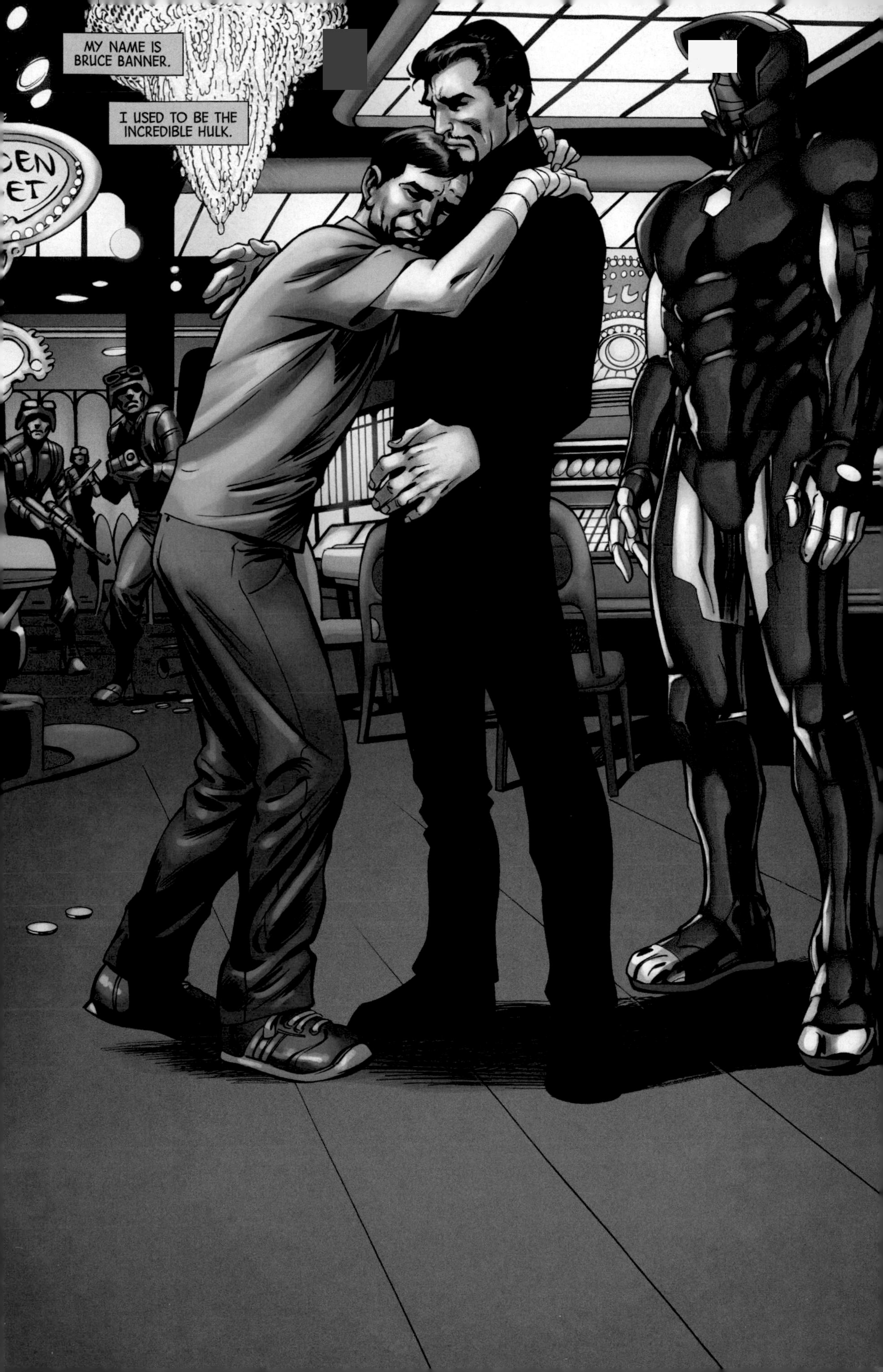
MY NAME IS BRUCE BANNER.
I USED TO BE THE INCREDIBLE HULK.

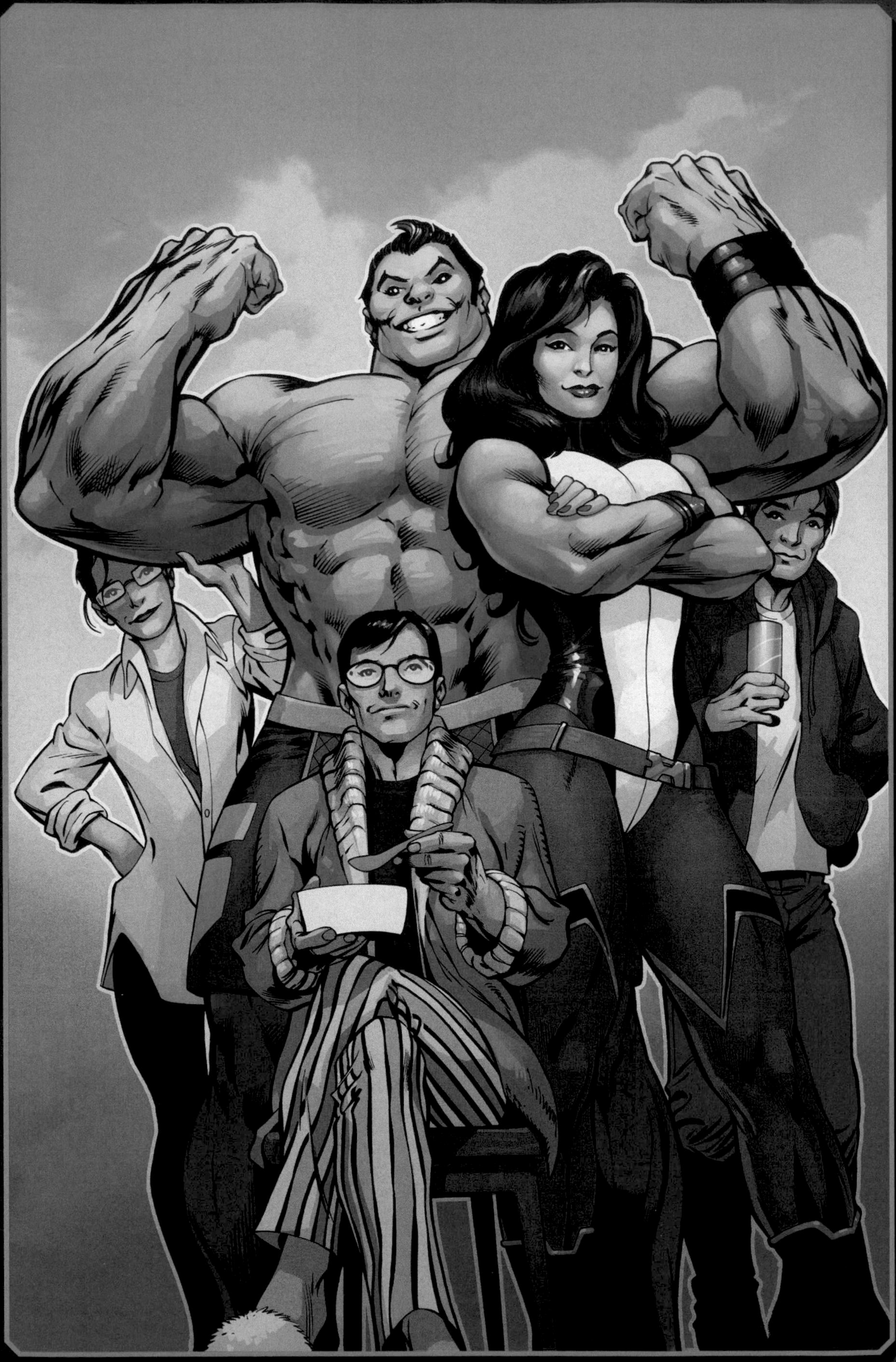

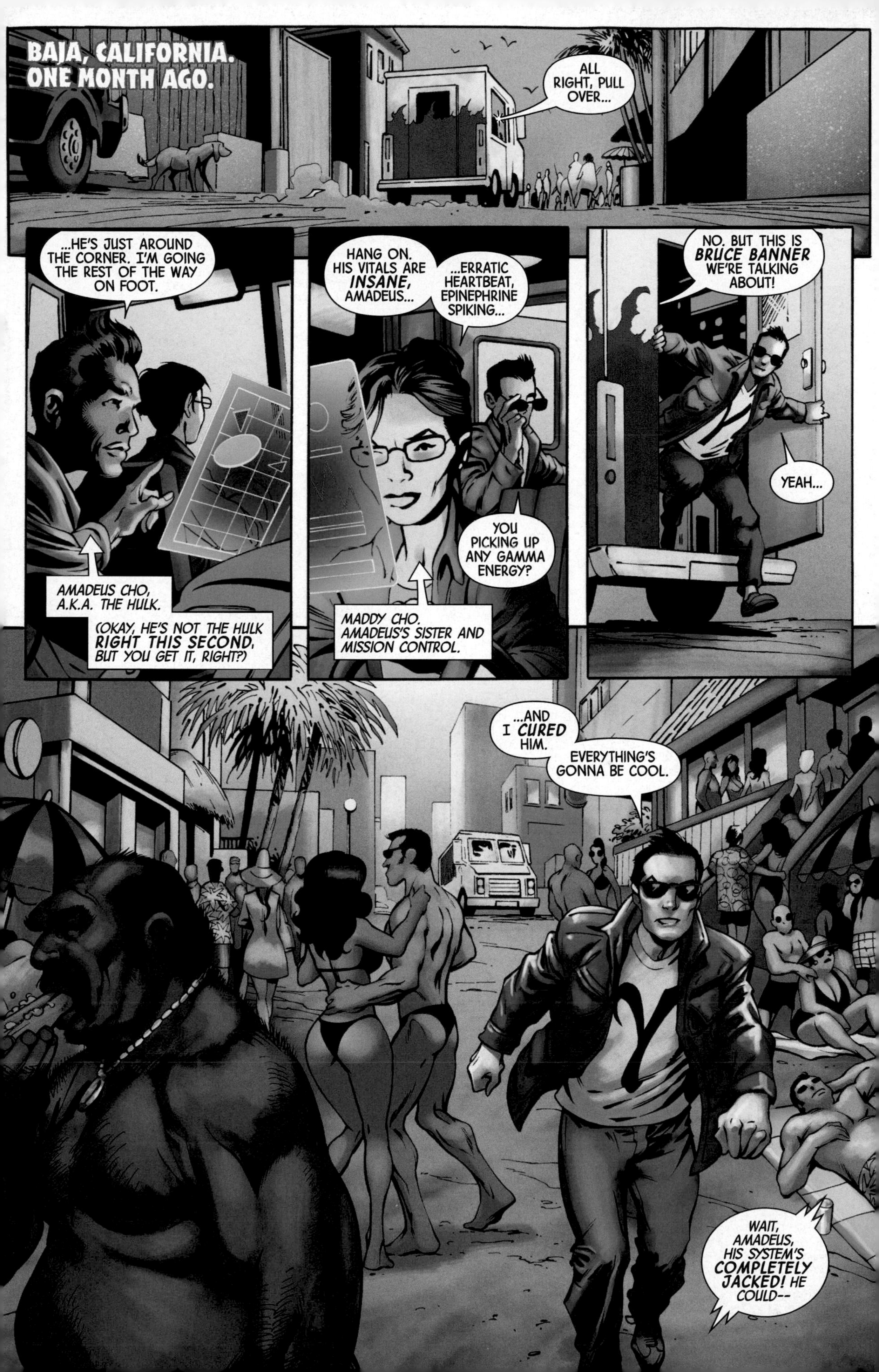
BAJA, CALIFORNIA. ONE MONTH AGO.
ALL RIGHT, PULL OVER...
...HE'S JUST AROUND THE CORNER. I'M GOING THE REST OF THE WAY ON FOOT.
AMADEUS CHO, A.K.A. THE HULK.
(OKAY, HE'S NOT THE HULK RIGHT THIS SECOND, BUT YOU GET IT, RIGHT?)
HANG ON. HIS VITALS ARE INSANE, AMADEUS...
...ERRATIC HEARTBEAT, EPINEPHRINE SPIKING...
YOU PICKING UP ANY GAMMA ENERGY?
MADDY CHO. AMADEUS'S SISTER AND MISSION CONTROL.
NO. BUT THIS IS BRUCE BANNER WE'RE TALKING ABOUT!
YEAH...
...AND I CURED HIM.
EVERYTHING'S GONNA BE COOL.
WAIT, AMADEUS, HIS SYSTEM'S COMPLETELY JACKED! HE COULD--

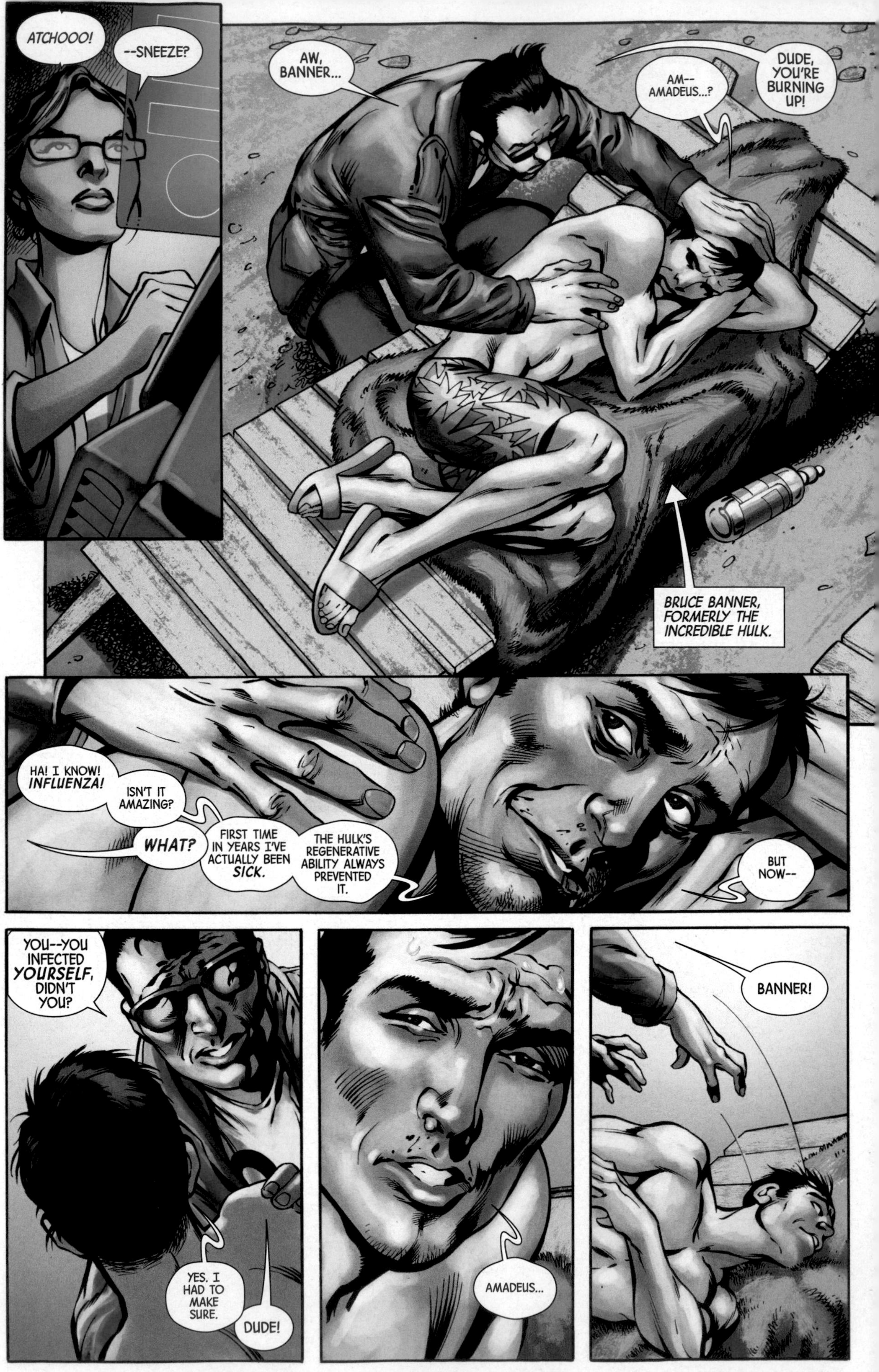

ATCHOOO!
--SNEEZE?
AW, BANNER...
AM-- AMADEUS...?
DUDE, YOU'RE BURNING UP!
BRUCE BANNER, FORMERLY THE INCREDIBLE HULK.
HA! I KNOW! INFLUENZA!
ISN'T IT AMAZING?
WHAT?
FIRST TIME IN YEARS I'VE ACTUALLY BEEN SICK.
THE HULK'S REGENERATIVE ABILITY ALWAYS PREVENTED IT.
BUT NOW--
YOU--YOU INFECTED YOURSELF, DIDN'T YOU?
YES. I HAD TO MAKE SURE.
DUDE!
AMADEUS...
BANNER!

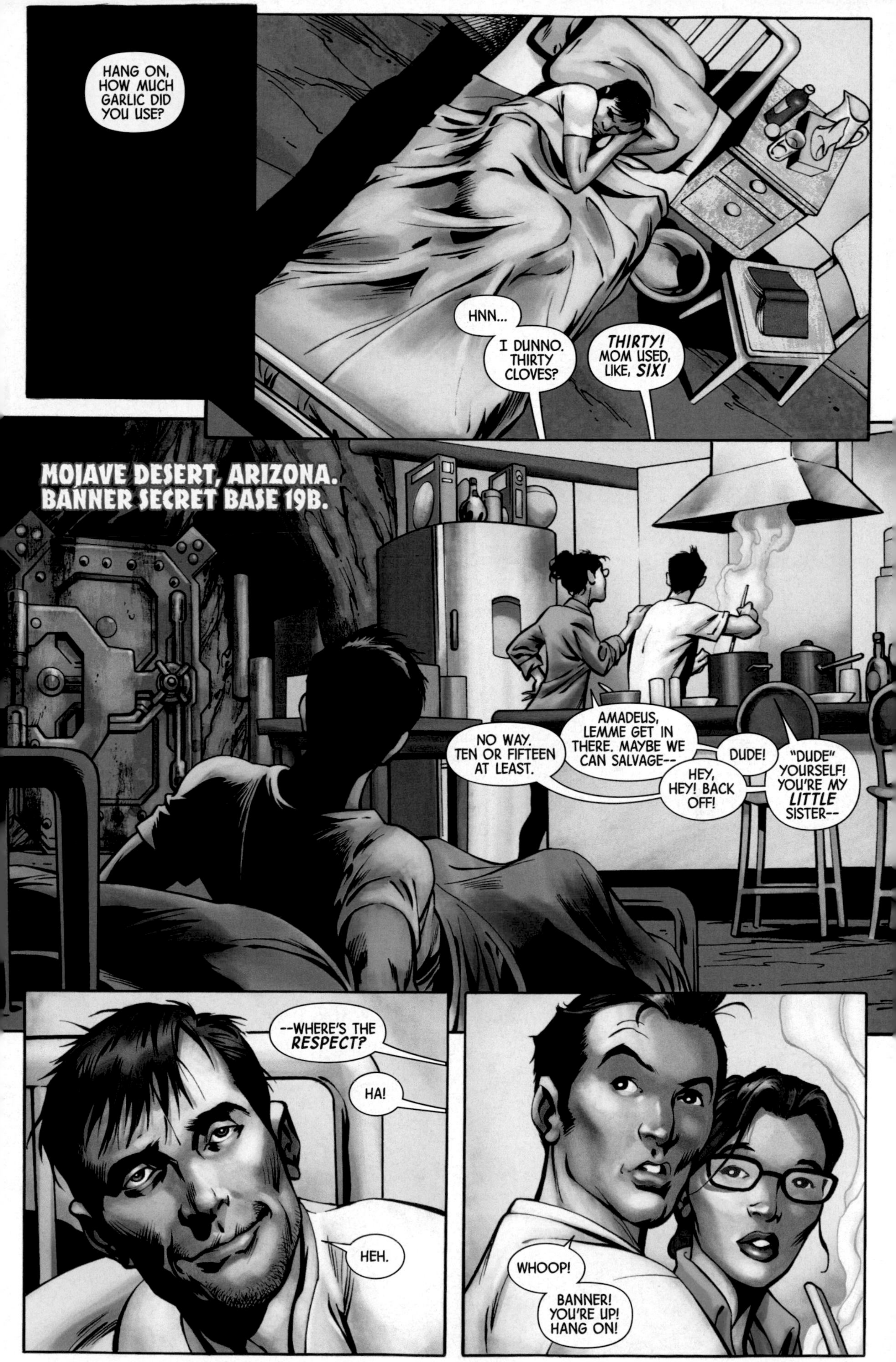
HANG ON, HOW MUCH GARLIC DID YOU USE?
HNN...
I DUNNO. THIRTY CLOVES?
THIRTY! MOM USED, LIKE, SIX!
MOJAVE DESERT, ARIZONA. BANNER SECRET BASE 19B.
NO WAY. TEN OR FIFTEEN AT LEAST.
AMADEUS, LEMME GET IN THERE. MAYBE WE CAN SALVAGE--
DUDE!
HEY, HEY! BACK OFF!
"DUDE" YOURSELF! YOU'RE MY LITTLE SISTER--
--WHERE'S THE RESPECT?
HA!
HEH.
WHOOP!
BANNER! YOU'RE UP! HANG ON!

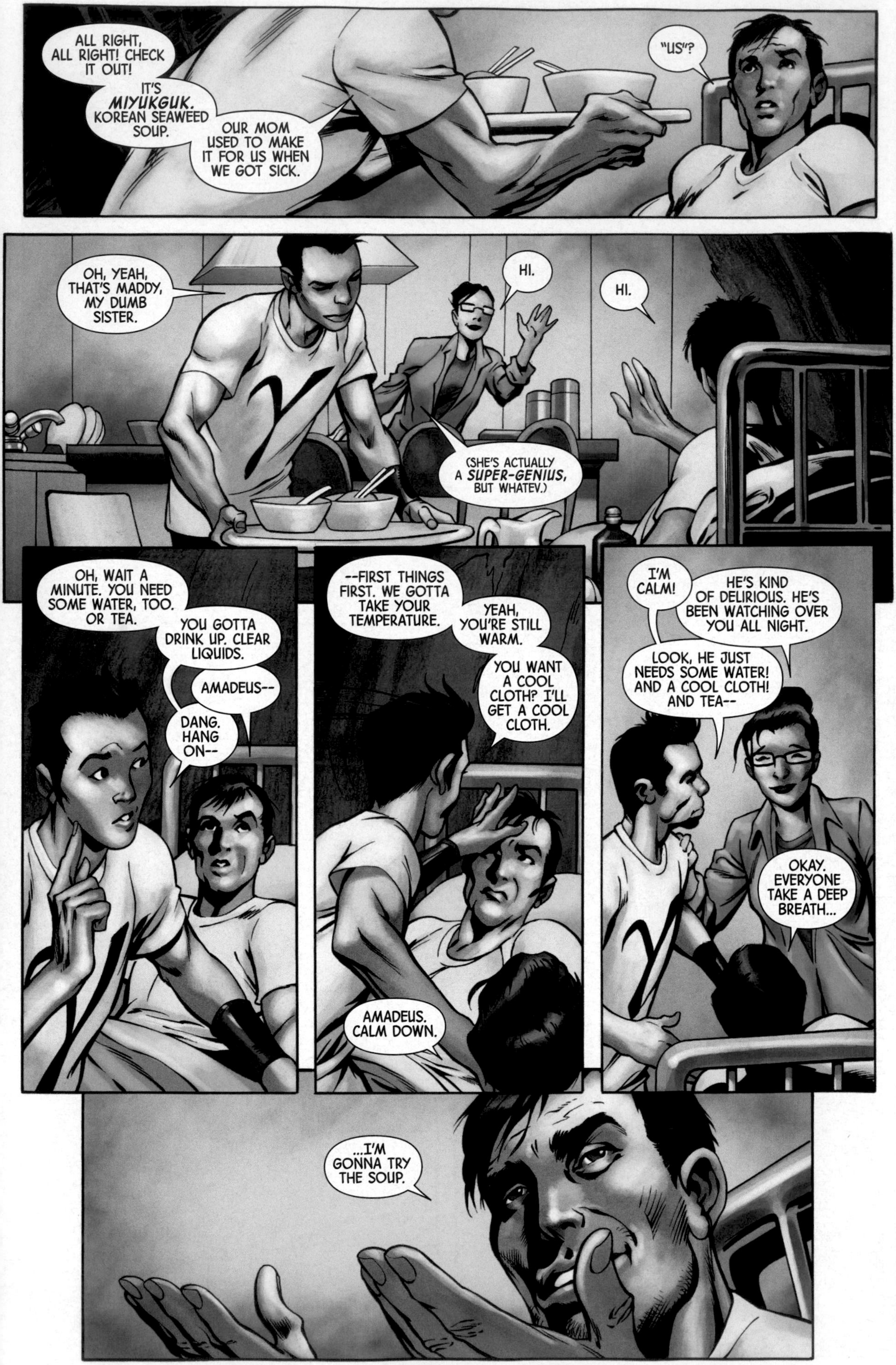
ALL RIGHT, ALL RIGHT! CHECK IT OUT!
IT'S *MIYUKGUK.* KOREAN SEAWEED SOUP.
OUR MOM USED TO MAKE IT FOR US WHEN WE GOT SICK.
"US"?
OH, YEAH, THAT'S MADDY, MY DUMB SISTER.
HI.
HI.
(SHE'S ACTUALLY A *SUPER-GENIUS*, BUT WHATEV.)
OH, WAIT A MINUTE. YOU NEED SOME WATER, TOO. OR TEA.
YOU GOTTA DRINK UP. CLEAR LIQUIDS.
AMADEUS--
DANG. HANG ON--
--FIRST THINGS FIRST. WE GOTTA TAKE YOUR TEMPERATURE.
YEAH, YOU'RE STILL WARM.
YOU WANT A COOL CLOTH? I'LL GET A COOL CLOTH.
AMADEUS. CALM DOWN.
I'M CALM!
HE'S KIND OF DELIRIOUS. HE'S BEEN WATCHING OVER YOU ALL NIGHT.
LOOK, HE JUST NEEDS SOME WATER! AND A COOL CLOTH! AND TEA--
OKAY. EVERYONE TAKE A DEEP BREATH...
...I'M GONNA TRY THE SOUP.

>SIP<

OH. THAT'S GOOD.

THAT'S... VERY GOOD.

THIRTY CLOVES, HUH?

DAMN STRAIGHT.

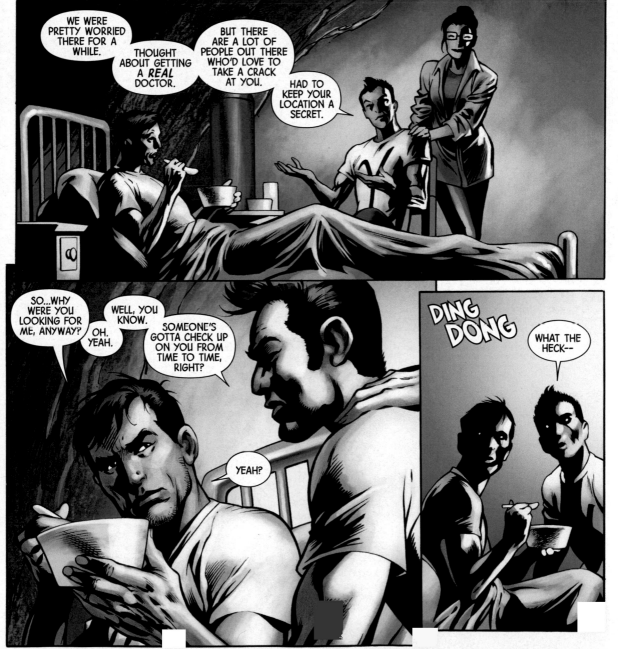

WE WERE PRETTY WORRIED THERE FOR A WHILE.

THOUGHT ABOUT GETTING A *REAL* DOCTOR.

BUT THERE ARE A LOT OF PEOPLE OUT THERE WHO'D LOVE TO TAKE A CRACK AT YOU.

HAD TO KEEP YOUR LOCATION A SECRET.

SO...WHY WERE YOU LOOKING FOR ME, ANYWAY?

WELL, YOU KNOW.

OH. YEAH.

SOMEONE'S GOTTA CHECK UP ON YOU FROM TIME TO TIME, RIGHT?

YEAH?

DING DONG

WHAT THE HECK--

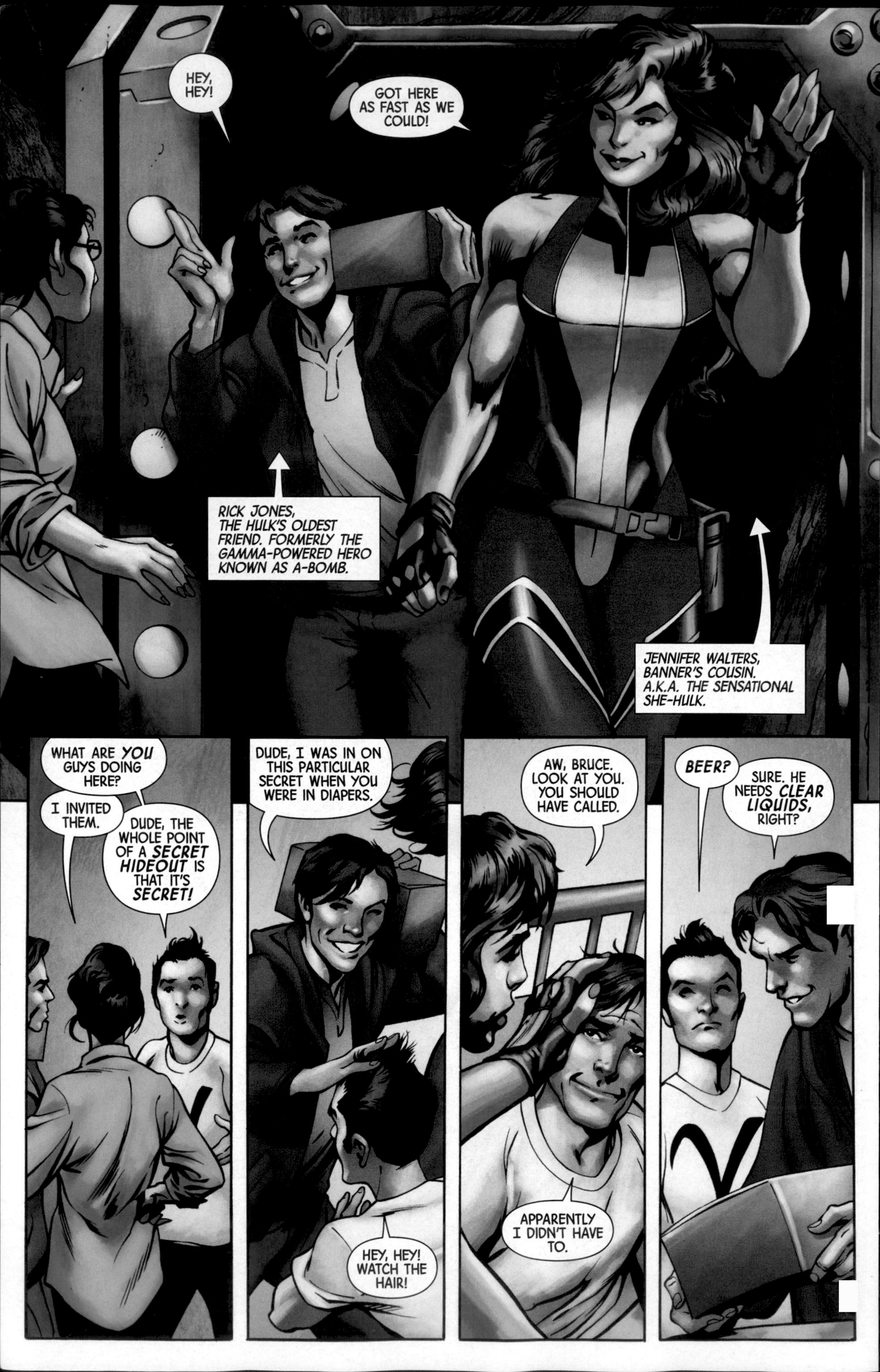
HEY, HEY!
GOT HERE AS FAST AS WE COULD!
RICK JONES, THE HULK'S OLDEST FRIEND. FORMERLY THE GAMMA-POWERED HERO KNOWN AS A-BOMB.
JENNIFER WALTERS, BANNER'S COUSIN. A.K.A. THE SENSATIONAL SHE-HULK.
WHAT ARE *YOU* GUYS DOING HERE?
I INVITED THEM.
DUDE, THE WHOLE POINT OF A ***SECRET HIDEOUT*** IS THAT IT'S ***SECRET!***
DUDE, I WAS IN ON THIS PARTICULAR SECRET WHEN YOU WERE IN DIAPERS.
HEY, HEY! WATCH THE HAIR!
AW, BRUCE. LOOK AT YOU. YOU SHOULD HAVE CALLED.
APPARENTLY I DIDN'T HAVE TO.
BEER?
SURE. HE NEEDS ***CLEAR LIQUIDS,*** RIGHT?

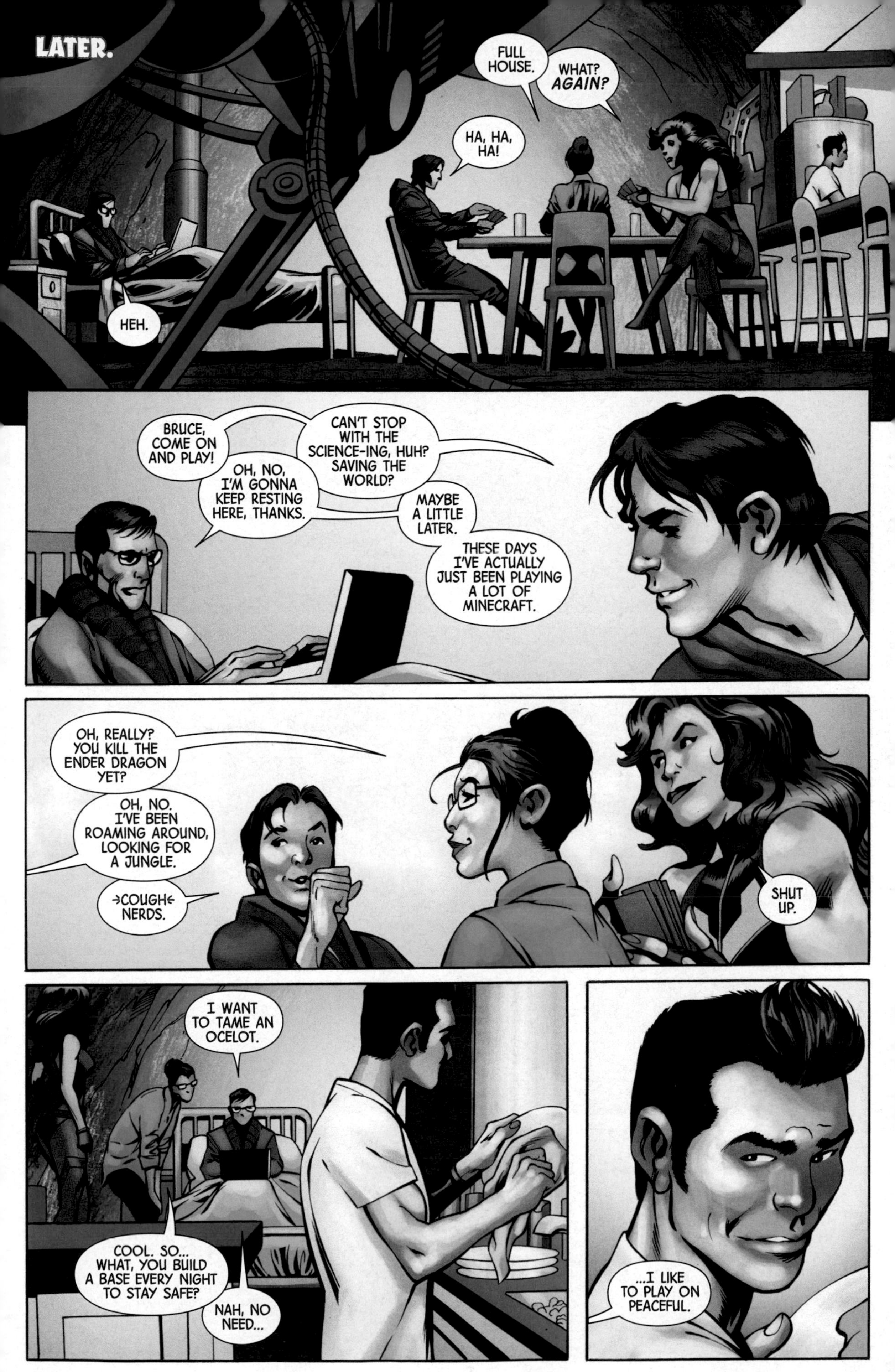
LATER.
FULL HOUSE.
WHAT? AGAIN?
HA, HA, HA!
HEH.
BRUCE, COME ON AND PLAY!
CAN'T STOP WITH THE SCIENCE-ING, HUH? SAVING THE WORLD?
OH, NO, I'M GONNA KEEP RESTING HERE, THANKS.
MAYBE A LITTLE LATER.
THESE DAYS I'VE ACTUALLY JUST BEEN PLAYING A LOT OF MINECRAFT.
OH, REALLY? YOU KILL THE ENDER DRAGON YET?
OH, NO. I'VE BEEN ROAMING AROUND, LOOKING FOR A JUNGLE.
COUGH NERDS.
SHUT UP.
I WANT TO TAME AN OCELOT.
COOL. SO... WHAT, YOU BUILD A BASE EVERY NIGHT TO STAY SAFE?
NAH, NO NEED...
...I LIKE TO PLAY ON PEACEFUL.

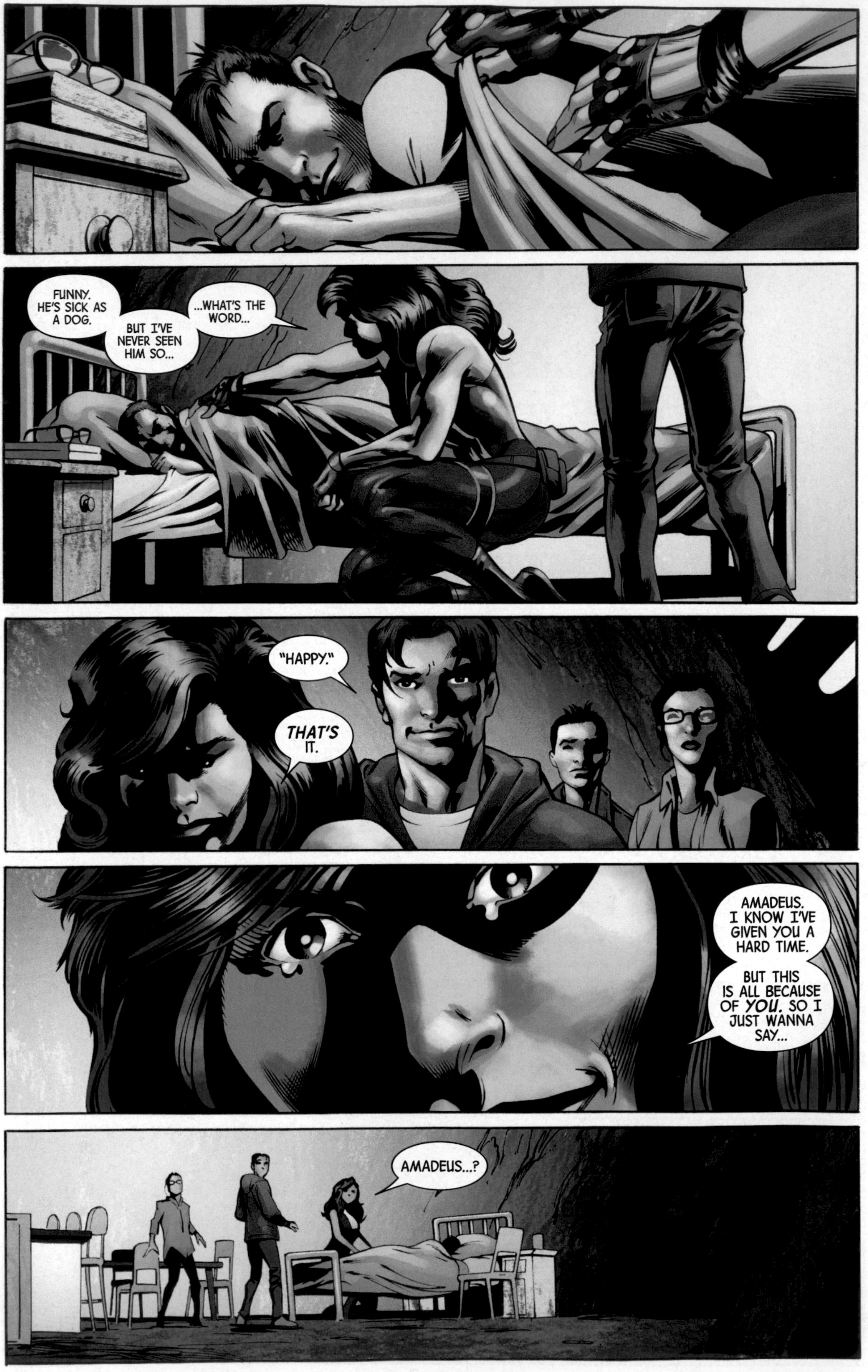

FUNNY. HE'S SICK AS A DOG.
BUT I'VE NEVER SEEN HIM SO...
...WHAT'S THE WORD...
"HAPPY."
THAT'S IT.
AMADEUS. I KNOW I'VE GIVEN YOU A HARD TIME.
BUT THIS IS ALL BECAUSE OF YOU. SO I JUST WANNA SAY...
AMADEUS...?

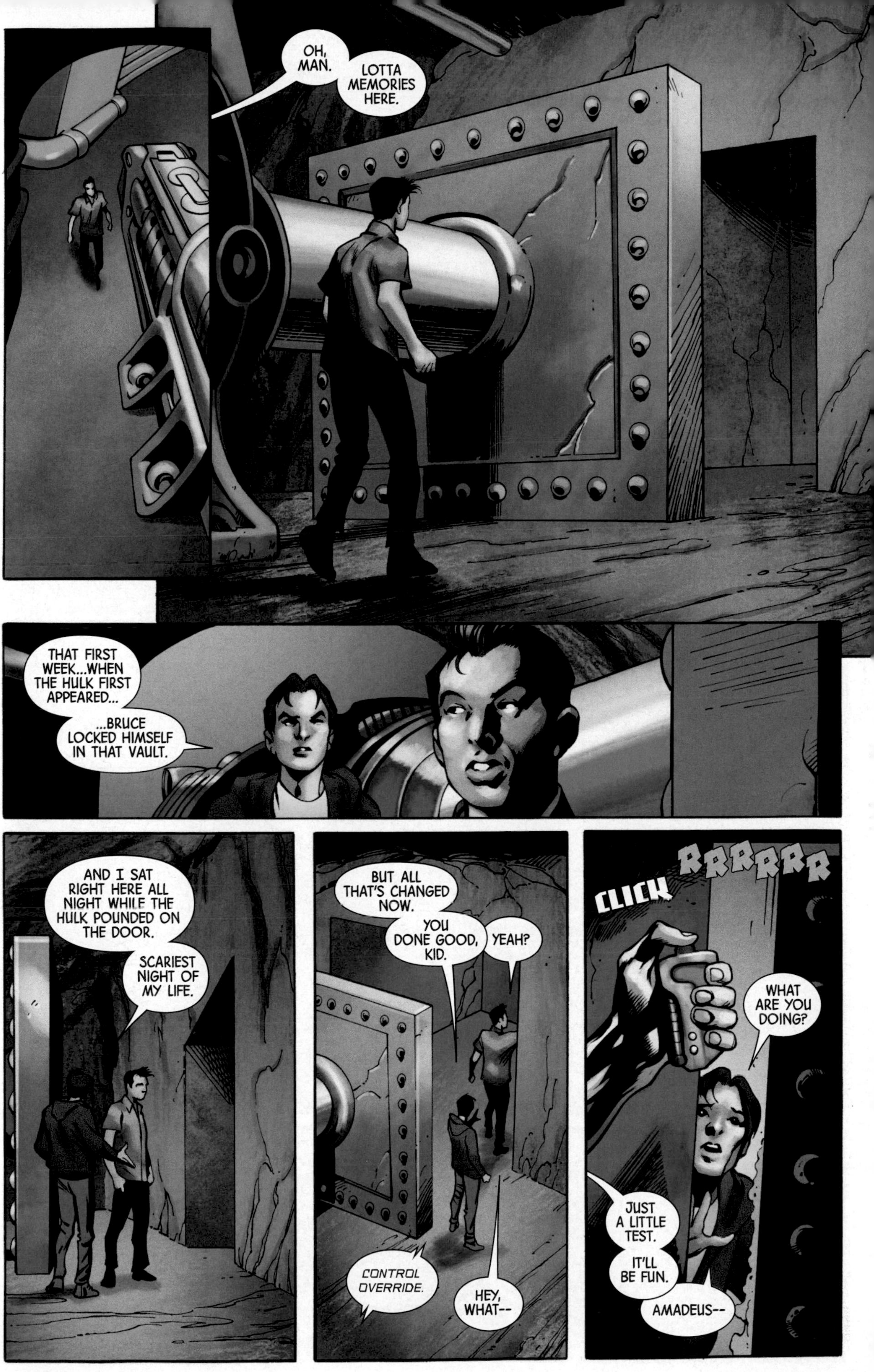
OH, MAN.
LOTTA MEMORIES HERE.
THAT FIRST WEEK...WHEN THE HULK FIRST APPEARED...
...BRUCE LOCKED HIMSELF IN THAT VAULT.
AND I SAT RIGHT HERE ALL NIGHT WHILE THE HULK POUNDED ON THE DOOR.
SCARIEST NIGHT OF MY LIFE.
BUT ALL THAT'S CHANGED NOW.
YOU DONE GOOD, KID.
YEAH?
CONTROL OVERRIDE.
HEY, WHAT--
CLICK
RRRRRRR
WHAT ARE YOU DOING?
JUST A LITTLE TEST.
IT'LL BE FUN.
AMADEUS--

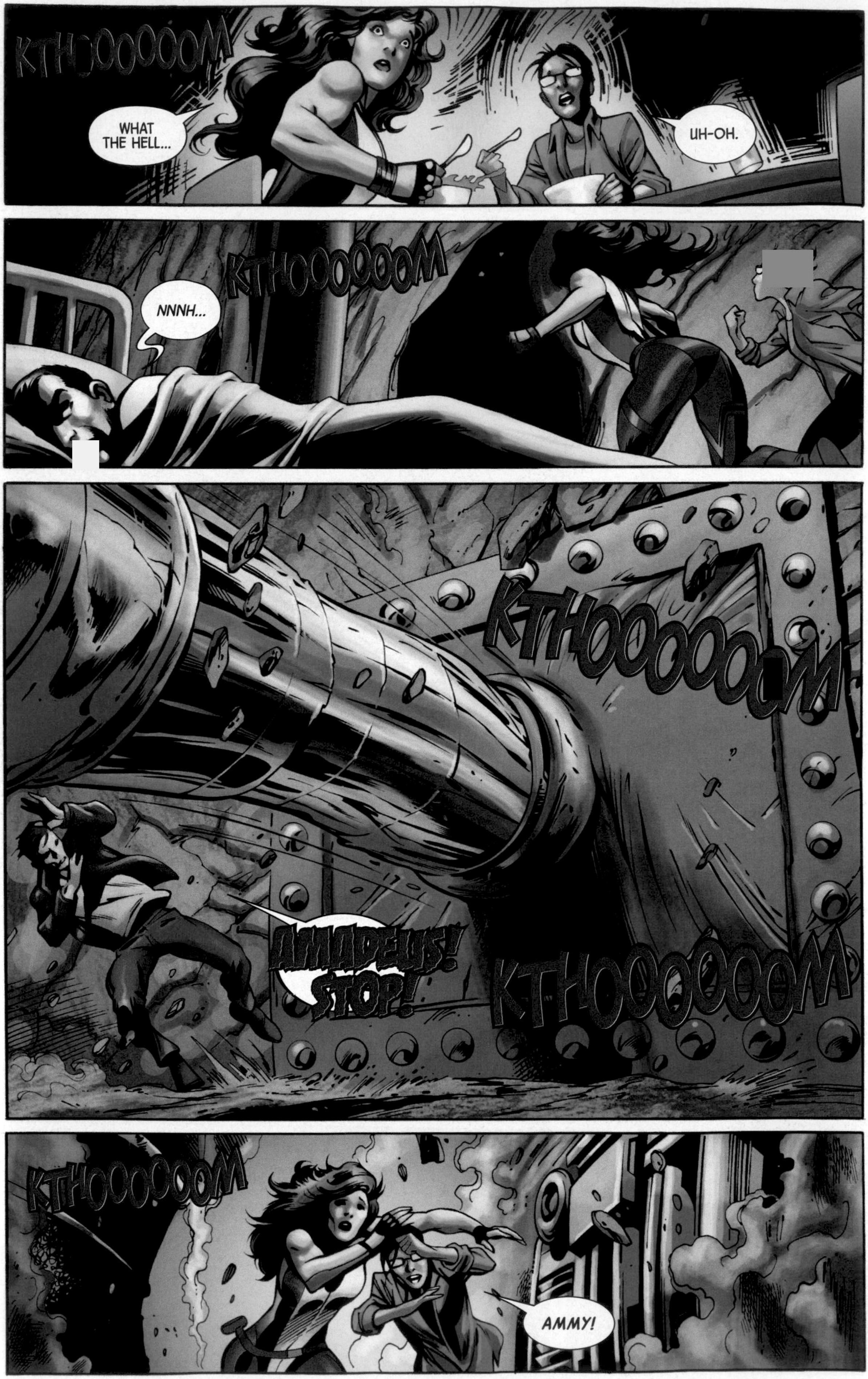
KTHOOOOOOM
WHAT THE HELL...
UH-OH.
KTHOOOOOOM
NNNH...
KTHOOOOOOOM
AMADEUS! STOP!
KTHOOOOOOM
KTHOOOOOOM
AMMY!

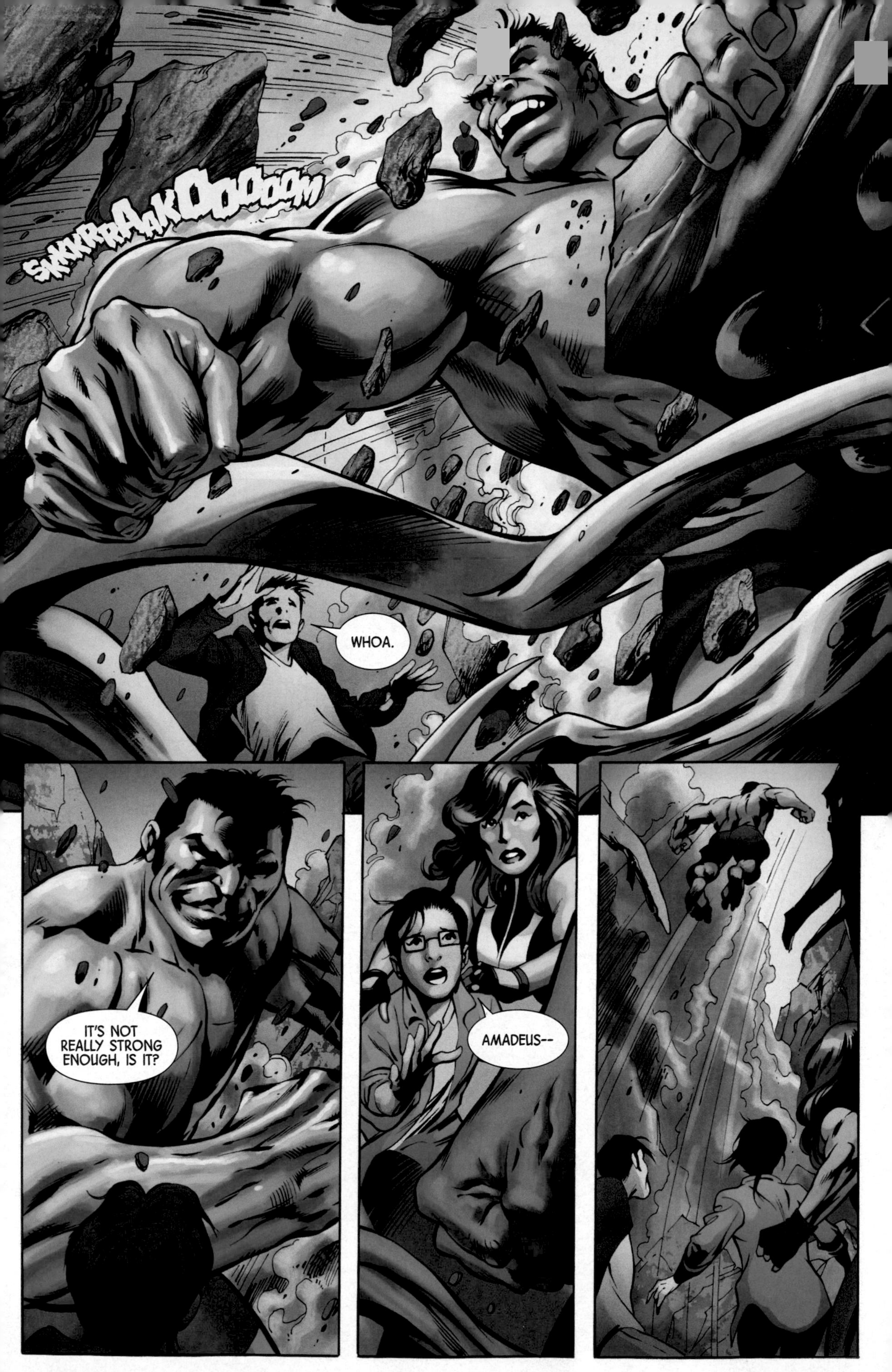
SKKRRAAKOOOOOM
WHOA.
IT'S NOT REALLY STRONG ENOUGH, IS IT?
AMADEUS--

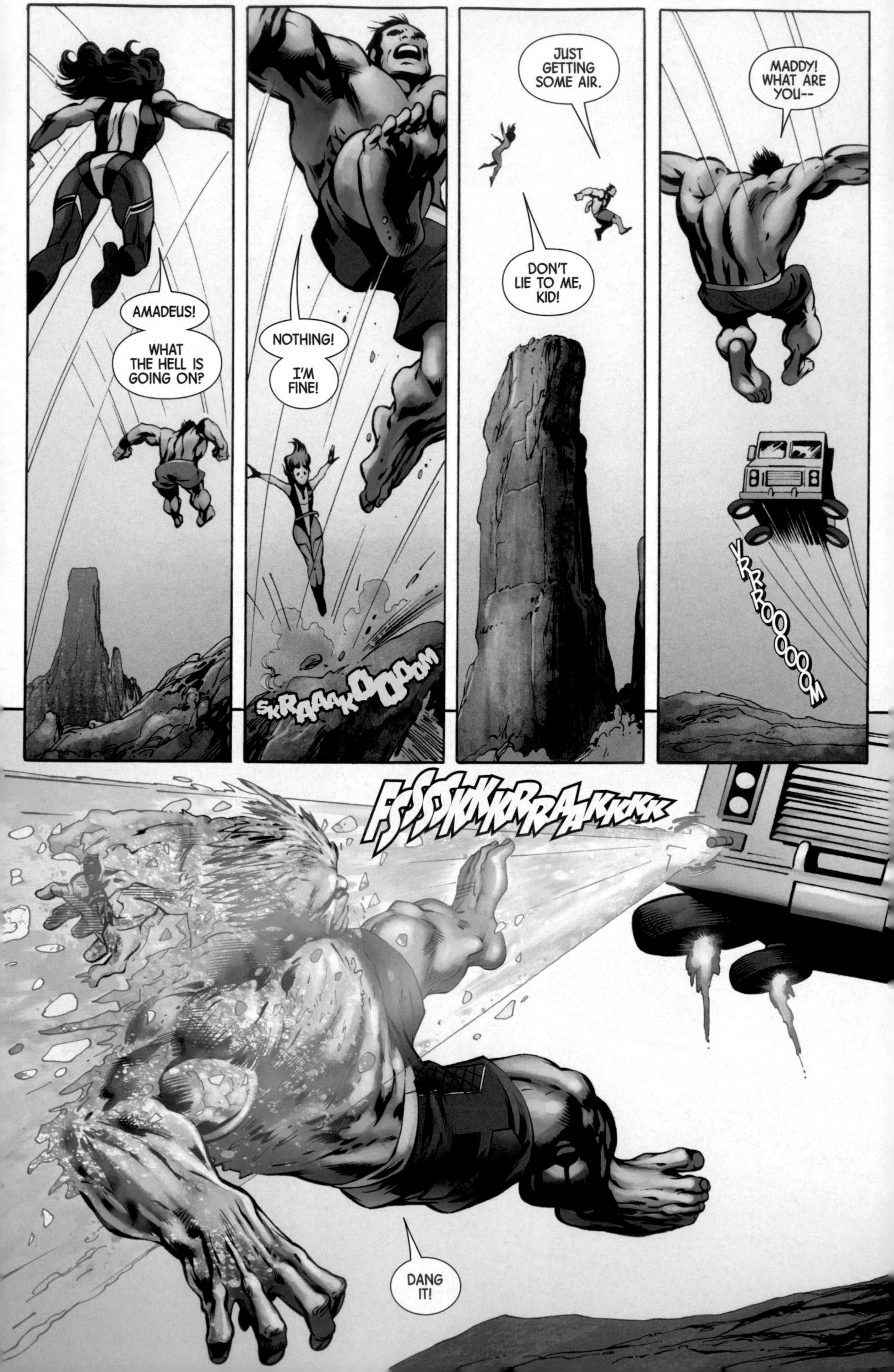
AMADEUS!
WHAT THE HELL IS GOING ON?
NOTHING!
I'M FINE!
SKRAAAKOOOOM
JUST GETTING SOME AIR.
DON'T LIE TO ME, KID!
MADDY! WHAT ARE YOU--
VRRROOOOOOM
FSSSKKKRRAKKKK
DANG IT!

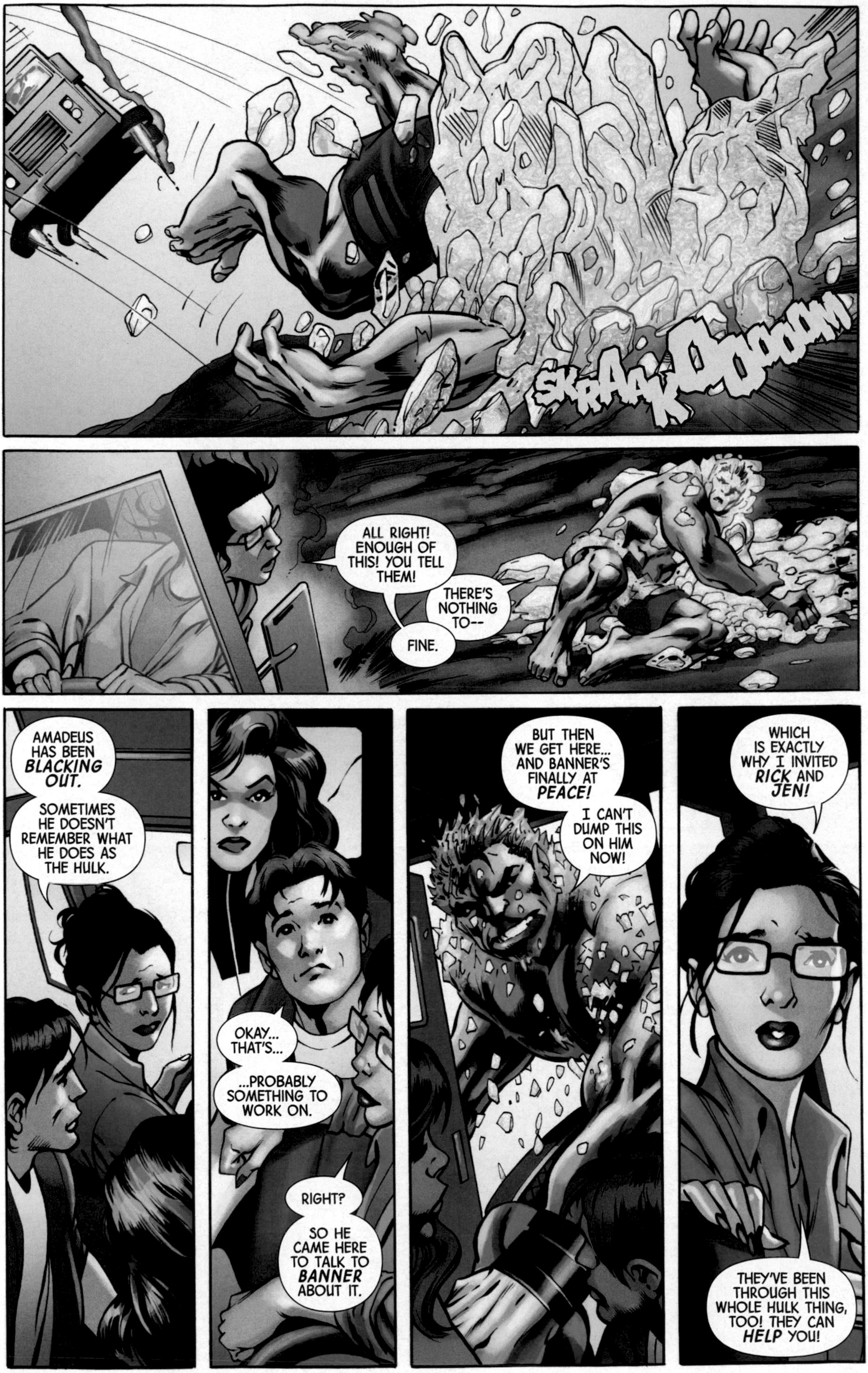
SKRAAKOOOOOOM
ALL RIGHT! ENOUGH OF THIS! YOU TELL THEM!
THERE'S NOTHING TO--
FINE.
AMADEUS HAS BEEN BLACKING OUT.
SOMETIMES HE DOESN'T REMEMBER WHAT HE DOES AS THE HULK.
OKAY... THAT'S...
...PROBABLY SOMETHING TO WORK ON.
RIGHT?
SO HE CAME HERE TO TALK TO BANNER ABOUT IT.
BUT THEN WE GET HERE... AND BANNER'S FINALLY AT PEACE!
I CAN'T DUMP THIS ON HIM NOW!
WHICH IS EXACTLY WHY I INVITED RICK AND JEN!
THEY'VE BEEN THROUGH THIS WHOLE HULK THING, TOO! THEY CAN HELP YOU!

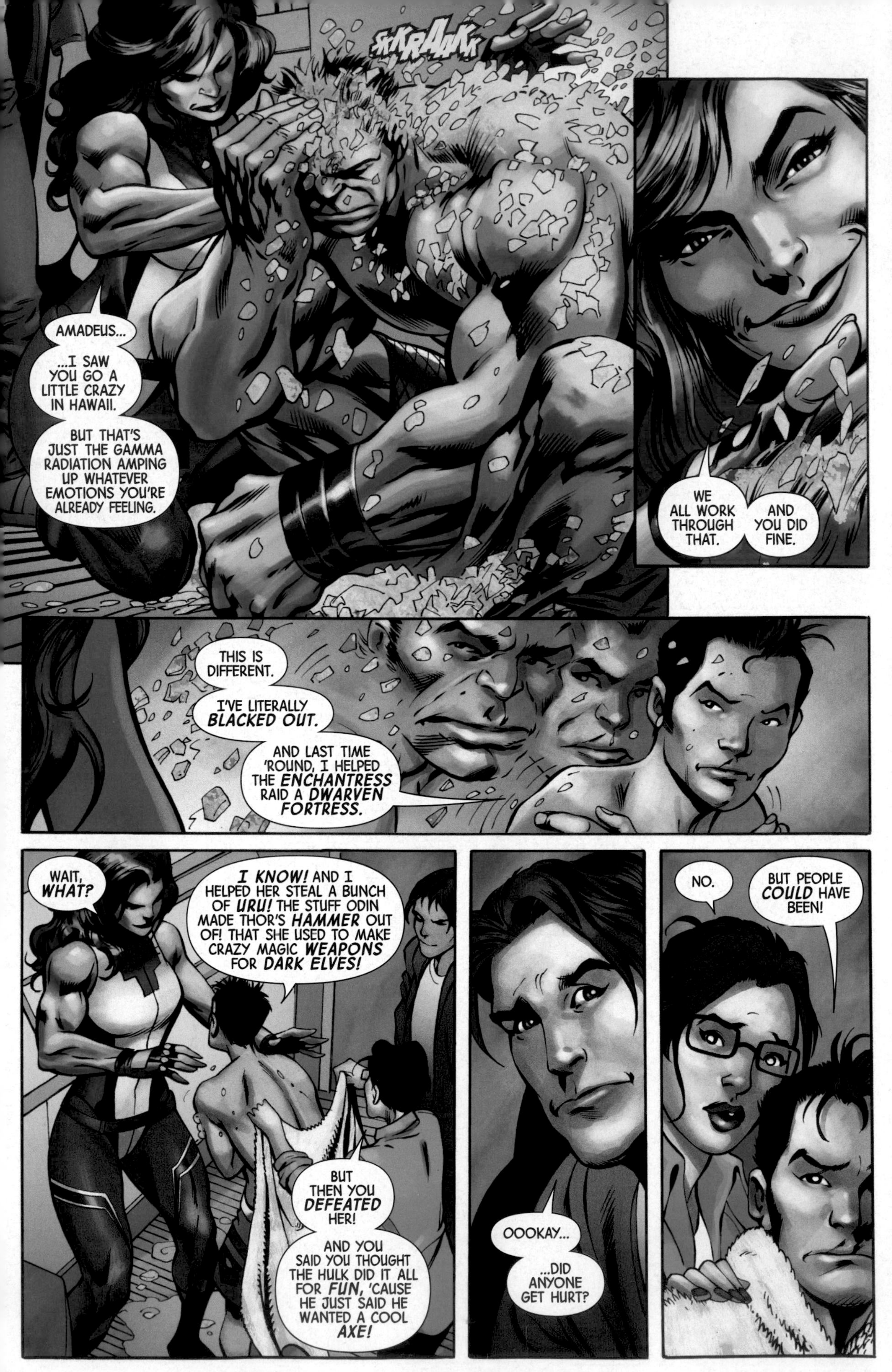
SKKRAAKK
AMADEUS...
...I SAW YOU GO A LITTLE CRAZY IN HAWAII.
BUT THAT'S JUST THE GAMMA RADIATION AMPING UP WHATEVER EMOTIONS YOU'RE ALREADY FEELING.
WE ALL WORK THROUGH THAT.
AND YOU DID FINE.
THIS IS DIFFERENT.
I'VE LITERALLY BLACKED OUT.
AND LAST TIME 'ROUND, I HELPED THE ENCHANTRESS RAID A DWARVEN FORTRESS.
WAIT, WHAT?
I KNOW! AND I HELPED HER STEAL A BUNCH OF URU! THE STUFF ODIN MADE THOR'S HAMMER OUT OF! THAT SHE USED TO MAKE CRAZY MAGIC WEAPONS FOR DARK ELVES!
BUT THEN YOU DEFEATED HER!
AND YOU SAID YOU THOUGHT THE HULK DID IT ALL FOR FUN, 'CAUSE HE JUST SAID HE WANTED A COOL AXE!
OOOKAY...
...DID ANYONE GET HURT?
NO.
BUT PEOPLE COULD HAVE BEEN!

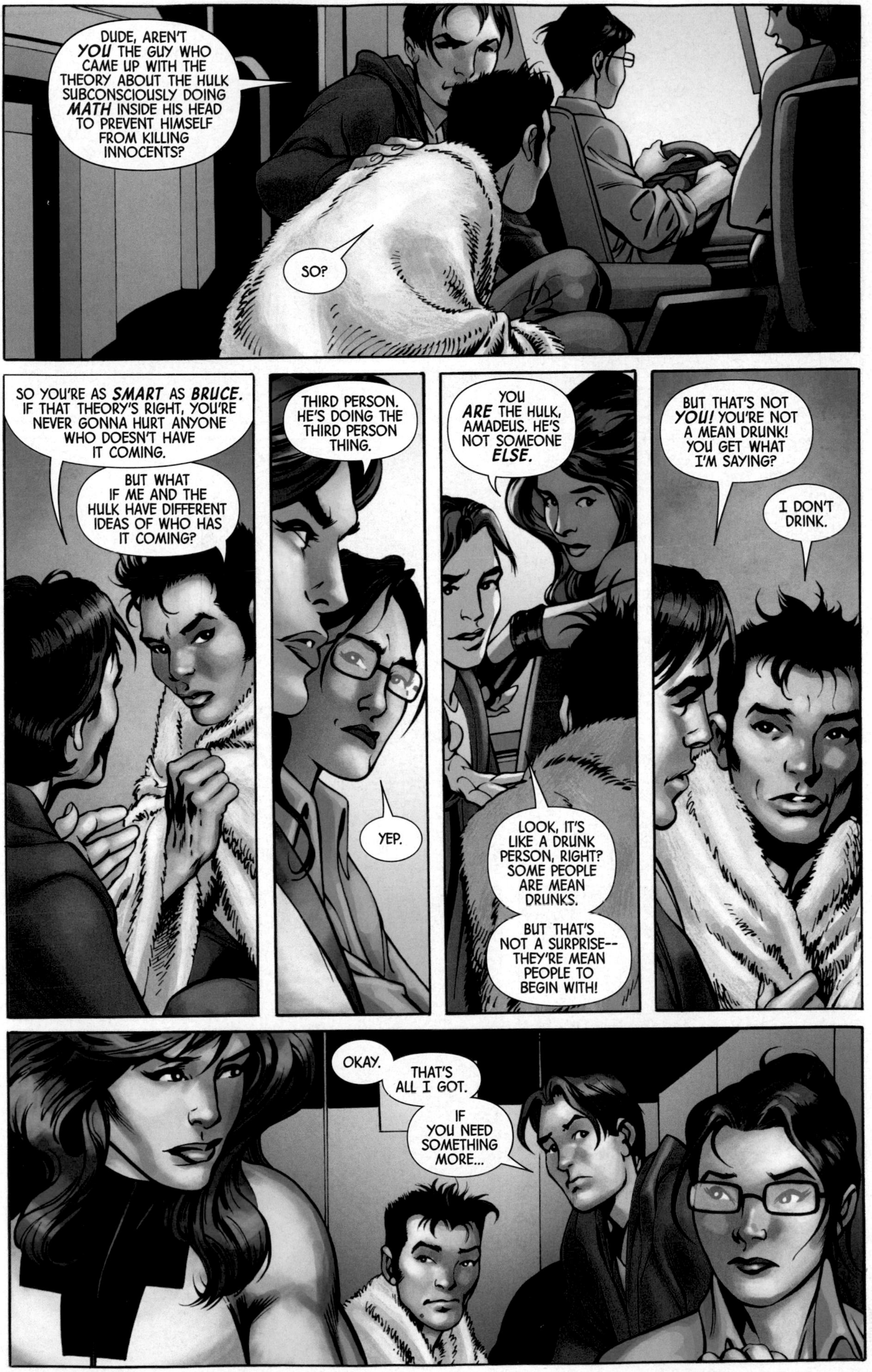
DUDE, AREN'T YOU THE GUY WHO CAME UP WITH THE THEORY ABOUT THE HULK SUBCONSCIOUSLY DOING MATH INSIDE HIS HEAD TO PREVENT HIMSELF FROM KILLING INNOCENTS?
SO?
SO YOU'RE AS SMART AS BRUCE. IF THAT THEORY'S RIGHT, YOU'RE NEVER GONNA HURT ANYONE WHO DOESN'T HAVE IT COMING.
BUT WHAT IF ME AND THE HULK HAVE DIFFERENT IDEAS OF WHO HAS IT COMING?
THIRD PERSON. HE'S DOING THE THIRD PERSON THING.
YEP.
YOU ARE THE HULK, AMADEUS. HE'S NOT SOMEONE ELSE.
LOOK, IT'S LIKE A DRUNK PERSON, RIGHT? SOME PEOPLE ARE MEAN DRUNKS.
BUT THAT'S NOT A SURPRISE-- THEY'RE MEAN PEOPLE TO BEGIN WITH!
BUT THAT'S NOT YOU! YOU'RE NOT A MEAN DRUNK! YOU GET WHAT I'M SAYING?
I DON'T DRINK.
OKAY.
THAT'S ALL I GOT.
IF YOU NEED SOMETHING MORE...

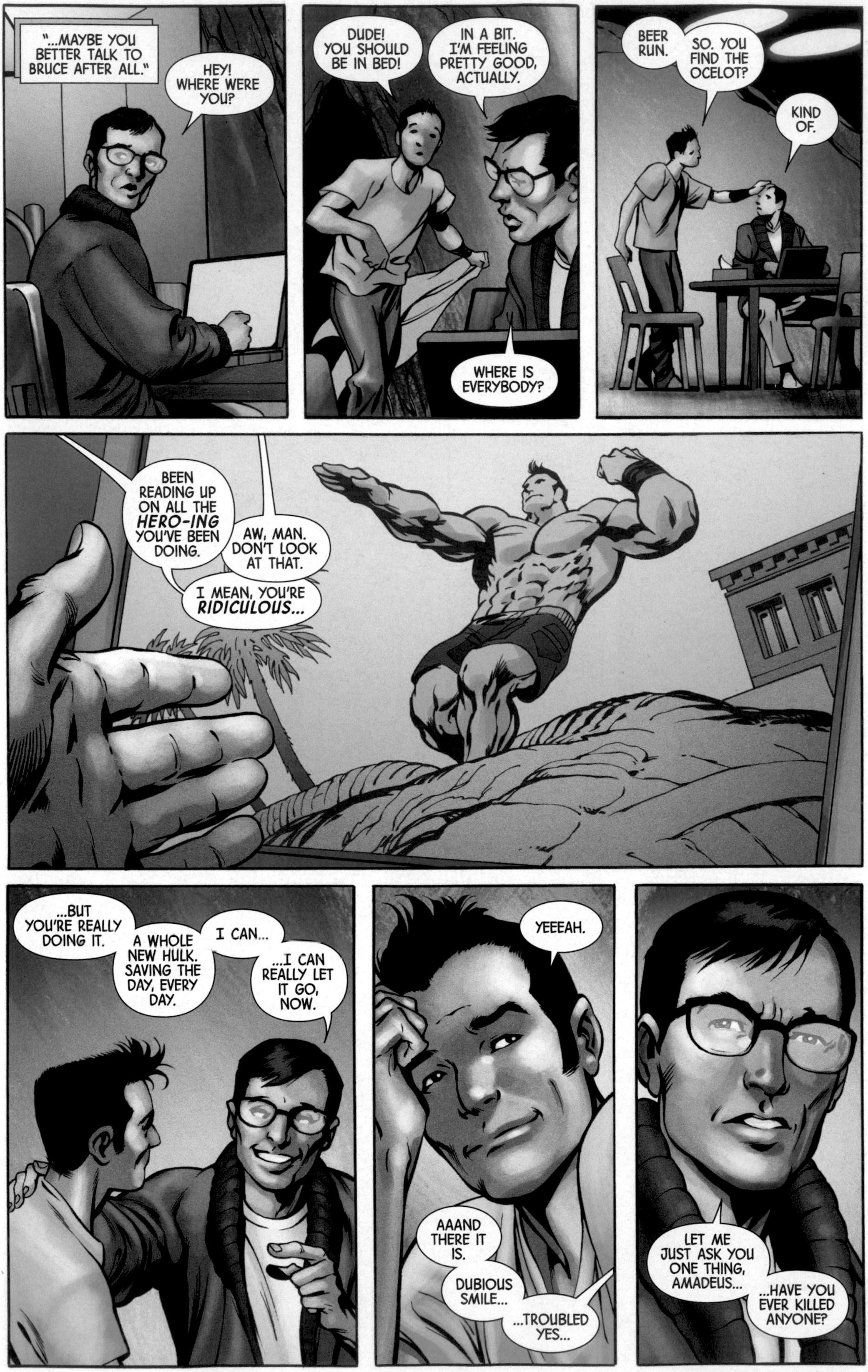
"...MAYBE YOU BETTER TALK TO BRUCE AFTER ALL."
HEY! WHERE WERE YOU?
DUDE! YOU SHOULD BE IN BED!
IN A BIT. I'M FEELING PRETTY GOOD, ACTUALLY.
WHERE IS EVERYBODY?
BEER RUN.
SO. YOU FIND THE OCELOT?
KIND OF.
BEEN READING UP ON ALL THE HERO-ING YOU'VE BEEN DOING.
AW, MAN. DON'T LOOK AT THAT.
I MEAN, YOU'RE RIDICULOUS...
...BUT YOU'RE REALLY DOING IT.
A WHOLE NEW HULK. SAVING THE DAY, EVERY DAY.
I CAN...
...I CAN REALLY LET IT GO, NOW.
YEEEAH.
AAAND THERE IT IS.
DUBIOUS SMILE...
...TROUBLED YES...
LET ME JUST ASK YOU ONE THING, AMADEUS...
...HAVE YOU EVER KILLED ANYONE?

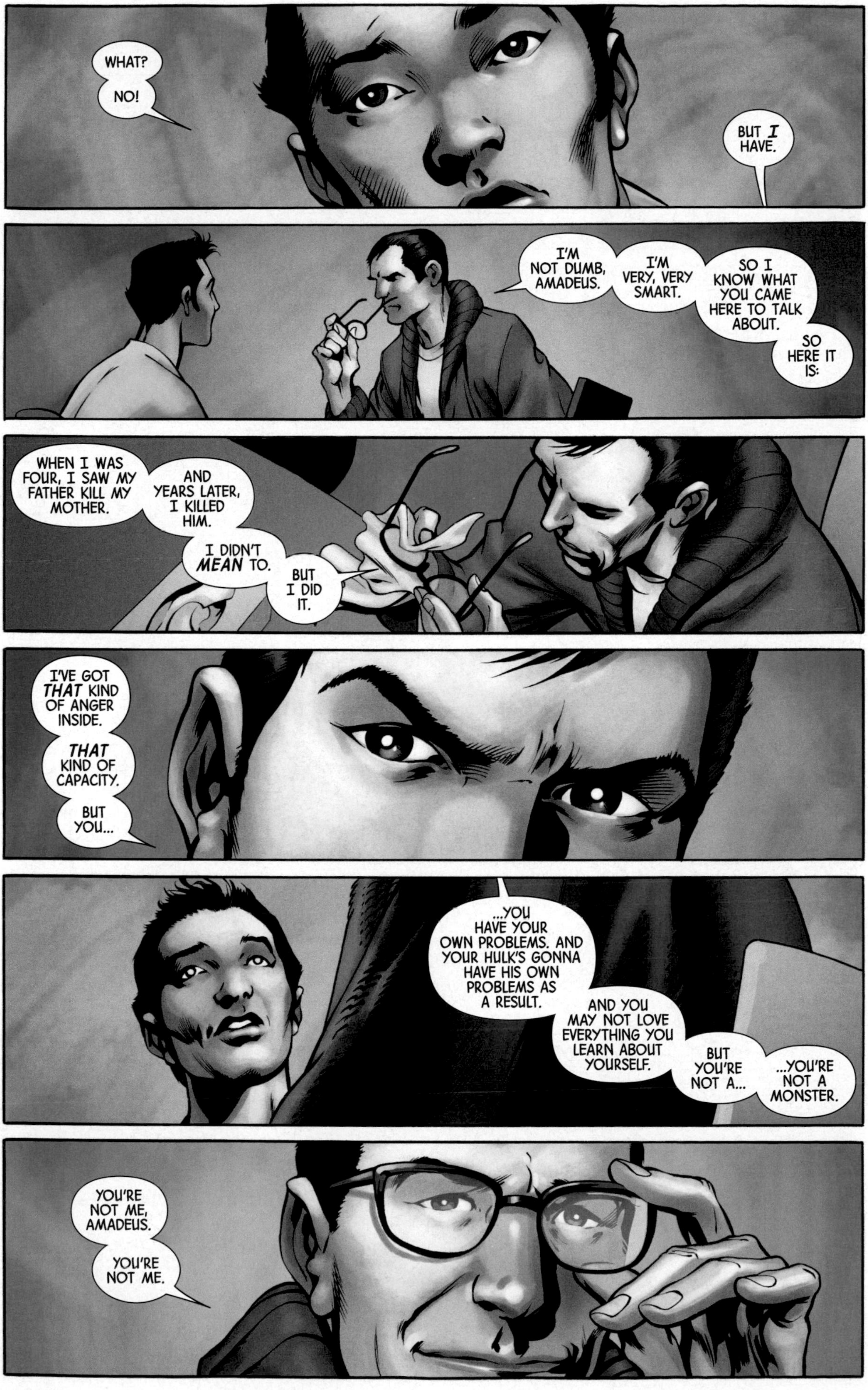
WHAT?
NO!
BUT I HAVE.
I'M NOT DUMB, AMADEUS.
I'M VERY, VERY SMART.
SO I KNOW WHAT YOU CAME HERE TO TALK ABOUT.
SO HERE IT IS:
WHEN I WAS FOUR, I SAW MY FATHER KILL MY MOTHER.
AND YEARS LATER, I KILLED HIM.
I DIDN'T MEAN TO.
BUT I DID IT.
I'VE GOT THAT KIND OF ANGER INSIDE.
THAT KIND OF CAPACITY.
BUT YOU...
...YOU HAVE YOUR OWN PROBLEMS. AND YOUR HULK'S GONNA HAVE HIS OWN PROBLEMS AS A RESULT.
AND YOU MAY NOT LOVE EVERYTHING YOU LEARN ABOUT YOURSELF.
BUT YOU'RE NOT A...
...YOU'RE NOT A MONSTER.
YOU'RE NOT ME, AMADEUS.
YOU'RE NOT ME.

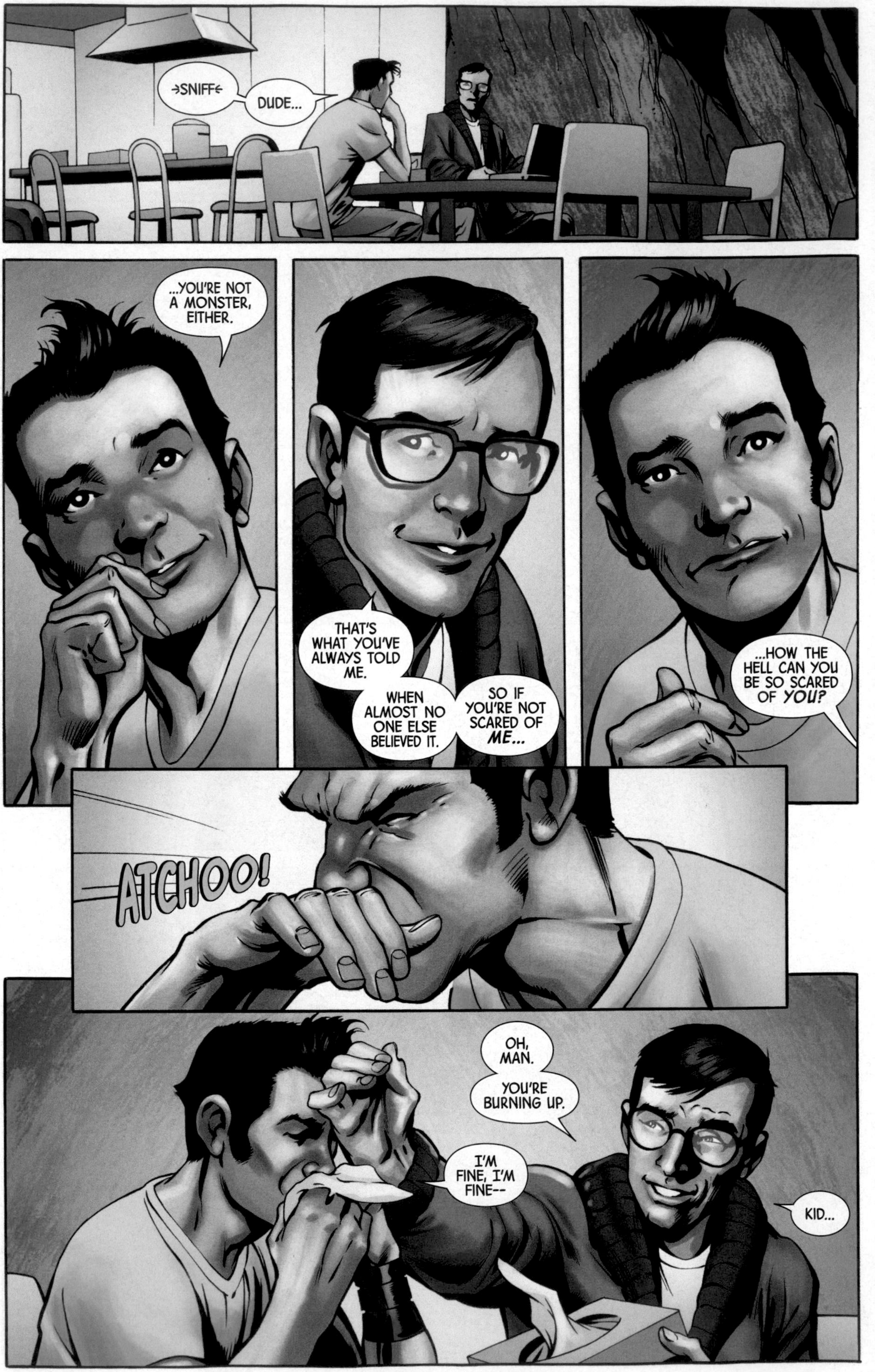

>SNIFF<
DUDE...
...YOU'RE NOT A MONSTER, EITHER.
THAT'S WHAT YOU'VE ALWAYS TOLD ME.
WHEN ALMOST NO ONE ELSE BELIEVED IT.
SO IF YOU'RE NOT SCARED OF ME...
...HOW THE HELL CAN YOU BE SO SCARED OF YOU?
ATCHOO!
OH, MAN.
YOU'RE BURNING UP.
I'M FINE, I'M FINE--
KID...

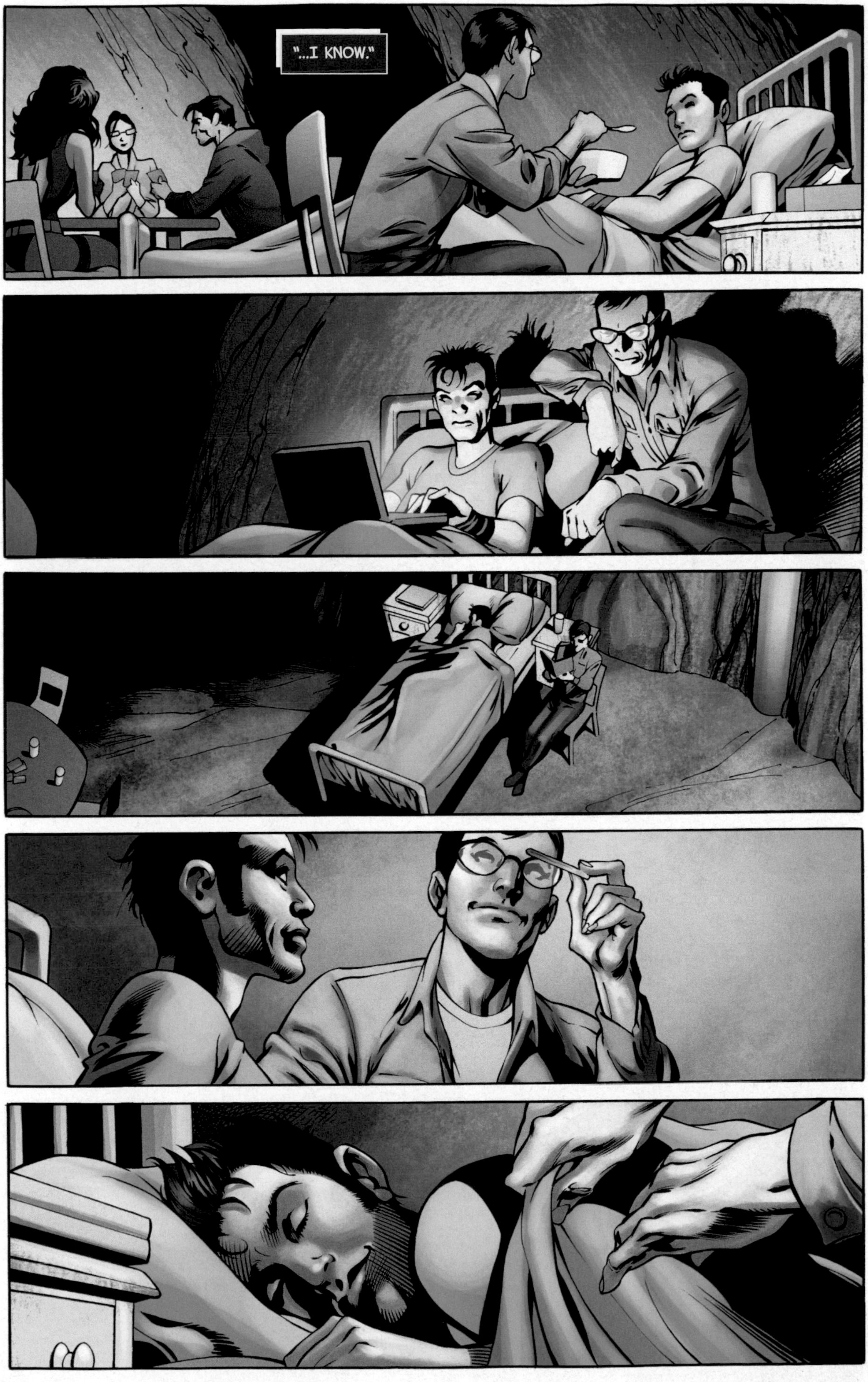
"...I KNOW."

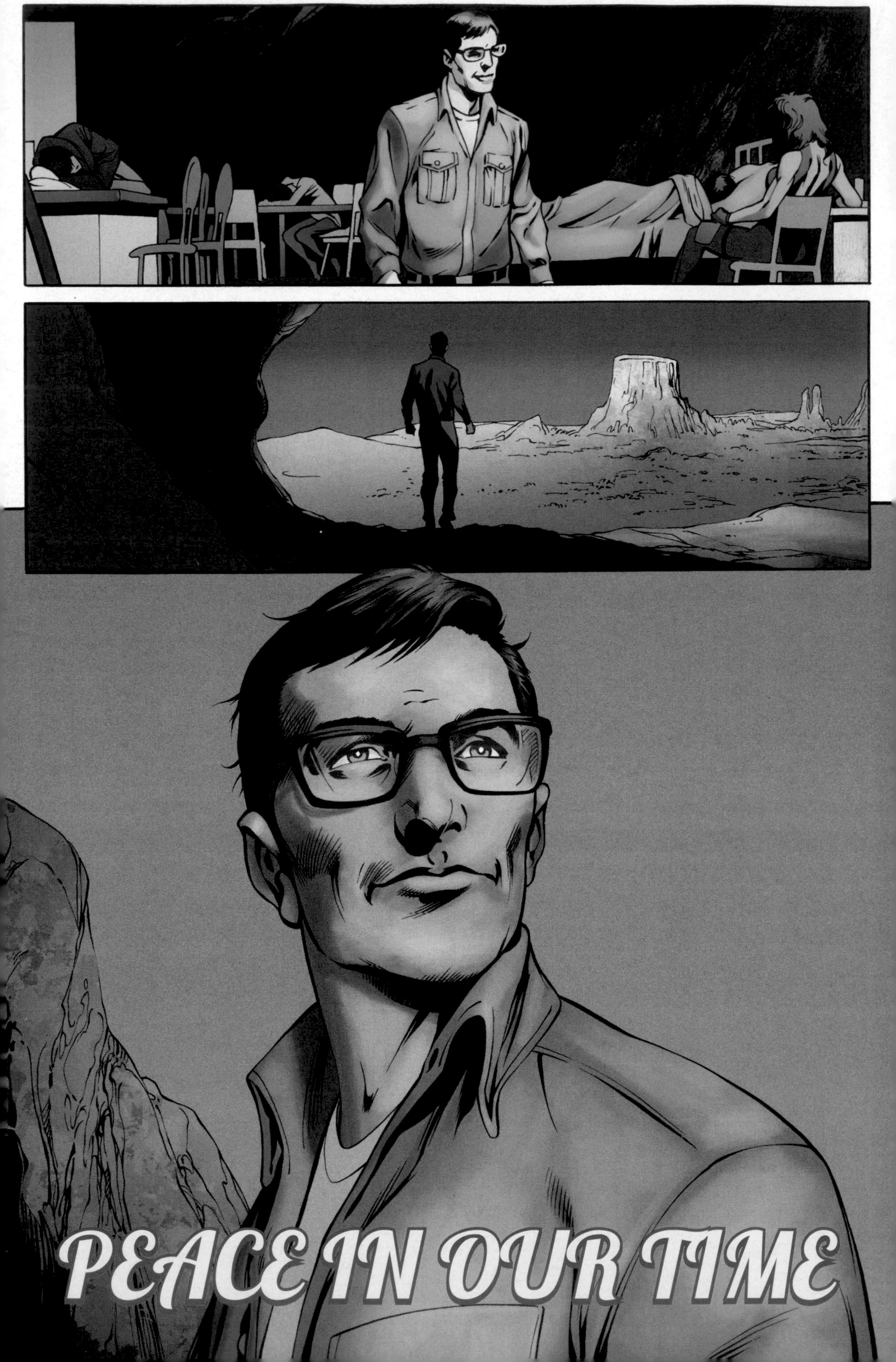
PEACE IN OUR TIME

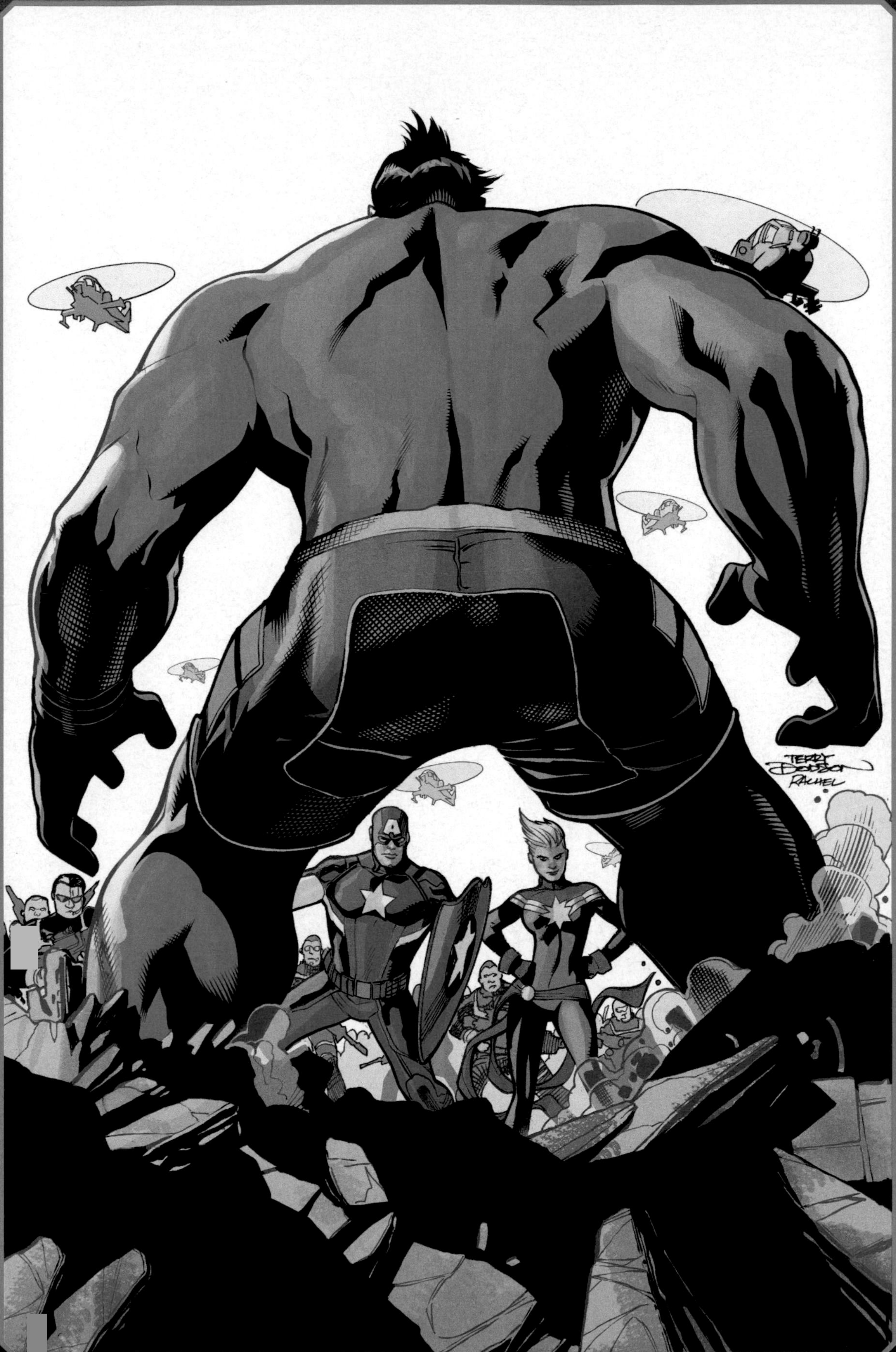
TERRY DODSON
RACHEL

CIVIL WAR II

THE TOTALLY AWESOME HULK

SUPER-GENIUS TEENAGER AMADEUS CHO CURED BRUCE BANNER AND TOOK ON
THE MANTLE OF THE HULK.

IN NEW YORK, AN INHUMAN NAMED ULYSSES HAS BEEN USING HIS PREDICTIVE
POWERS TO AID EARTH'S HEROES IN IDENTIFYING LIKELY DISASTERS AND
AVERTING THEM BEFORE THEY CAN OCCUR.

RECENTLY, ULYSSES HAD A VISION OF NUMEROUS CASUALTIES AND WANTON
DESTRUCTION CAUSED BY THE BRUCE BANNER-HULK. IN RESPONSE, CLINT
BARTON, A.K.A. HAWKEYE, HAS EXECUTED BANNER.

AMADEUS HAS JUST HEARD THE NEWS.

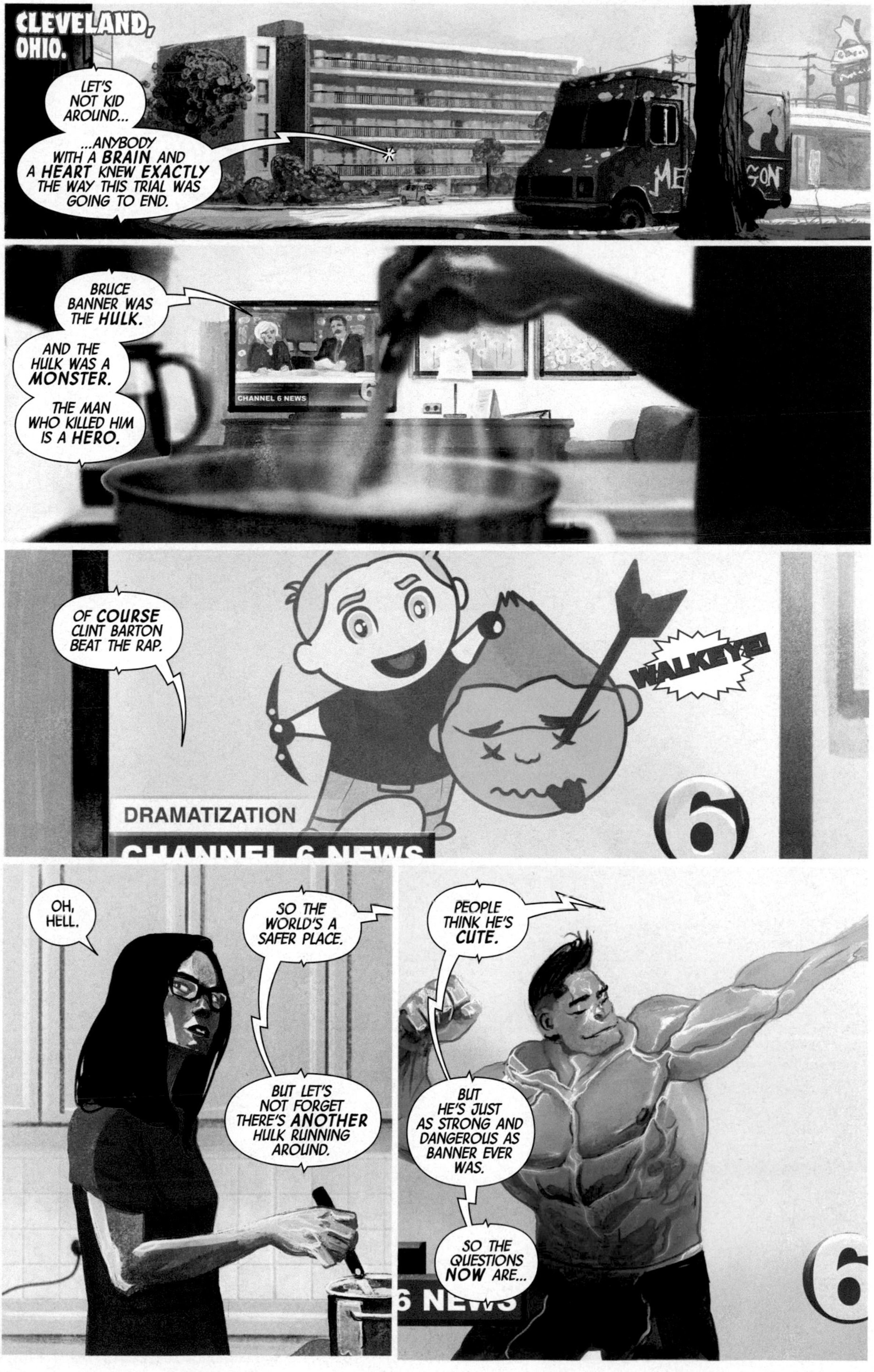
CLEVELAND, OHIO.
LET'S NOT KID AROUND...
...ANYBODY WITH A BRAIN AND A HEART KNEW EXACTLY THE WAY THIS TRIAL WAS GOING TO END.
BRUCE BANNER WAS THE HULK.
AND THE HULK WAS A MONSTER.
THE MAN WHO KILLED HIM IS A HERO.
CHANNEL 6 NEWS
OF COURSE CLINT BARTON BEAT THE RAP.
WALKEYE!
DRAMATIZATION
CHANNEL 6 NEWS
OH, HELL.
SO THE WORLD'S A SAFER PLACE.
BUT LET'S NOT FORGET THERE'S ANOTHER HULK RUNNING AROUND.
PEOPLE THINK HE'S CUTE.
BUT HE'S JUST AS STRONG AND DANGEROUS AS BANNER EVER WAS.
SO THE QUESTIONS NOW ARE...
6 NEWS

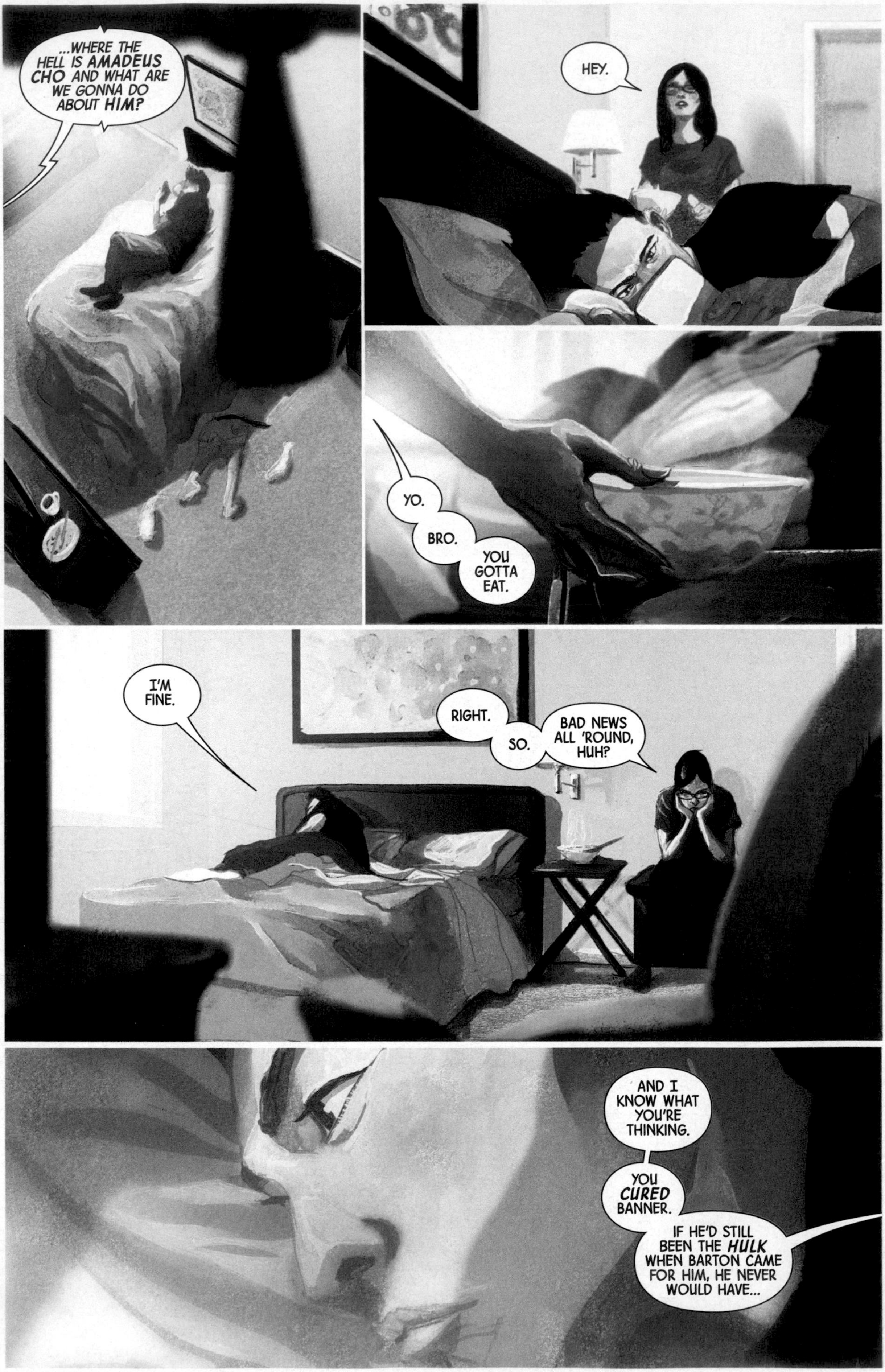
...WHERE THE HELL IS AMADEUS CHO AND WHAT ARE WE GONNA DO ABOUT HIM?
HEY.
YO.
BRO.
YOU GOTTA EAT.
I'M FINE.
RIGHT.
SO.
BAD NEWS ALL 'ROUND, HUH?
AND I KNOW WHAT YOU'RE THINKING.
YOU CURED BANNER.
IF HE'D STILL BEEN THE HULK WHEN BARTON CAME FOR HIM, HE NEVER WOULD HAVE...

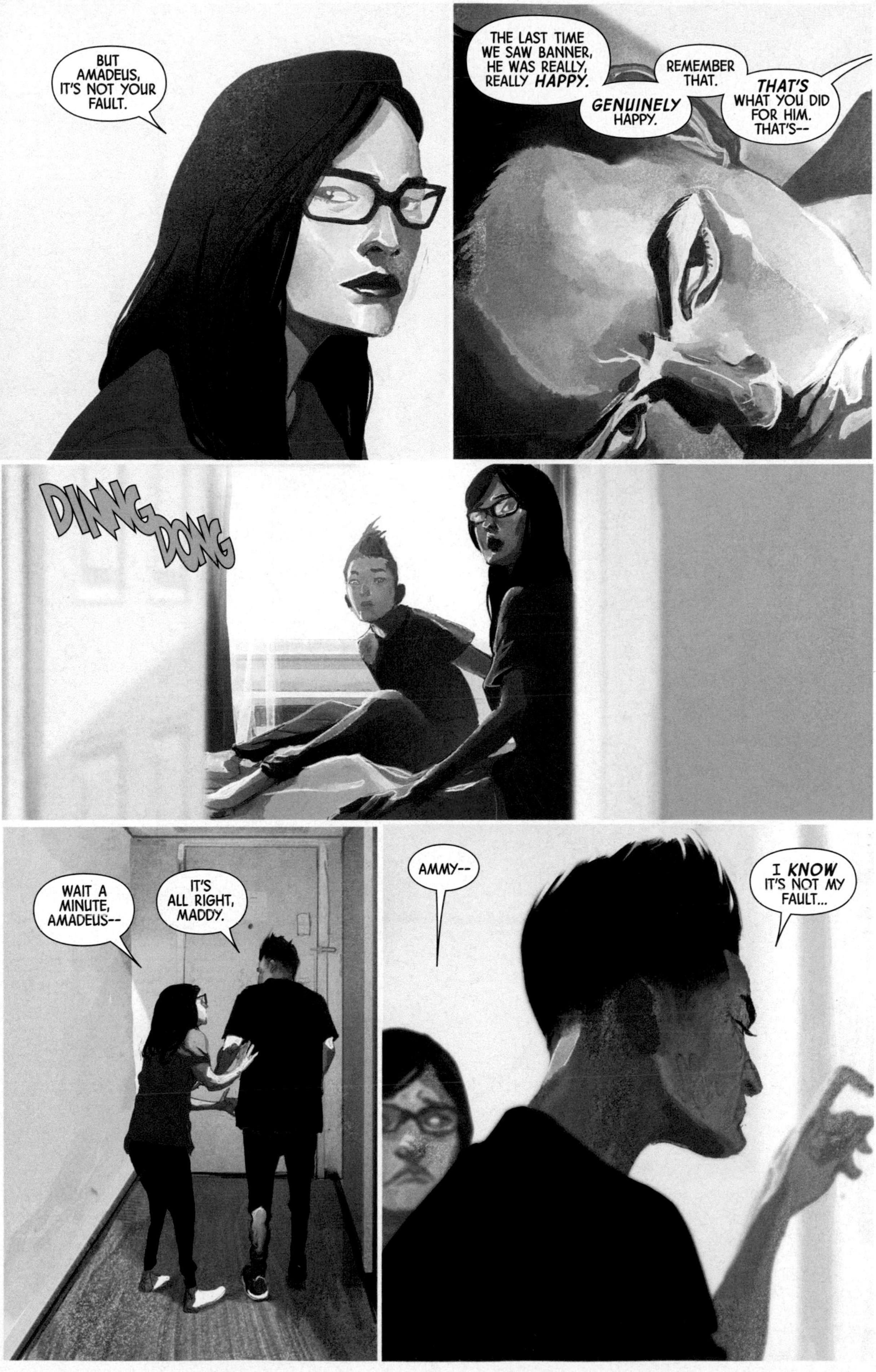
BUT AMADEUS, IT'S NOT YOUR FAULT.
THE LAST TIME WE SAW BANNER, HE WAS REALLY, REALLY HAPPY.
GENUINELY HAPPY.
REMEMBER THAT.
THAT'S WHAT YOU DID FOR HIM. THAT'S--
DING DONG
WAIT A MINUTE, AMADEUS--
IT'S ALL RIGHT, MADDY.
AMMY--
I KNOW IT'S NOT MY FAULT...

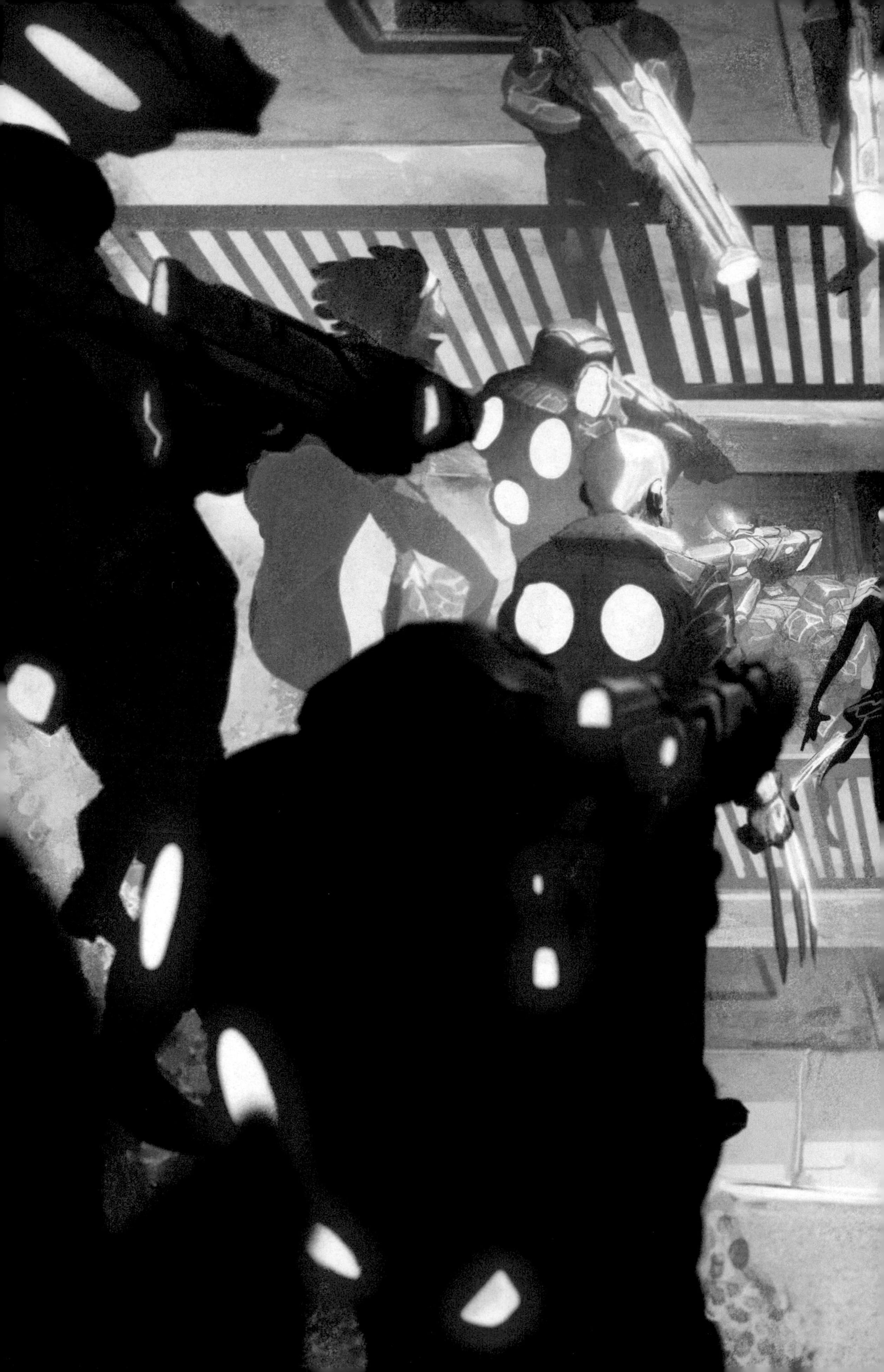

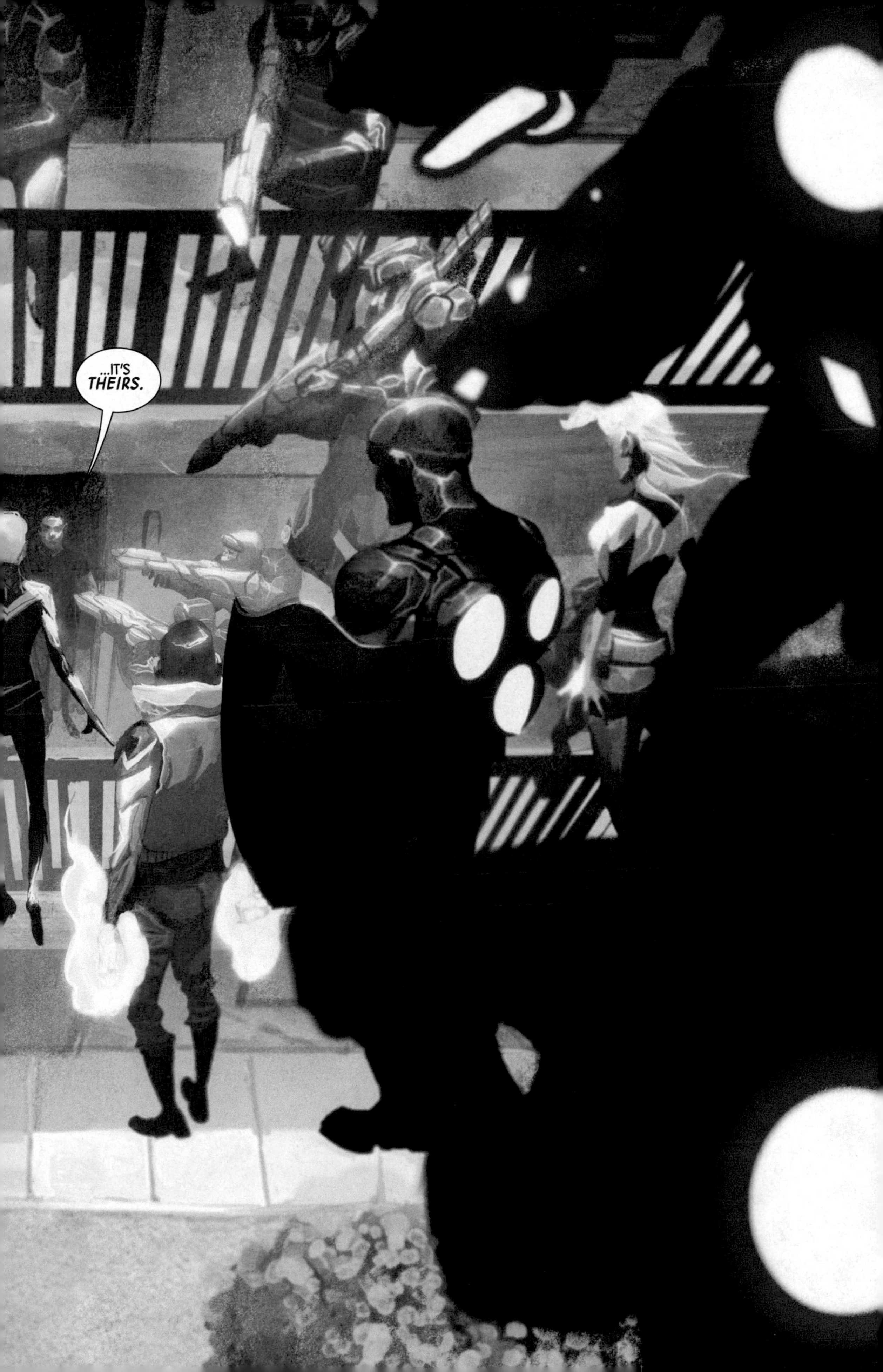
...IT'S THEIRS.

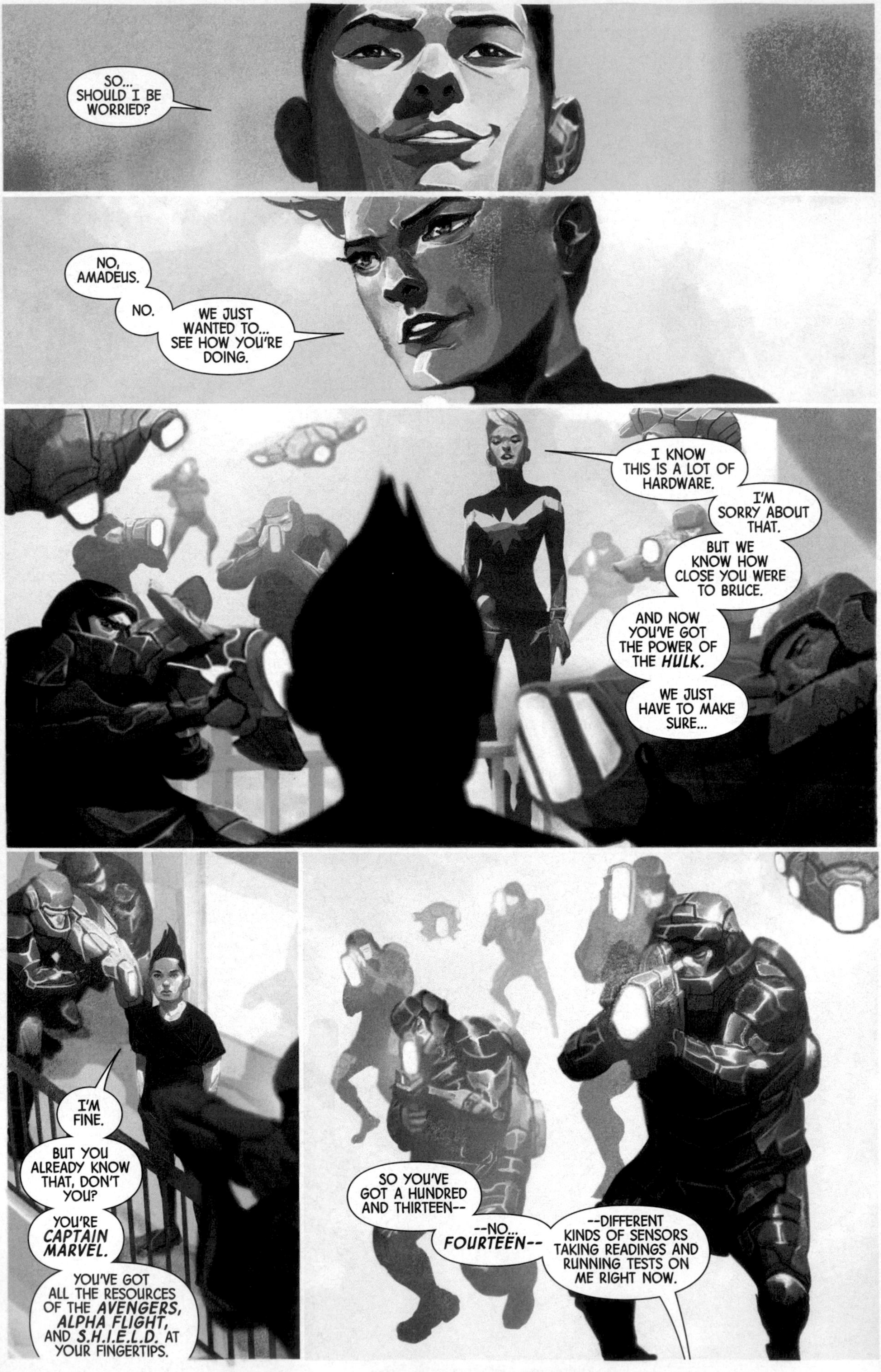
SO... SHOULD I BE WORRIED?
NO, AMADEUS.
NO.
WE JUST WANTED TO... SEE HOW YOU'RE DOING.
I KNOW THIS IS A LOT OF HARDWARE.
I'M SORRY ABOUT THAT.
BUT WE KNOW HOW CLOSE YOU WERE TO BRUCE.
AND NOW YOU'VE GOT THE POWER OF THE *HULK.*
WE JUST HAVE TO MAKE SURE...
I'M FINE.
BUT YOU ALREADY KNOW THAT, DON'T YOU?
YOU'RE *CAPTAIN MARVEL.*
YOU'VE GOT ALL THE RESOURCES OF THE *AVENGERS, ALPHA FLIGHT,* AND *S.H.I.E.L.D.* AT YOUR FINGERTIPS.
SO YOU'VE GOT A HUNDRED AND THIRTEEN--
--NO... *FOURTEEN*--
--DIFFERENT KINDS OF SENSORS TAKING READINGS AND RUNNING TESTS ON ME RIGHT NOW.

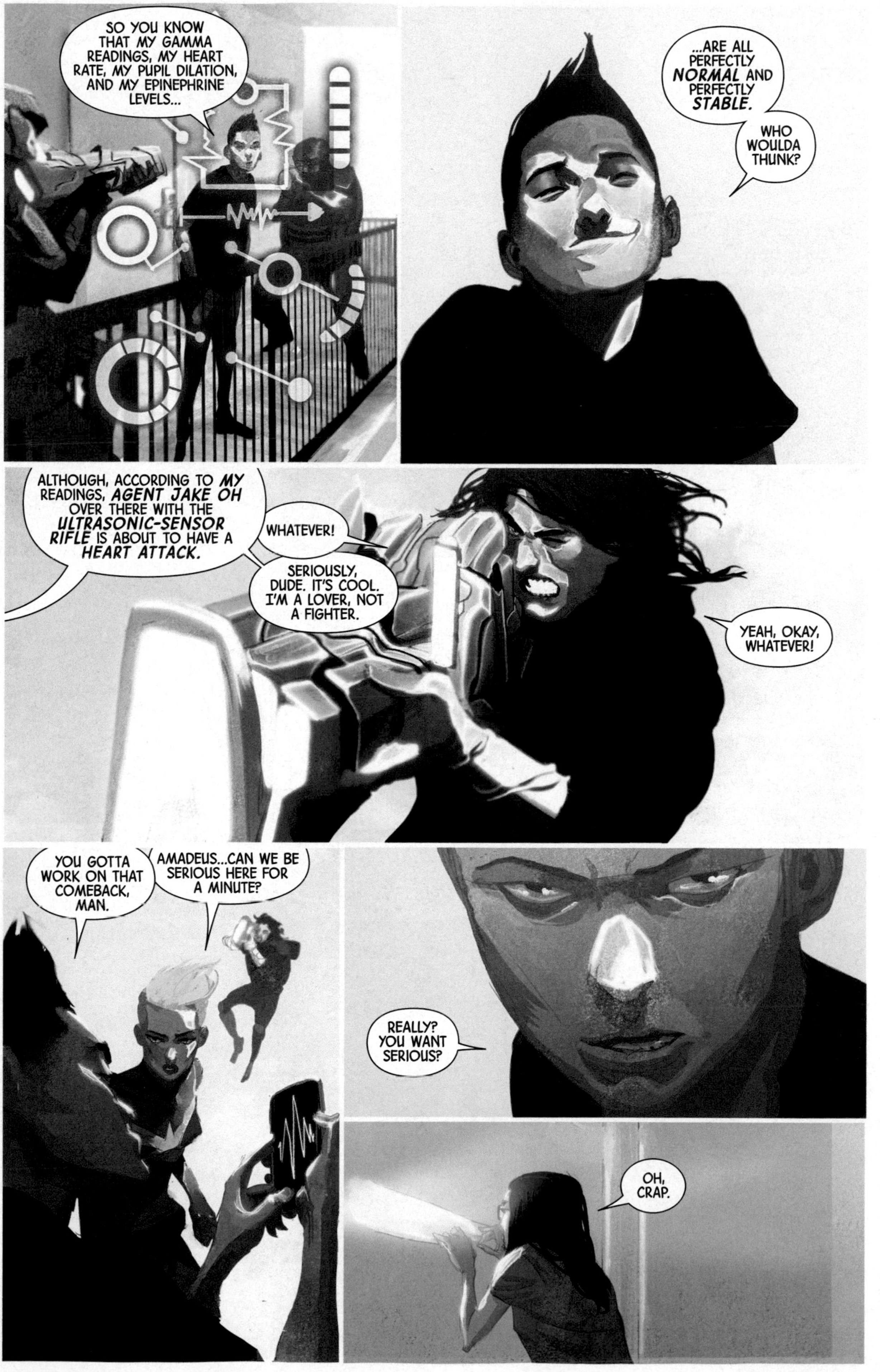
SO YOU KNOW THAT MY GAMMA READINGS, MY HEART RATE, MY PUPIL DILATION, AND MY EPINEPHRINE LEVELS...
...ARE ALL PERFECTLY NORMAL AND PERFECTLY STABLE.
WHO WOULDA THUNK?
ALTHOUGH, ACCORDING TO MY READINGS, AGENT JAKE OH OVER THERE WITH THE ULTRASONIC-SENSOR RIFLE IS ABOUT TO HAVE A HEART ATTACK.
WHATEVER!
SERIOUSLY, DUDE. IT'S COOL. I'M A LOVER, NOT A FIGHTER.
YEAH, OKAY, WHATEVER!
YOU GOTTA WORK ON THAT COMEBACK, MAN.
AMADEUS...CAN WE BE SERIOUS HERE FOR A MINUTE?
REALLY? YOU WANT SERIOUS?
OH, CRAP.

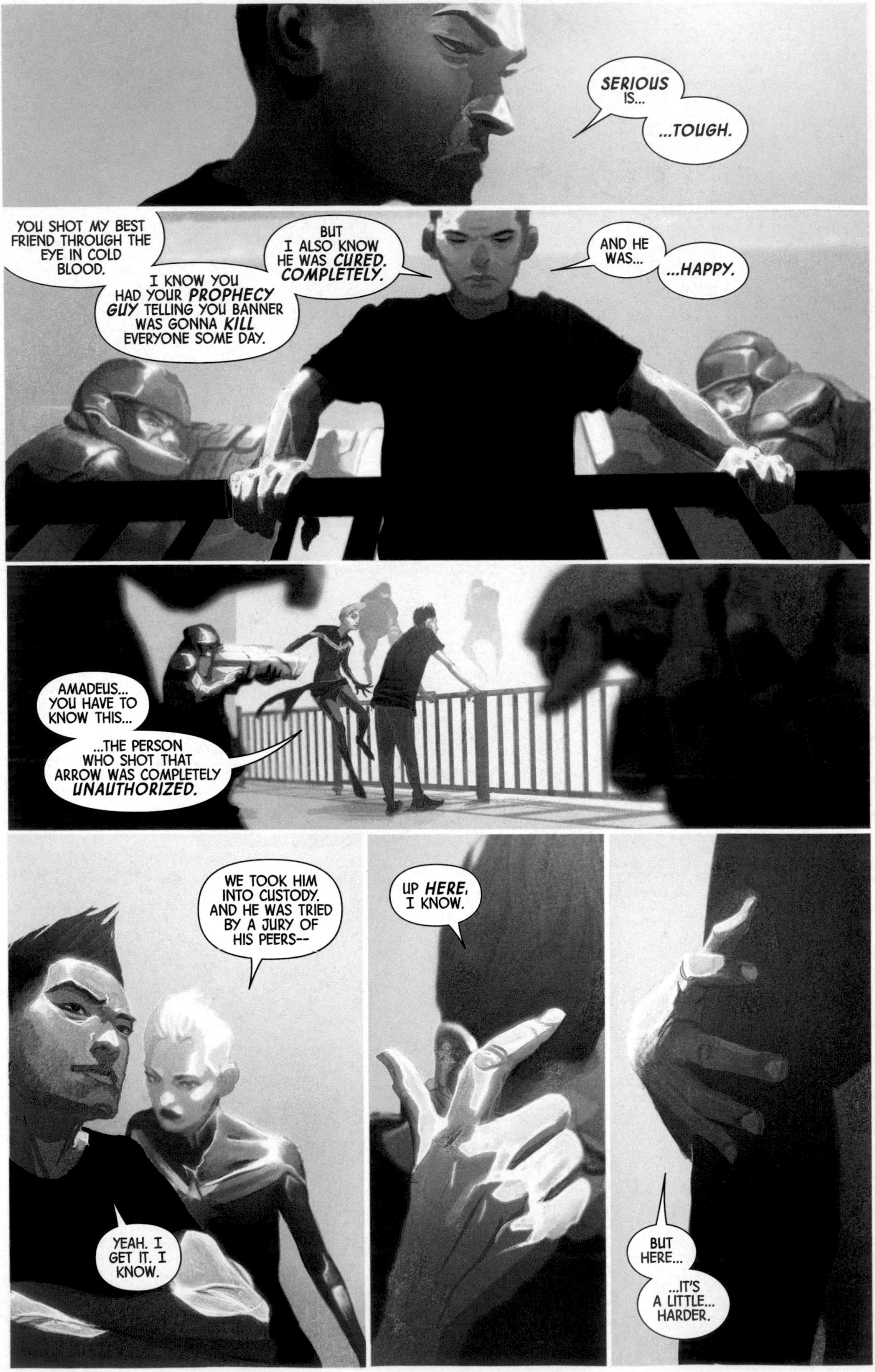
SERIOUS IS...
...TOUGH.
YOU SHOT MY BEST FRIEND THROUGH THE EYE IN COLD BLOOD.
I KNOW YOU HAD YOUR PROPHECY GUY TELLING YOU BANNER WAS GONNA KILL EVERYONE SOME DAY.
BUT I ALSO KNOW HE WAS CURED. COMPLETELY.
AND HE WAS...
...HAPPY.
AMADEUS... YOU HAVE TO KNOW THIS...
...THE PERSON WHO SHOT THAT ARROW WAS COMPLETELY UNAUTHORIZED.
WE TOOK HIM INTO CUSTODY. AND HE WAS TRIED BY A JURY OF HIS PEERS--
YEAH. I GET IT. I KNOW.
UP HERE, I KNOW.
BUT HERE...
...IT'S A LITTLE... HARDER.

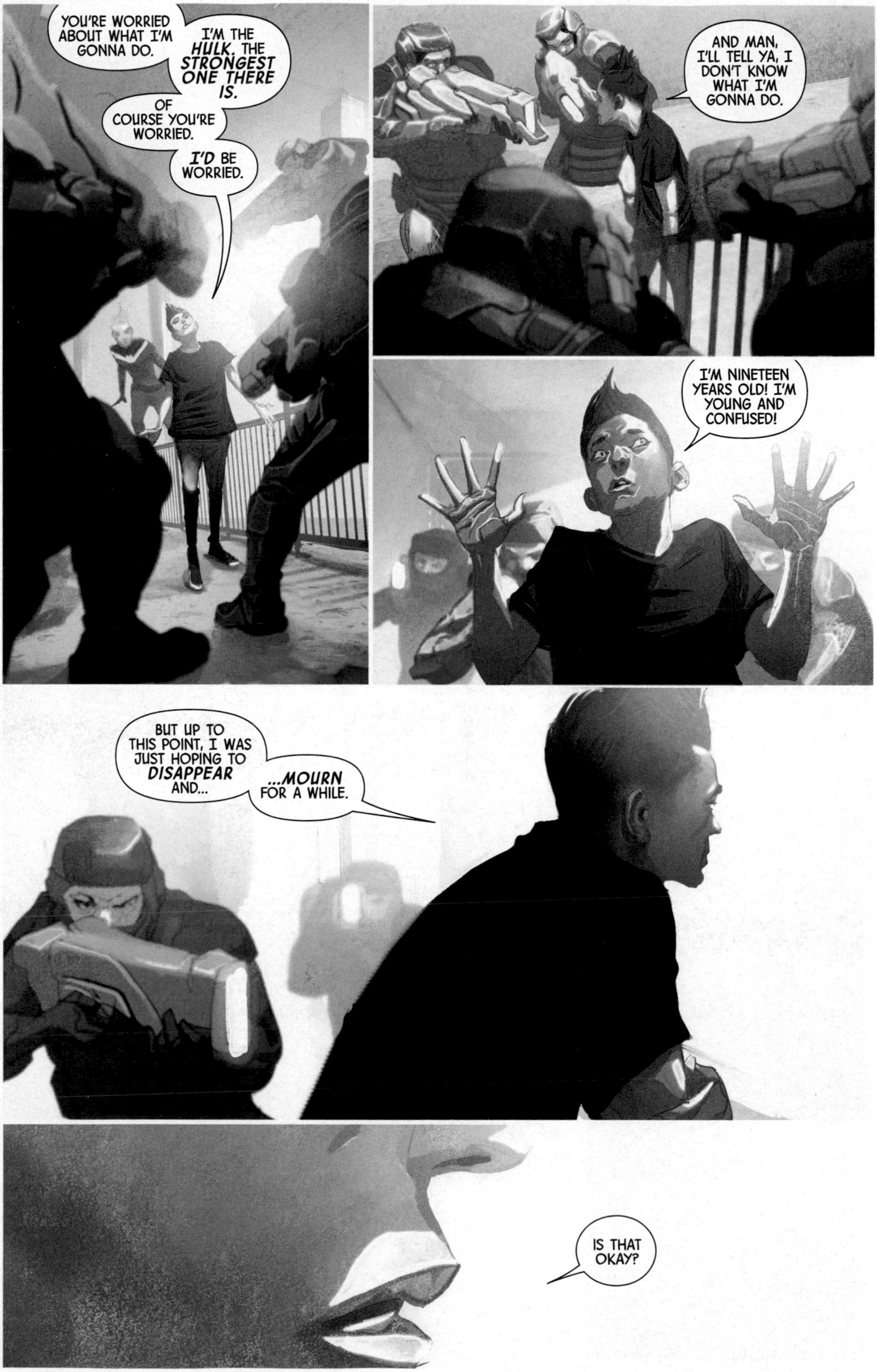
YOU'RE WORRIED ABOUT WHAT I'M GONNA DO.
I'M THE *HULK*. THE *STRONGEST ONE THERE IS.*
OF COURSE YOU'RE WORRIED.
I'D BE WORRIED.
AND MAN, I'LL TELL YA, I DON'T KNOW WHAT I'M GONNA DO.
I'M NINETEEN YEARS OLD! I'M YOUNG AND CONFUSED!
BUT UP TO THIS POINT, I WAS JUST HOPING TO *DISAPPEAR* AND...
...*MOURN* FOR A WHILE.
IS THAT OKAY?

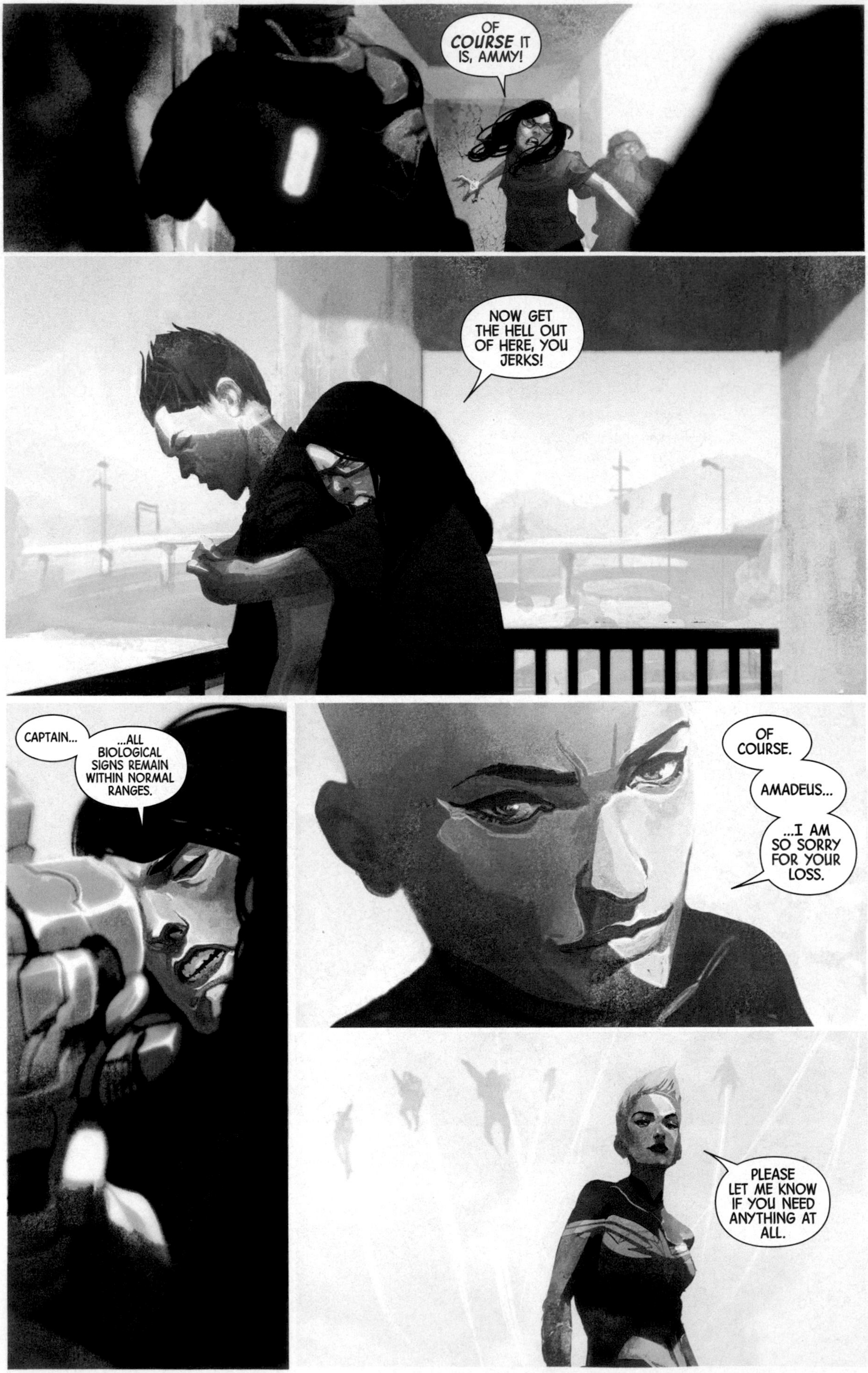
OF *COURSE* IT IS, AMMY!
NOW GET THE HELL OUT OF HERE, YOU JERKS!
CAPTAIN...
...ALL BIOLOGICAL SIGNS REMAIN WITHIN NORMAL RANGES.
OF COURSE.
AMADEUS...
...I AM SO SORRY FOR YOUR LOSS.
PLEASE LET ME KNOW IF YOU NEED ANYTHING AT ALL.

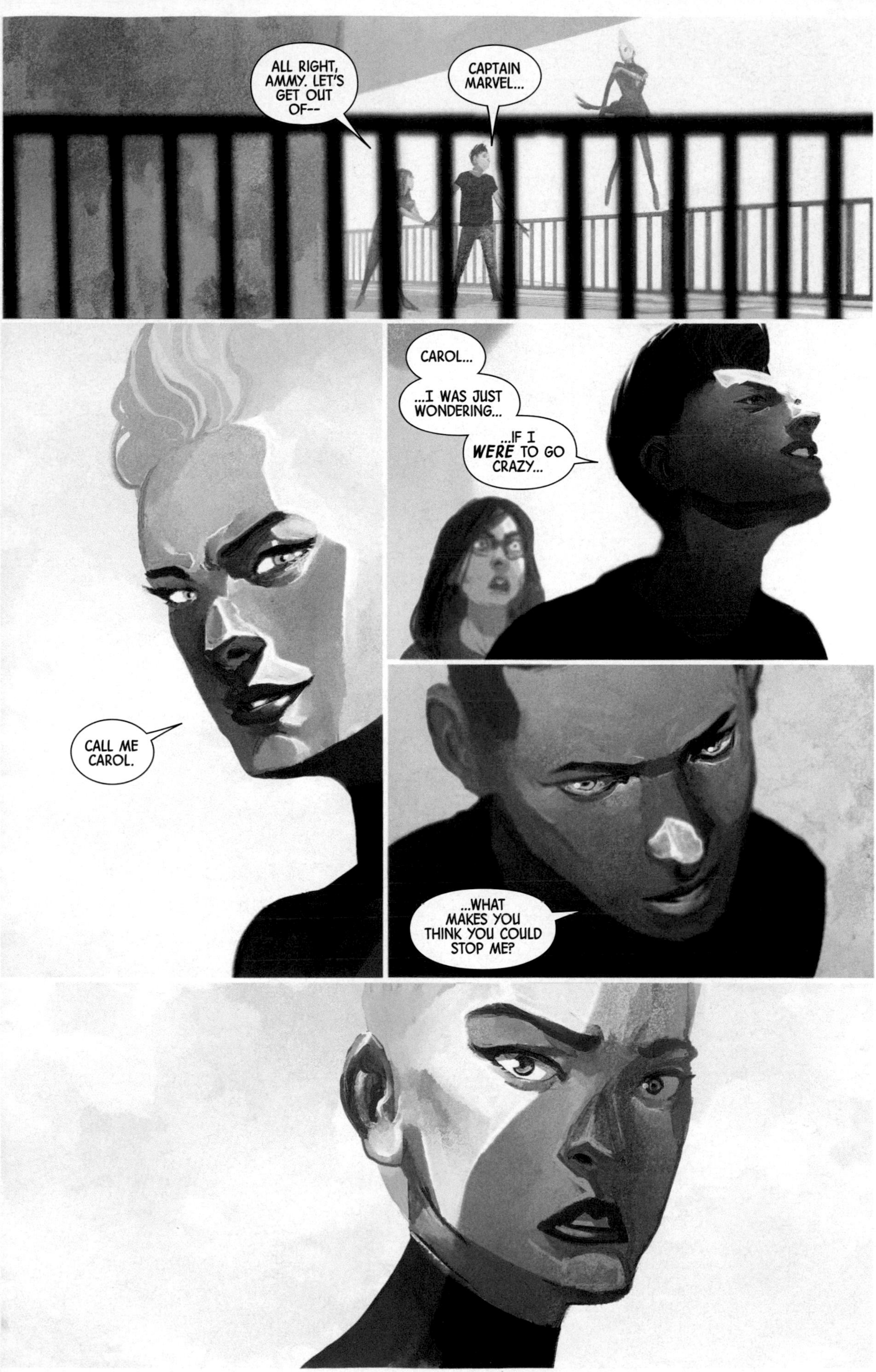
ALL RIGHT, AMMY. LET'S GET OUT OF--
CAPTAIN MARVEL...
CALL ME CAROL.
CAROL...
...I WAS JUST WONDERING...
...IF I *WERE* TO GO CRAZY...
...WHAT MAKES YOU THINK YOU COULD STOP ME?

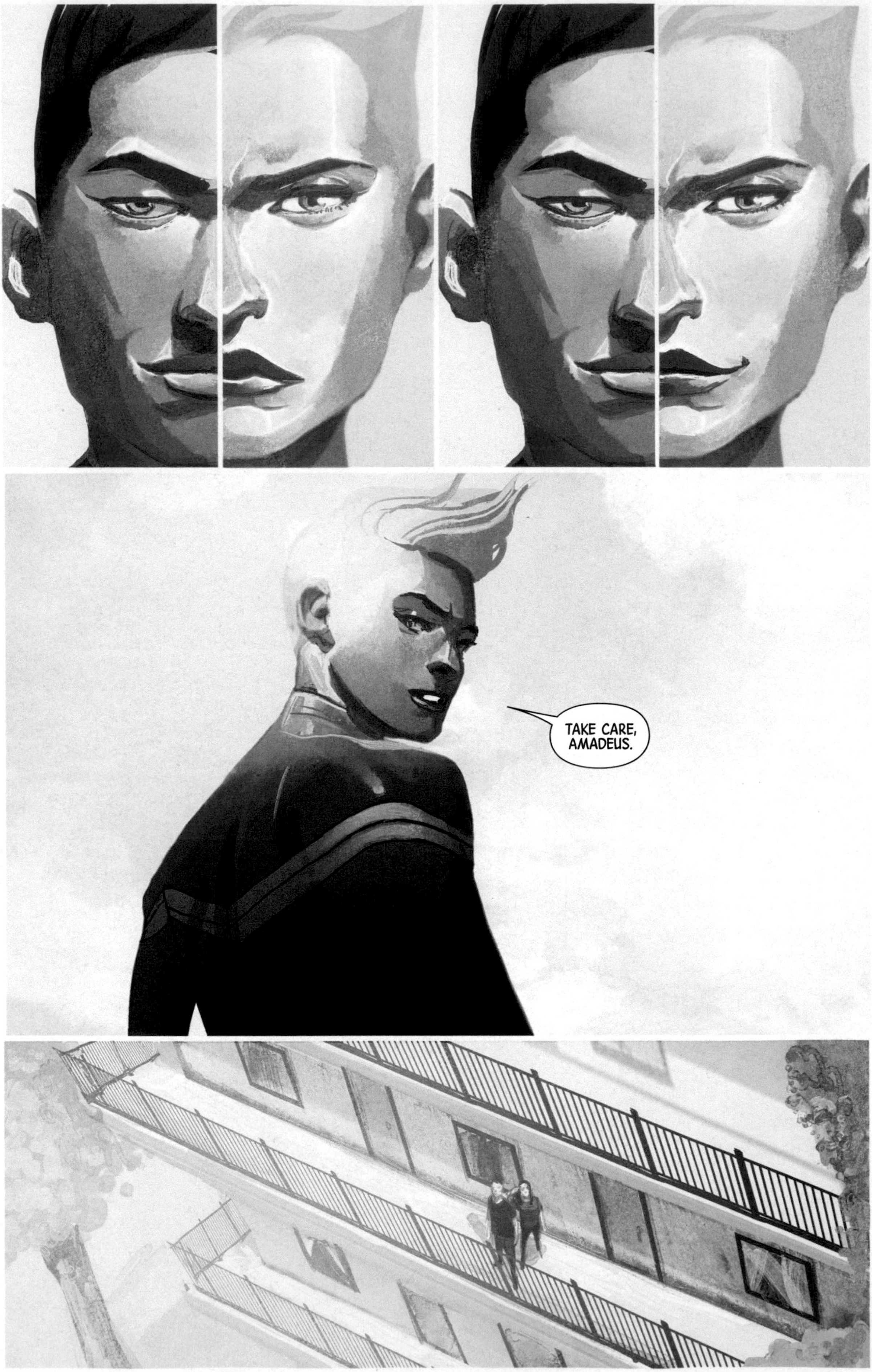
TAKE CARE, AMADEUS.

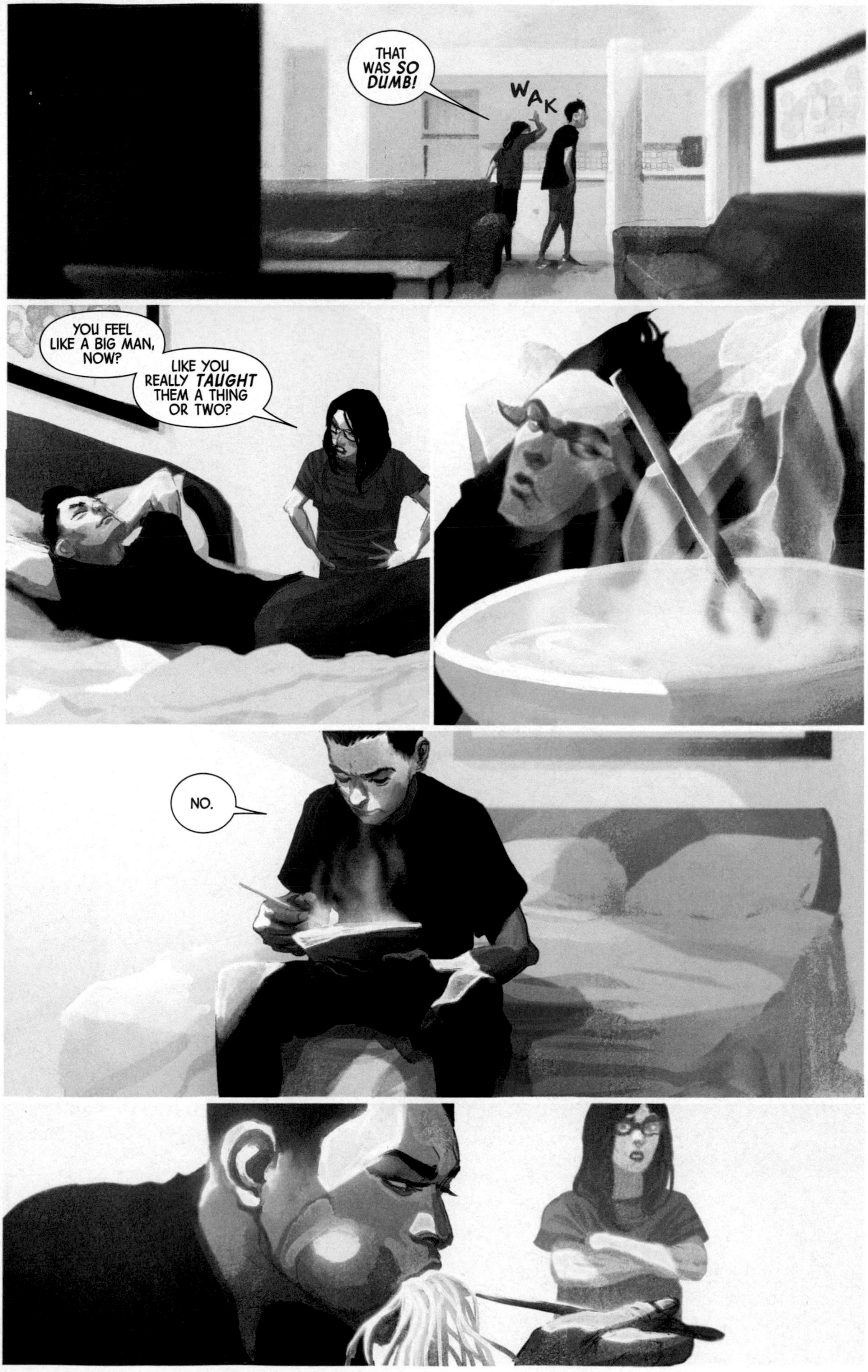
THAT WAS SO DUMB!
WAK
YOU FEEL LIKE A BIG MAN, NOW?
LIKE YOU REALLY TAUGHT THEM A THING OR TWO?
NO.

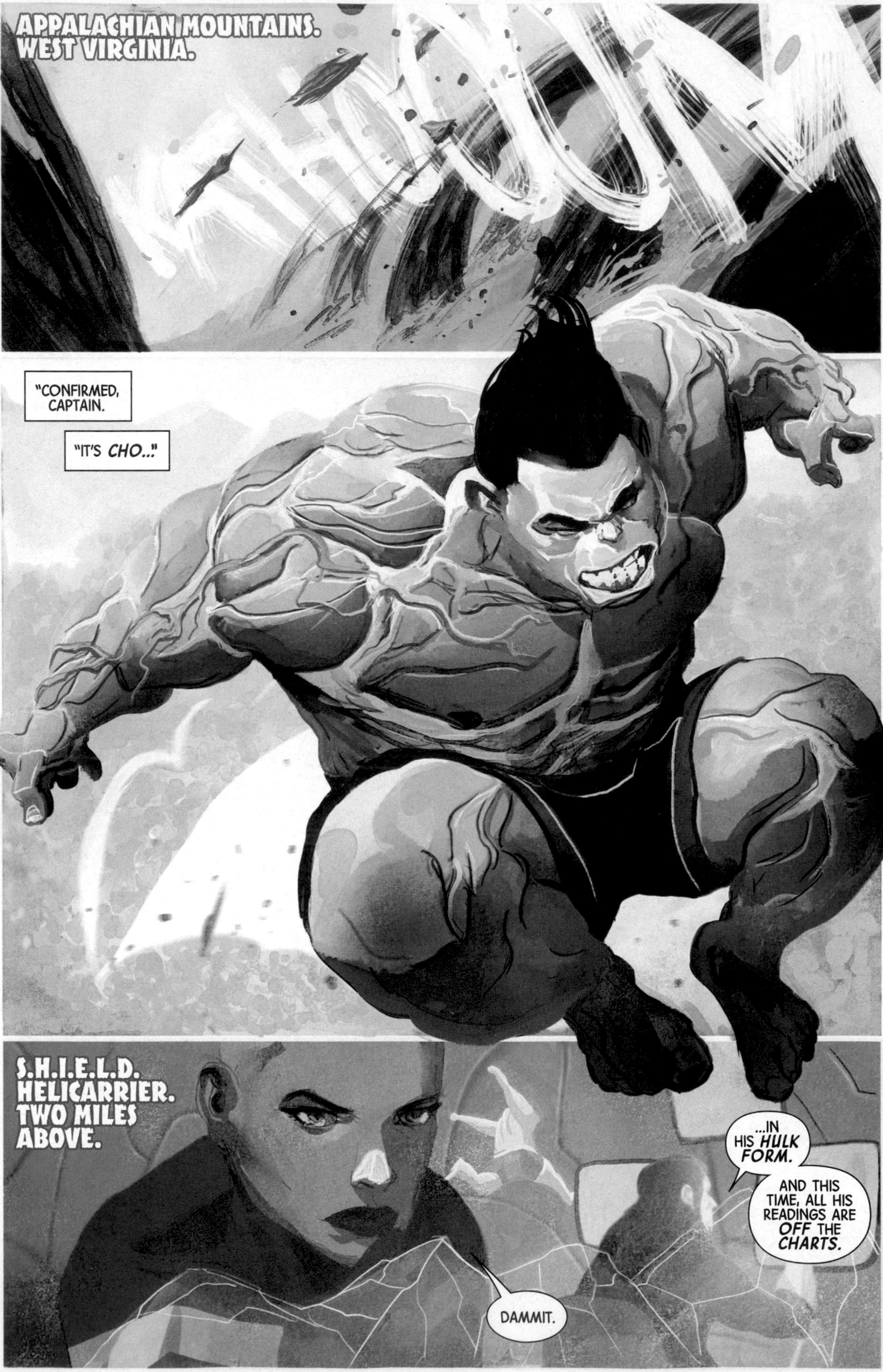
APPALACHIAN MOUNTAINS. WEST VIRGINIA.
"CONFIRMED, CAPTAIN.
"IT'S CHO..."
S.H.I.E.L.D. HELICARRIER. TWO MILES ABOVE.
...IN HIS HULK FORM.
AND THIS TIME, ALL HIS READINGS ARE OFF THE CHARTS.
DAMMIT.

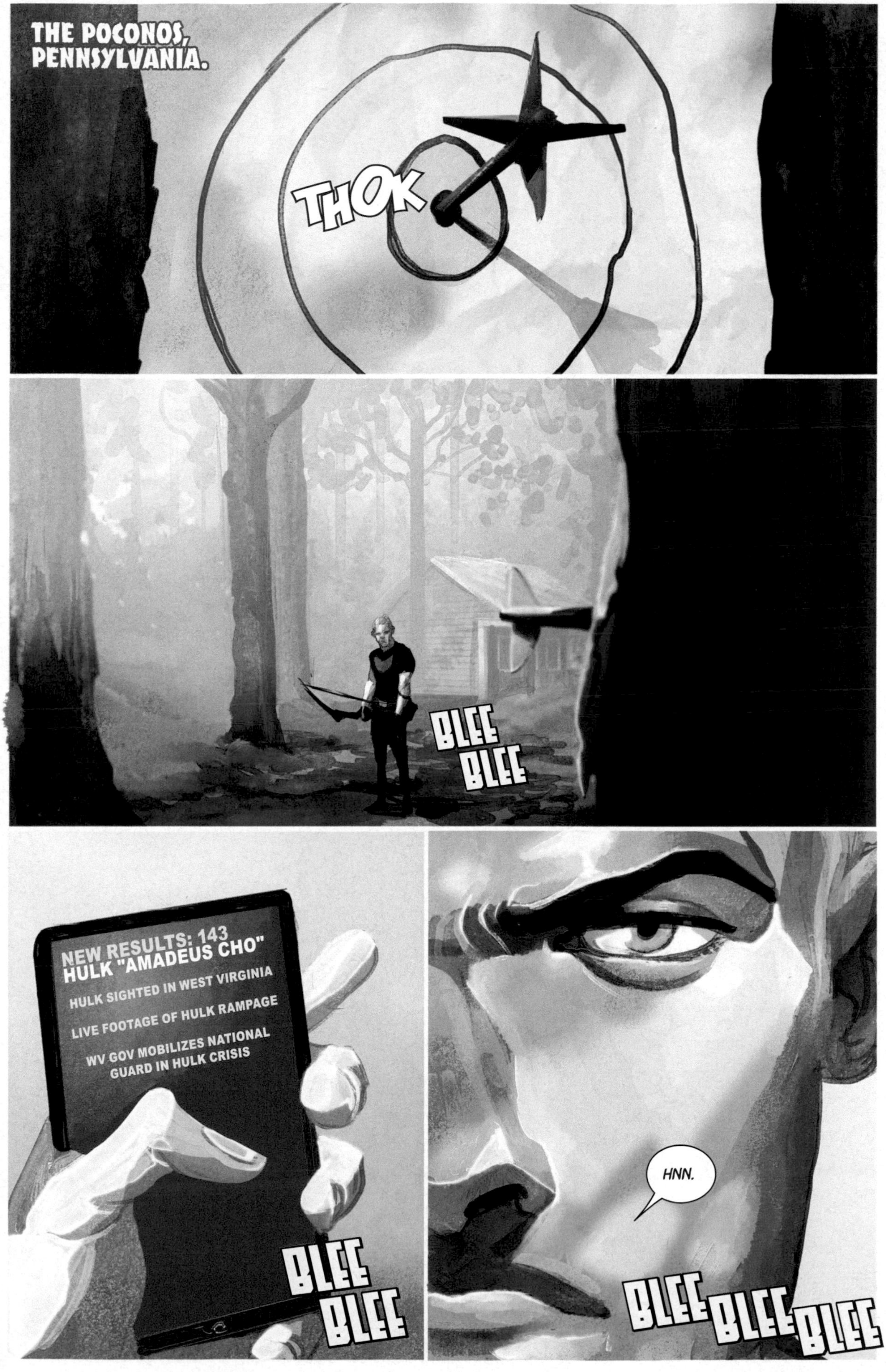
THE POCONOS, PENNSYLVANIA.
THOK
BLEE BLEE
NEW RESULTS: 143
HULK "AMADEUS CHO"
HULK SIGHTED IN WEST VIRGINIA
LIVE FOOTAGE OF HULK RAMPAGE
WV GOV MOBILIZES NATIONAL GUARD IN HULK CRISIS
BLEE BLEE
HNN.
BLEE BLEE BLEE

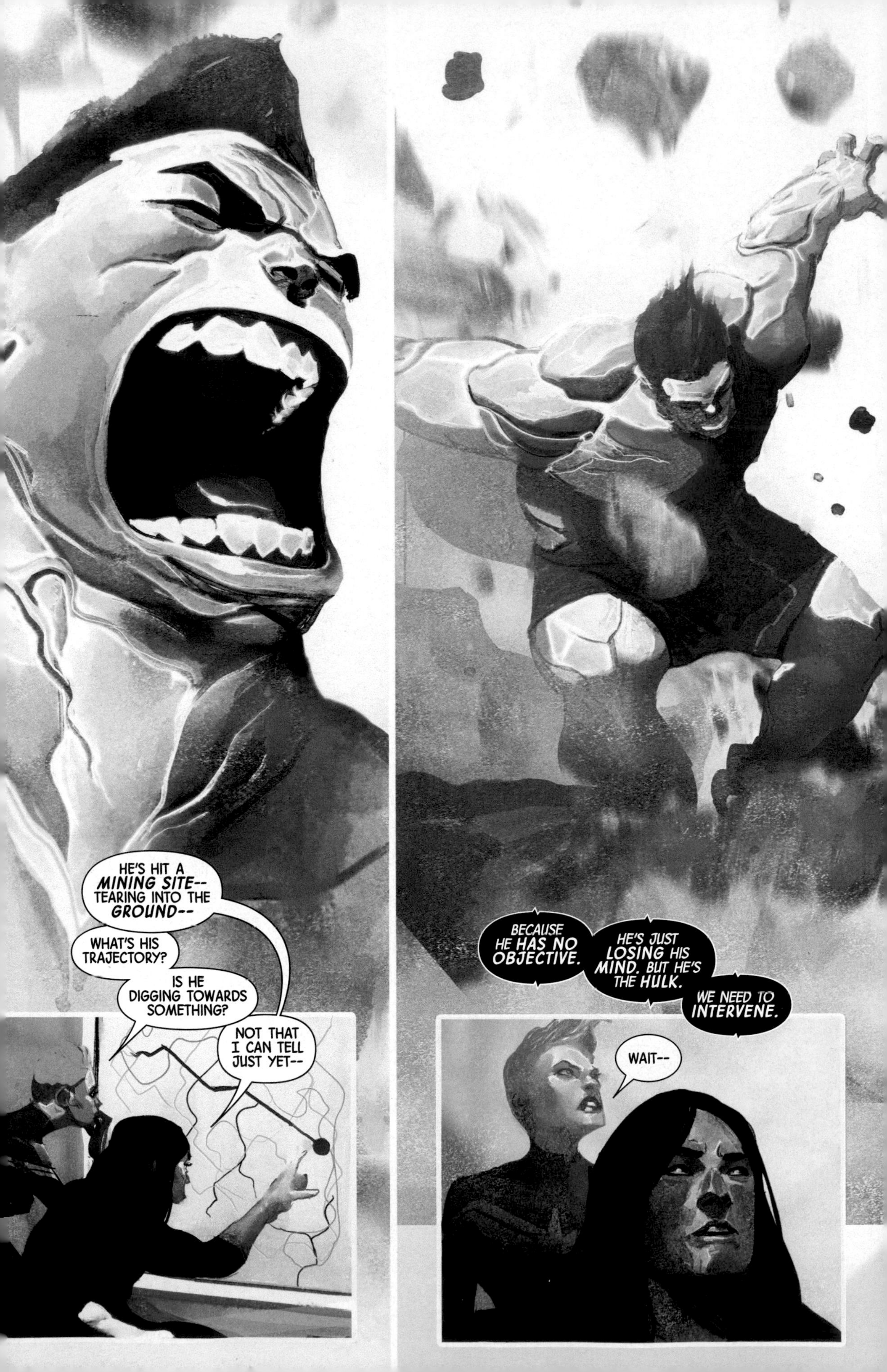
HE'S HIT A MINING SITE-- TEARING INTO THE GROUND--
WHAT'S HIS TRAJECTORY?
IS HE DIGGING TOWARDS SOMETHING?
NOT THAT I CAN TELL JUST YET--
BECAUSE HE HAS NO OBJECTIVE.
HE'S JUST LOSING HIS MIND. BUT HE'S THE HULK.
WE NEED TO INTERVENE.
WAIT--

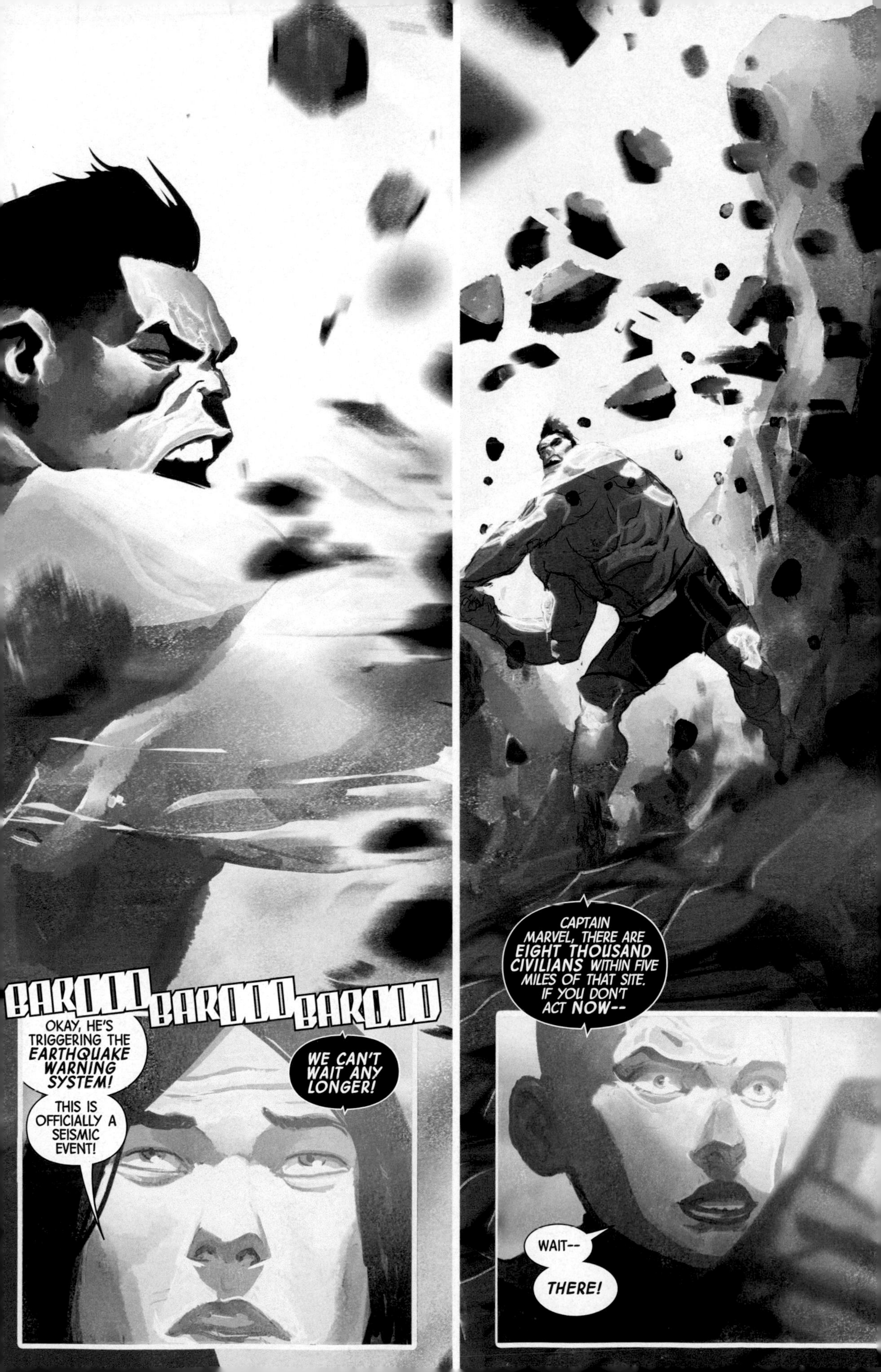
BAROOO BAROOO BAROOO
OKAY, HE'S TRIGGERING THE EARTHQUAKE WARNING SYSTEM!
THIS IS OFFICIALLY A SEISMIC EVENT!
WE CAN'T WAIT ANY LONGER!
CAPTAIN MARVEL, THERE ARE EIGHT THOUSAND CIVILIANS WITHIN FIVE MILES OF THAT SITE. IF YOU DON'T ACT NOW--
WAIT--
THERE!

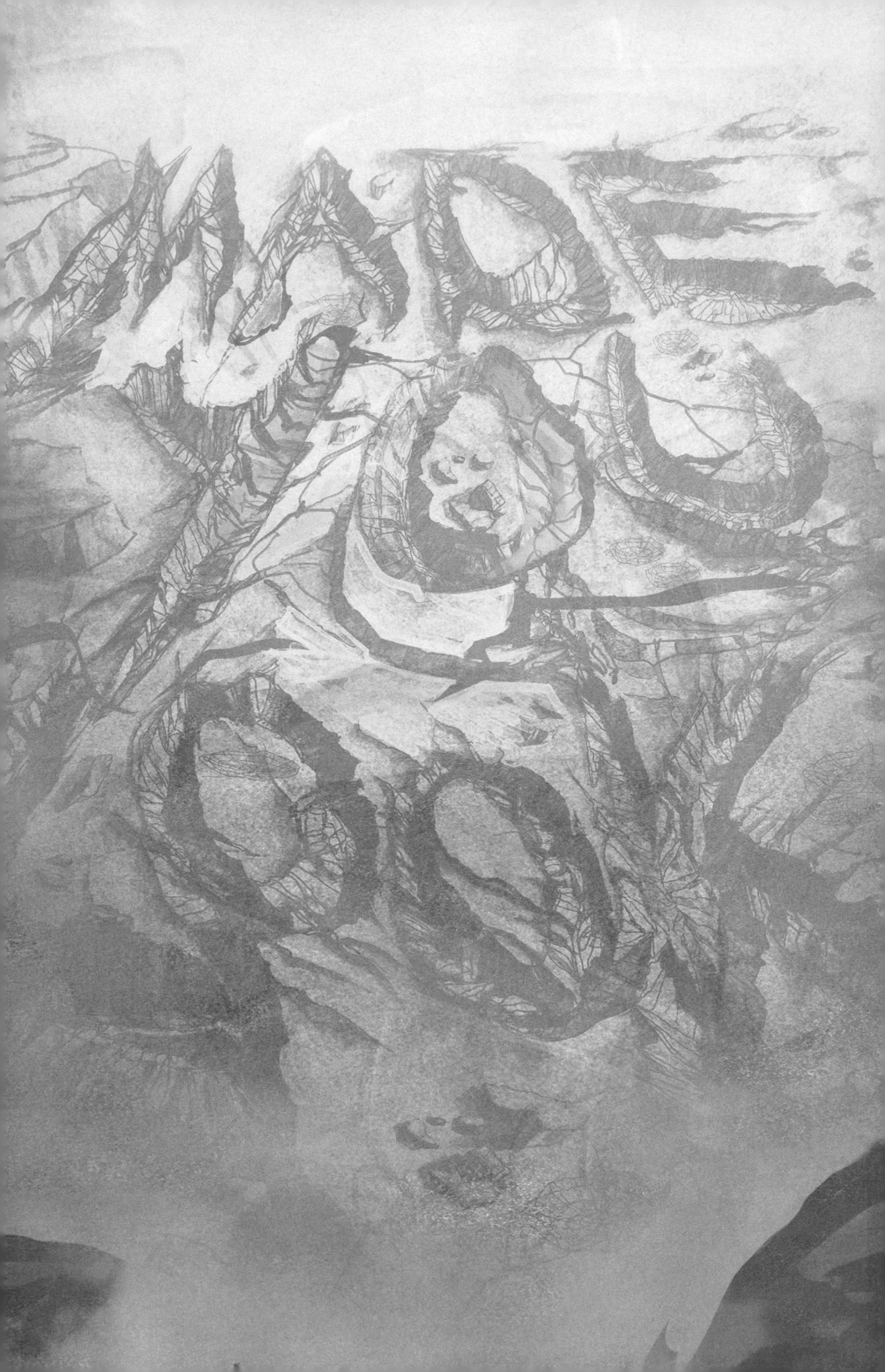

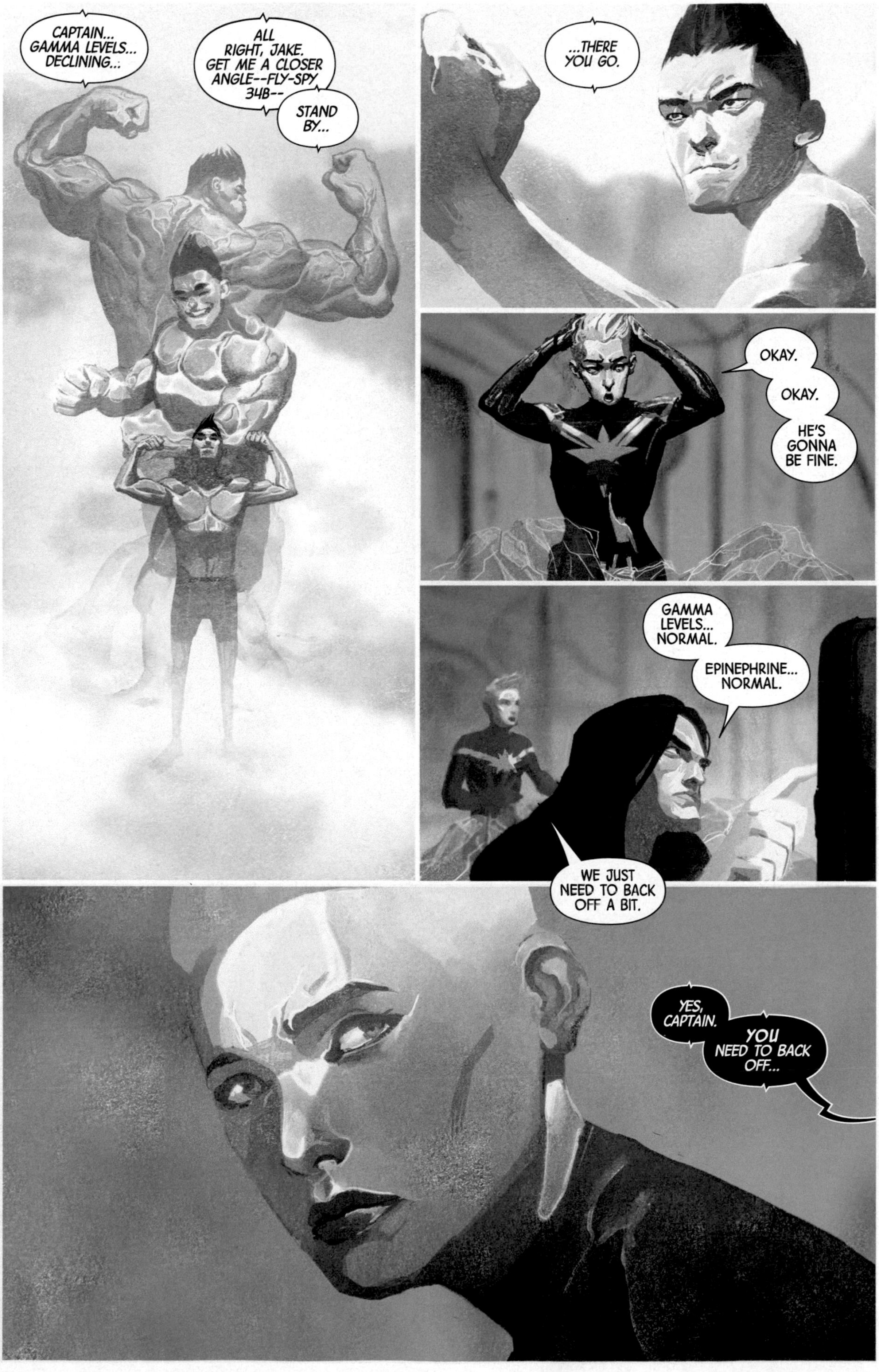
CAPTAIN... GAMMA LEVELS... DECLINING...
ALL RIGHT, JAKE. GET ME A CLOSER ANGLE--FLY-SPY 34B--
STAND BY...
...THERE YOU GO.
OKAY.
OKAY.
HE'S GONNA BE FINE.
GAMMA LEVELS... NORMAL.
EPINEPHRINE... NORMAL.
WE JUST NEED TO BACK OFF A BIT.
YES, CAPTAIN.
YOU NEED TO BACK OFF...

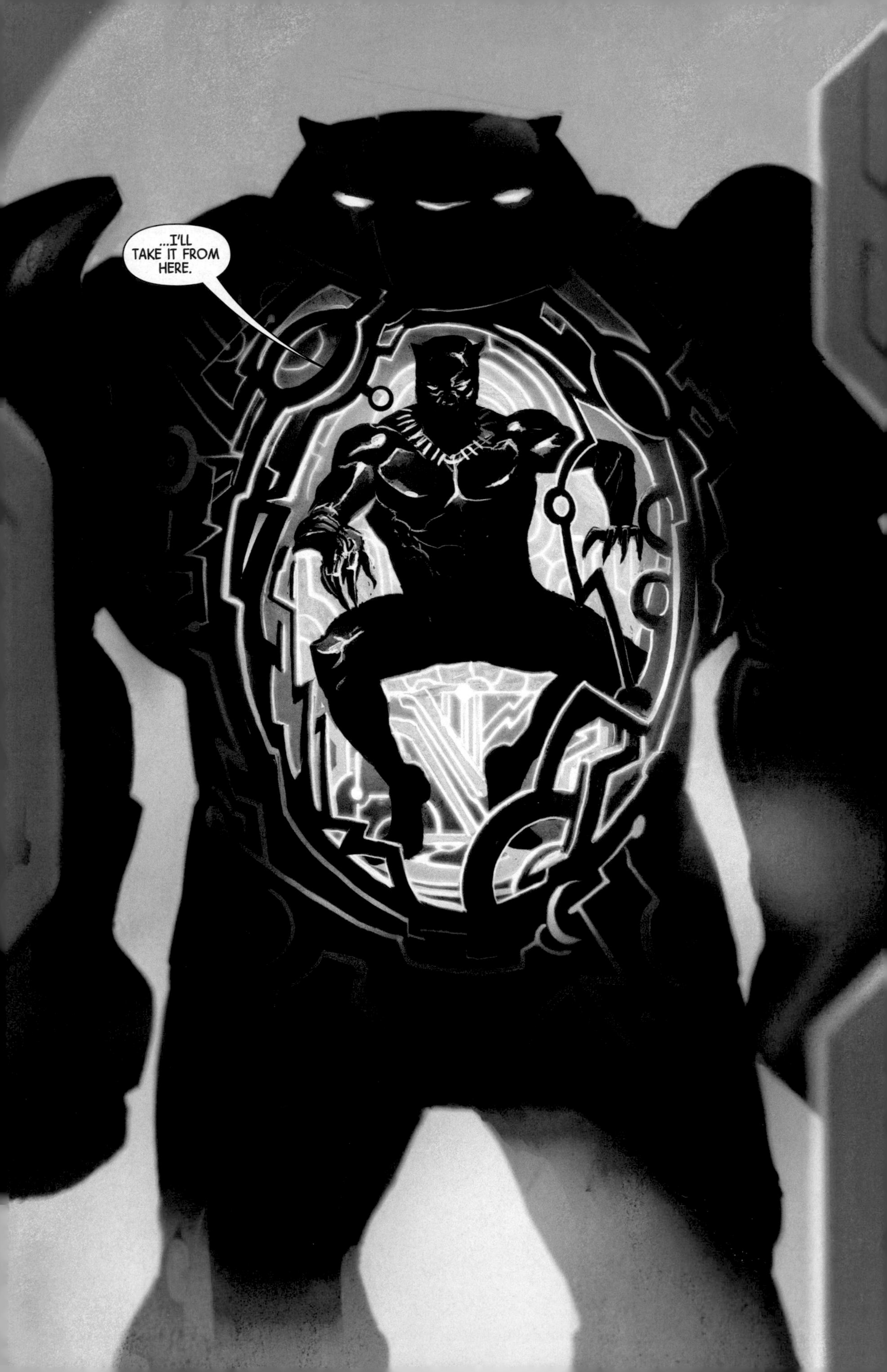
...I'LL TAKE IT FROM HERE.

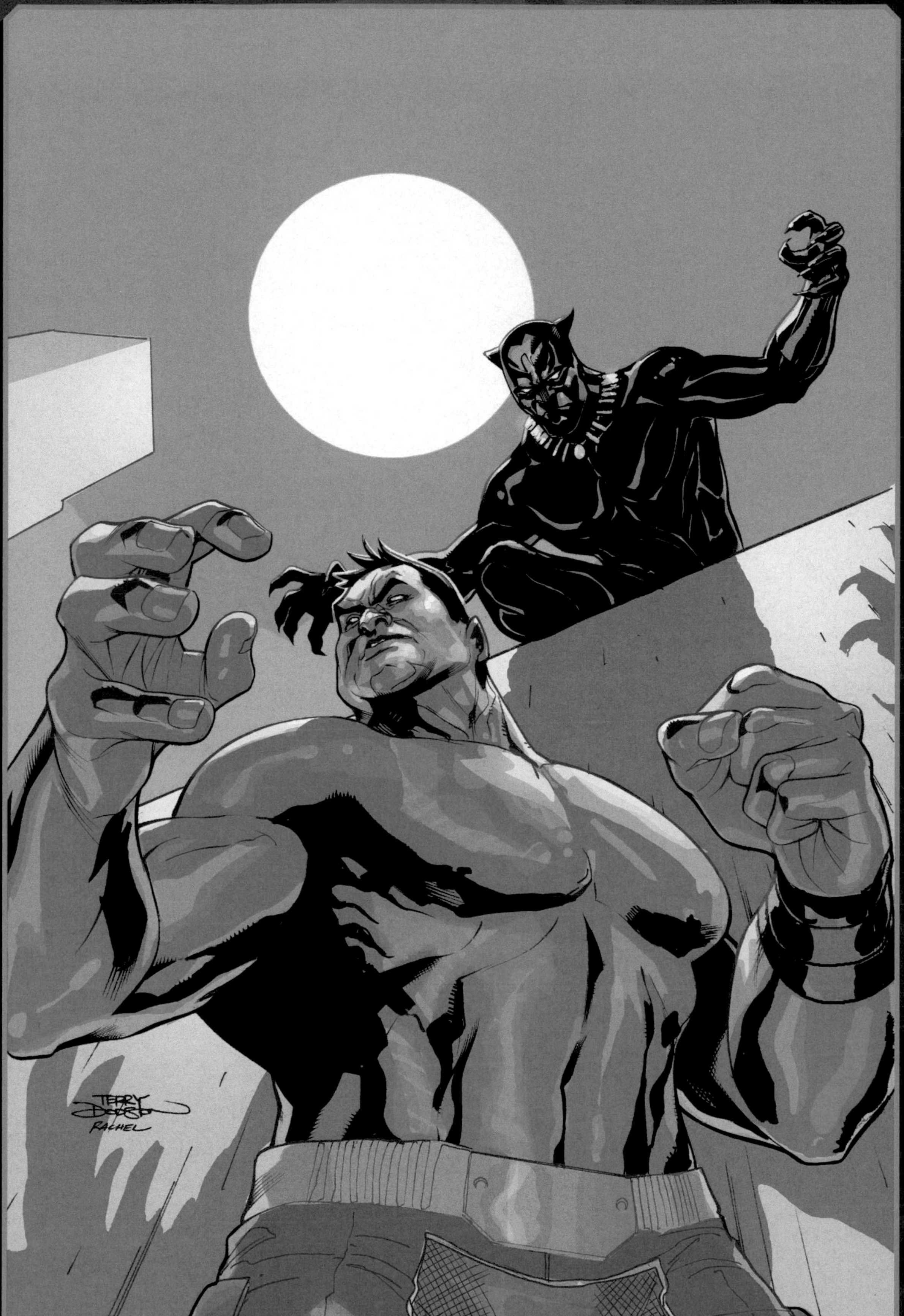
TERRY DODSON
RACHEL

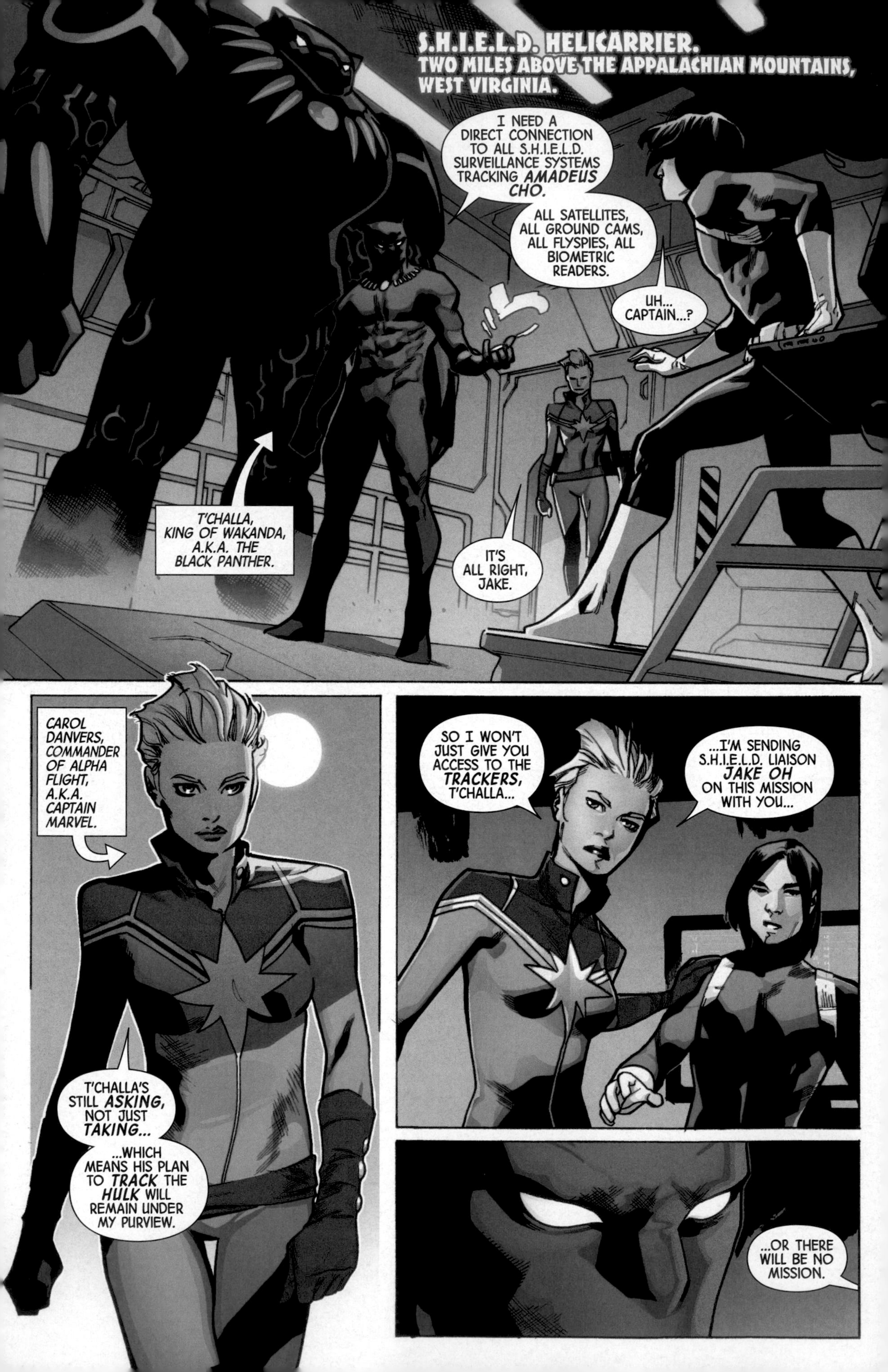
S.H.I.E.L.D. HELICARRIER.
TWO MILES ABOVE THE APPALACHIAN MOUNTAINS, WEST VIRGINIA.
I NEED A DIRECT CONNECTION TO ALL S.H.I.E.L.D. SURVEILLANCE SYSTEMS TRACKING AMADEUS CHO.
ALL SATELLITES, ALL GROUND CAMS, ALL FLYSPIES, ALL BIOMETRIC READERS.
UH... CAPTAIN...?
T'CHALLA, KING OF WAKANDA, A.K.A. THE BLACK PANTHER.
IT'S ALL RIGHT, JAKE.
CAROL DANVERS, COMMANDER OF ALPHA FLIGHT, A.K.A. CAPTAIN MARVEL.
T'CHALLA'S STILL ASKING, NOT JUST TAKING...
...WHICH MEANS HIS PLAN TO TRACK THE HULK WILL REMAIN UNDER MY PURVIEW.
SO I WON'T JUST GIVE YOU ACCESS TO THE TRACKERS, T'CHALLA...
...I'M SENDING S.H.I.E.L.D. LIAISON JAKE OH ON THIS MISSION WITH YOU...
...OR THERE WILL BE NO MISSION.

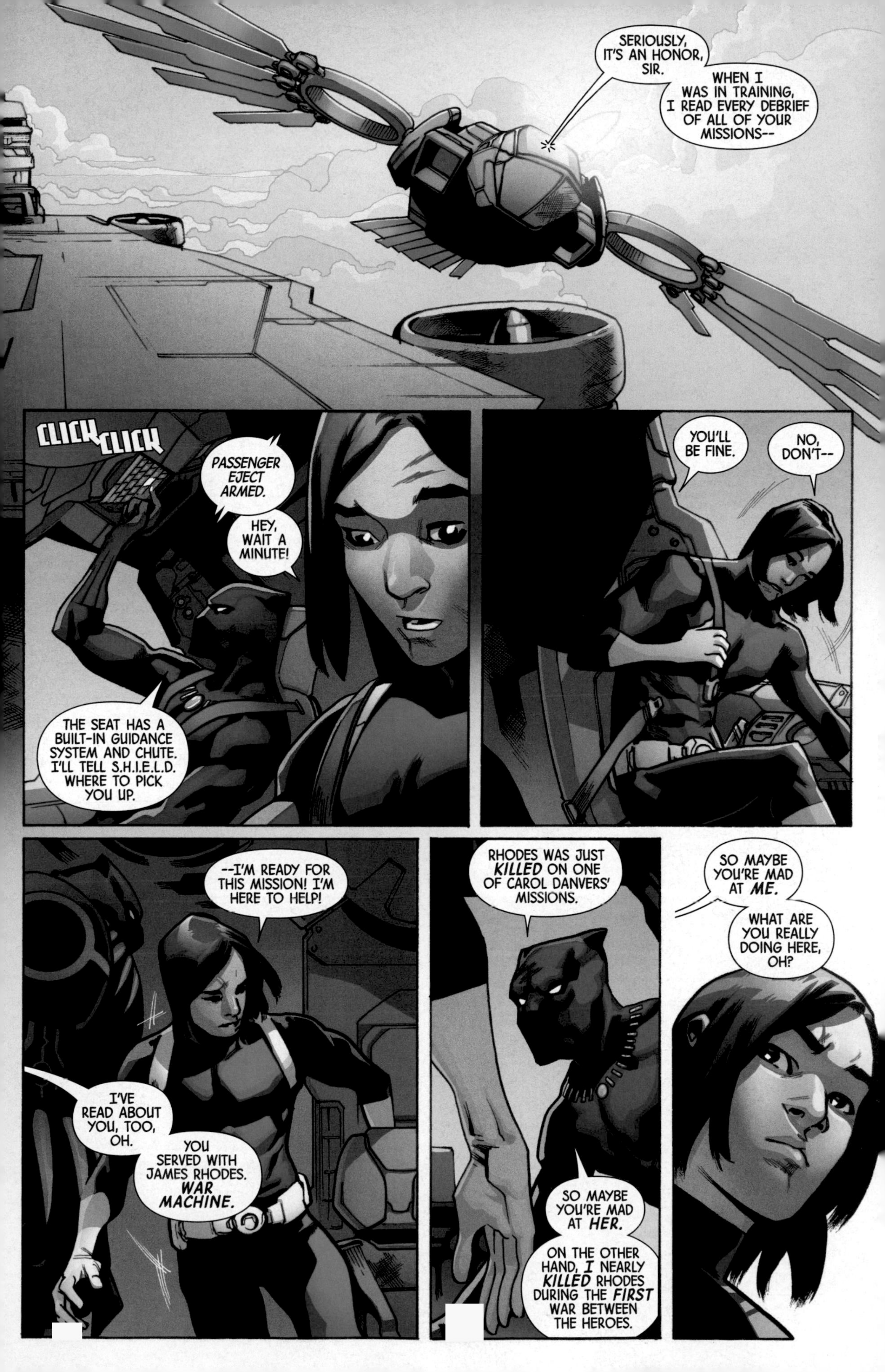
SERIOUSLY, IT'S AN HONOR, SIR.
WHEN I WAS IN TRAINING, I READ EVERY DEBRIEF OF ALL OF YOUR MISSIONS--
CLICK CLICK
PASSENGER EJECT ARMED.
HEY, WAIT A MINUTE!
THE SEAT HAS A BUILT-IN GUIDANCE SYSTEM AND CHUTE. I'LL TELL S.H.I.E.L.D. WHERE TO PICK YOU UP.
YOU'LL BE FINE.
NO, DON'T--
--I'M READY FOR THIS MISSION! I'M HERE TO HELP!
I'VE READ ABOUT YOU, TOO, OH.
YOU SERVED WITH JAMES RHODES. WAR MACHINE.
RHODES WAS JUST KILLED ON ONE OF CAROL DANVERS' MISSIONS.
SO MAYBE YOU'RE MAD AT HER.
ON THE OTHER HAND, I NEARLY KILLED RHODES DURING THE FIRST WAR BETWEEN THE HEROES.
SO MAYBE YOU'RE MAD AT ME.
WHAT ARE YOU REALLY DOING HERE, OH?

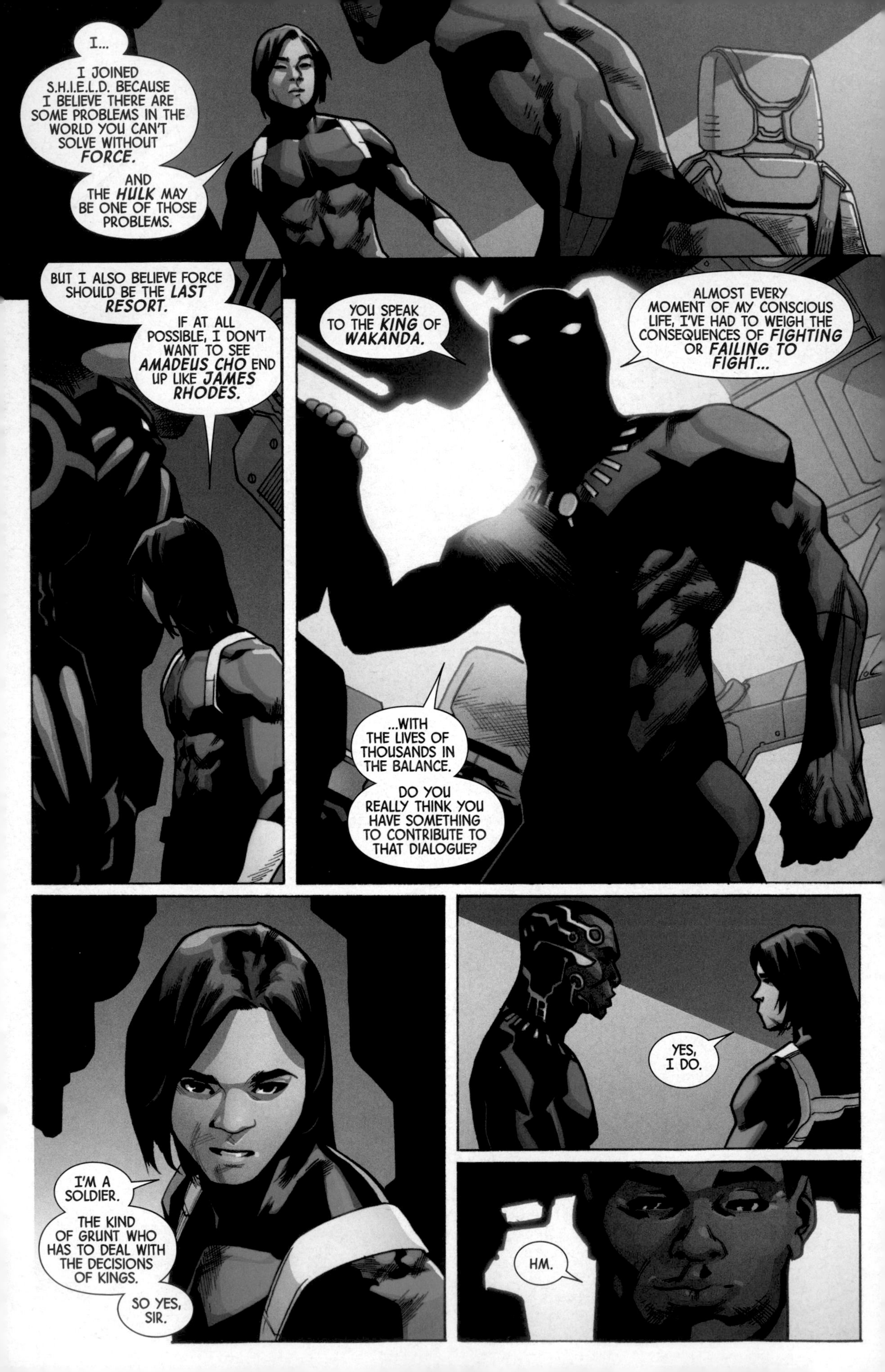
I...
I JOINED S.H.I.E.L.D. BECAUSE I BELIEVE THERE ARE SOME PROBLEMS IN THE WORLD YOU CAN'T SOLVE WITHOUT FORCE.
AND THE HULK MAY BE ONE OF THOSE PROBLEMS.
BUT I ALSO BELIEVE FORCE SHOULD BE THE LAST RESORT.
IF AT ALL POSSIBLE, I DON'T WANT TO SEE AMADEUS CHO END UP LIKE JAMES RHODES.
YOU SPEAK TO THE KING OF WAKANDA.
ALMOST EVERY MOMENT OF MY CONSCIOUS LIFE, I'VE HAD TO WEIGH THE CONSEQUENCES OF FIGHTING OR FAILING TO FIGHT...
...WITH THE LIVES OF THOUSANDS IN THE BALANCE.
DO YOU REALLY THINK YOU HAVE SOMETHING TO CONTRIBUTE TO THAT DIALOGUE?
I'M A SOLDIER.
THE KIND OF GRUNT WHO HAS TO DEAL WITH THE DECISIONS OF KINGS.
SO YES, SIR.
YES, I DO.
HM.

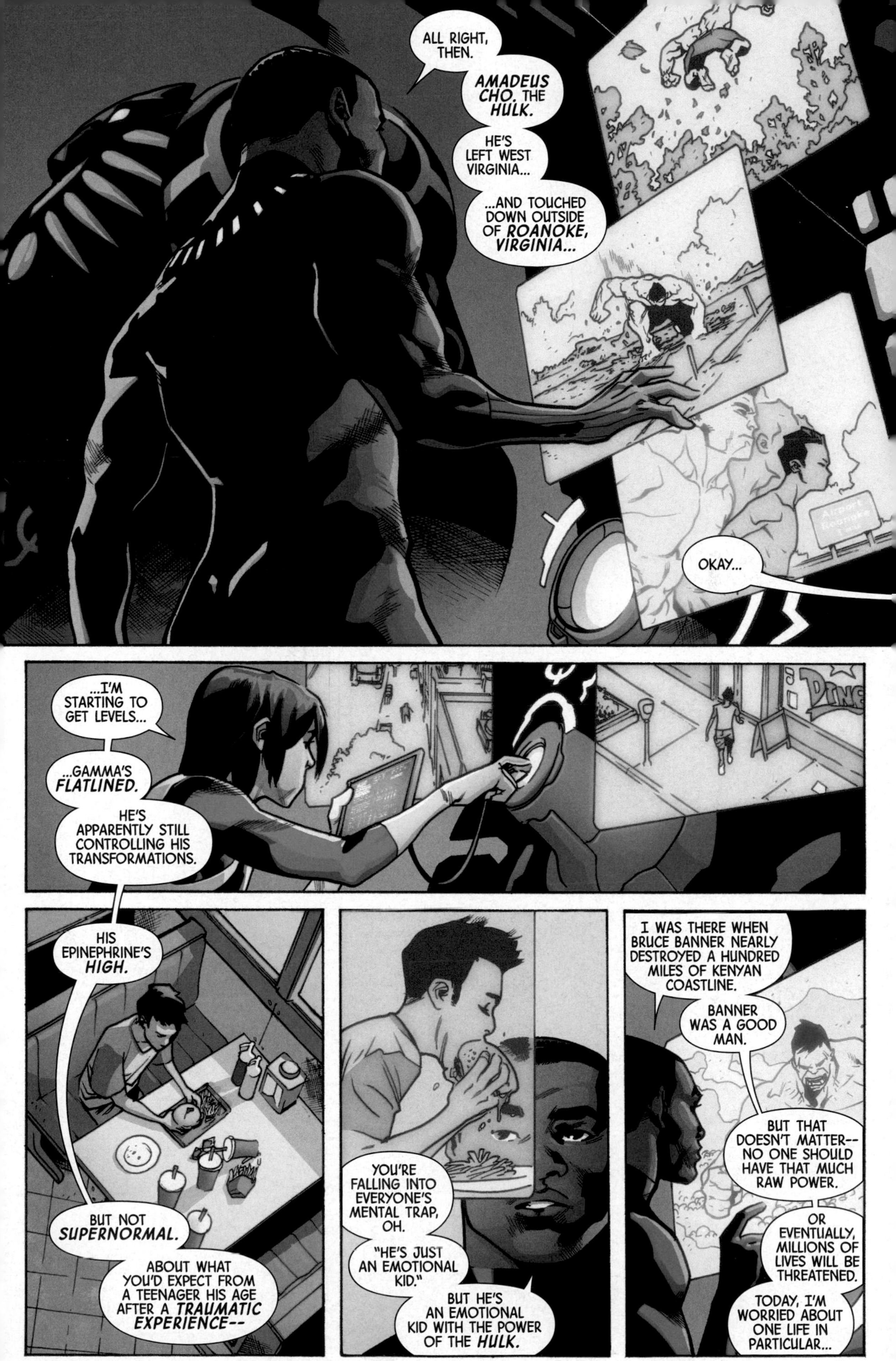

ALL RIGHT, THEN.
AMADEUS CHO, THE HULK.
HE'S LEFT WEST VIRGINIA...
...AND TOUCHED DOWN OUTSIDE OF ROANOKE, VIRGINIA...
OKAY...
...I'M STARTING TO GET LEVELS...
...GAMMA'S FLATLINED.
HE'S APPARENTLY STILL CONTROLLING HIS TRANSFORMATIONS.
HIS EPINEPHRINE'S HIGH.
BUT NOT SUPERNORMAL.
ABOUT WHAT YOU'D EXPECT FROM A TEENAGER HIS AGE AFTER A TRAUMATIC EXPERIENCE--
YOU'RE FALLING INTO EVERYONE'S MENTAL TRAP, OH.
"HE'S JUST AN EMOTIONAL KID."
BUT HE'S AN EMOTIONAL KID WITH THE POWER OF THE HULK.
I WAS THERE WHEN BRUCE BANNER NEARLY DESTROYED A HUNDRED MILES OF KENYAN COASTLINE.
BANNER WAS A GOOD MAN.
BUT THAT DOESN'T MATTER--NO ONE SHOULD HAVE THAT MUCH RAW POWER.
OR EVENTUALLY, MILLIONS OF LIVES WILL BE THREATENED.
TODAY, I'M WORRIED ABOUT ONE LIFE IN PARTICULAR...

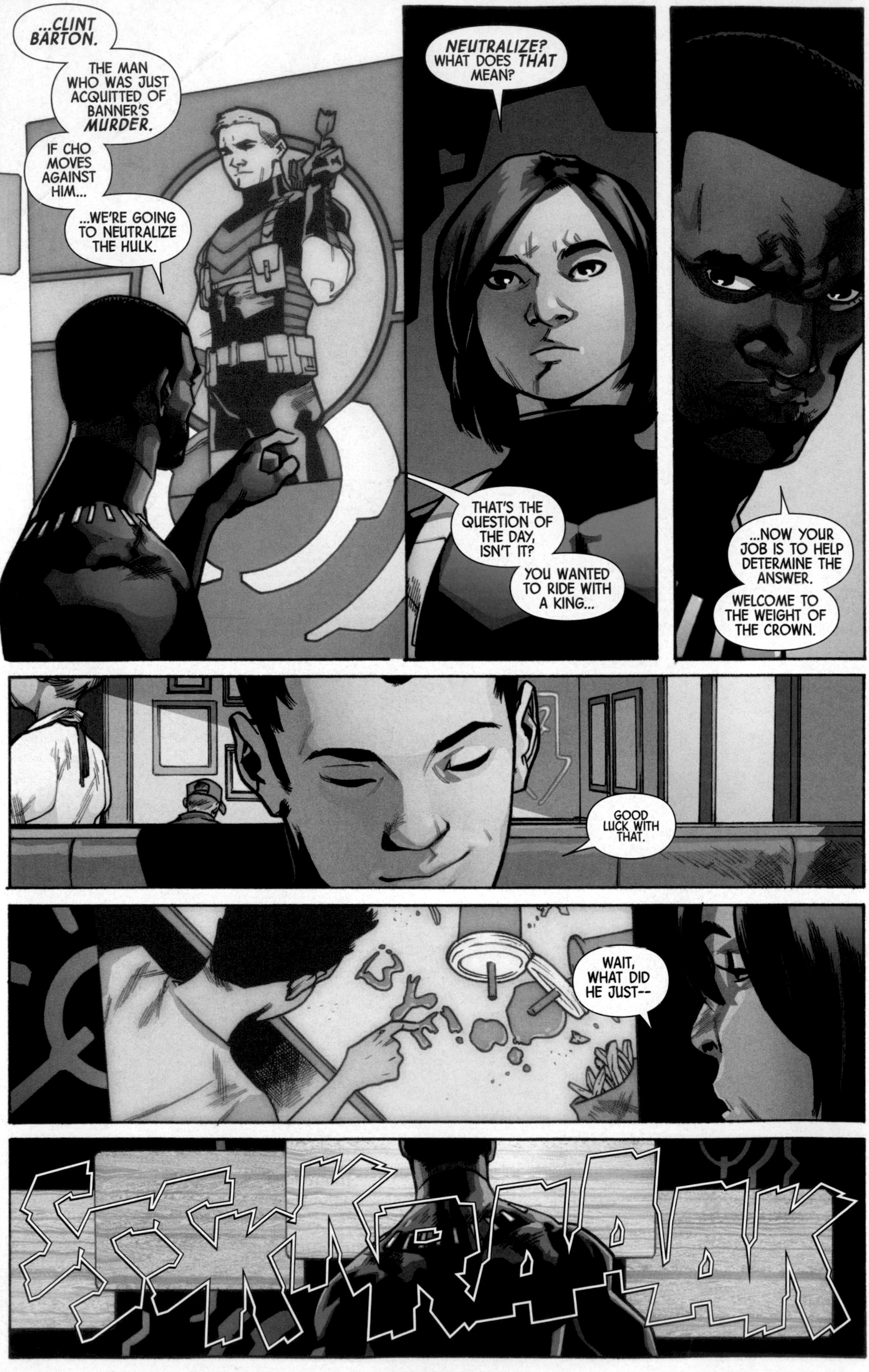
...CLINT BARTON.
THE MAN WHO WAS JUST ACQUITTED OF BANNER'S MURDER.
IF CHO MOVES AGAINST HIM...
...WE'RE GOING TO NEUTRALIZE THE HULK.
NEUTRALIZE? WHAT DOES THAT MEAN?
THAT'S THE QUESTION OF THE DAY, ISN'T IT?
YOU WANTED TO RIDE WITH A KING...
...NOW YOUR JOB IS TO HELP DETERMINE THE ANSWER.
WELCOME TO THE WEIGHT OF THE CROWN.
GOOD LUCK WITH THAT.
WAIT, WHAT DID HE JUST--
SKRAKADAK

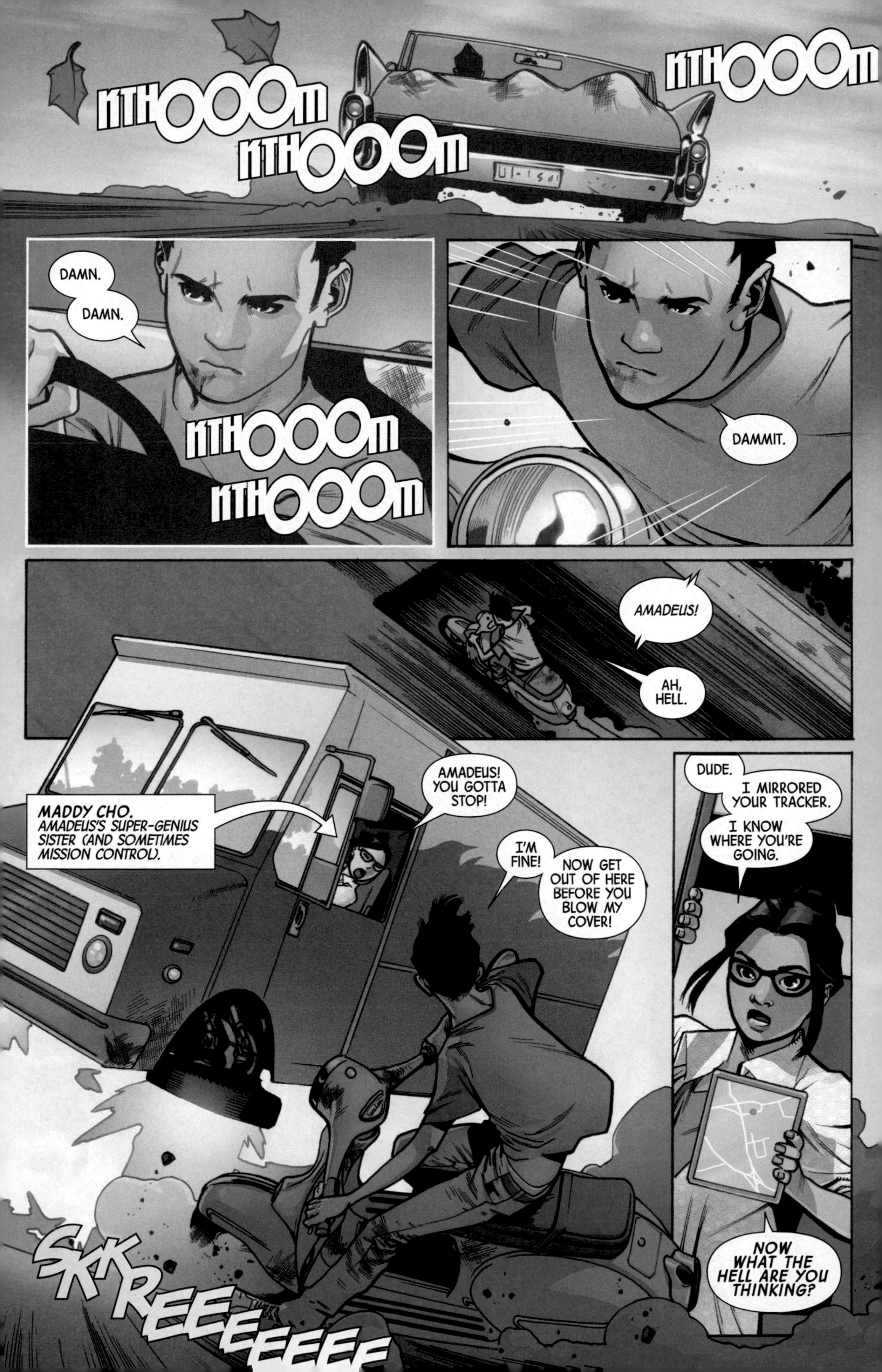
KTHOOOM
KTHOOOM
KTHOOOM
DAMN.
DAMN.
KTHOOOM
KTHOOOM
DAMMIT.
AMADEUS!
AH, HELL.
MADDY CHO. AMADEUS'S SUPER-GENIUS SISTER (AND SOMETIMES MISSION CONTROL).
AMADEUS! YOU GOTTA STOP!
I'M FINE!
NOW GET OUT OF HERE BEFORE YOU BLOW MY COVER!
SKKREEEEEEEF
DUDE.
I MIRRORED YOUR TRACKER.
I KNOW WHERE YOU'RE GOING.
NOW WHAT THE HELL ARE YOU THINKING?

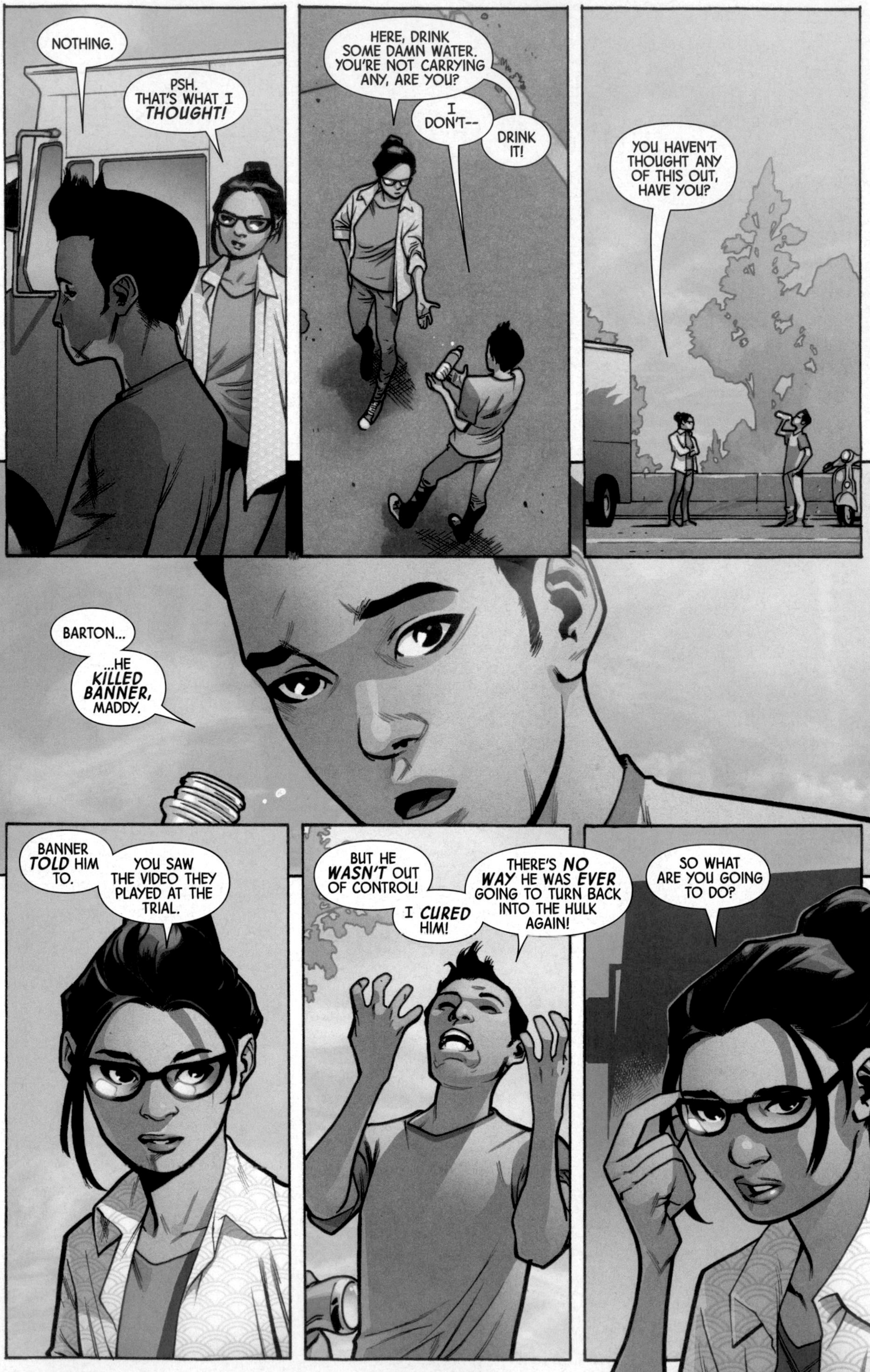
NOTHING.
PSH. THAT'S WHAT I *THOUGHT!*
HERE, DRINK SOME DAMN WATER. YOU'RE NOT CARRYING ANY, ARE YOU?
I DON'T--
DRINK IT!
YOU HAVEN'T THOUGHT ANY OF THIS OUT, HAVE YOU?
BARTON...
...HE *KILLED BANNER,* MADDY.
BANNER *TOLD* HIM TO.
YOU SAW THE VIDEO THEY PLAYED AT THE TRIAL.
BUT HE *WASN'T* OUT OF CONTROL!
I *CURED* HIM!
THERE'S *NO WAY* HE WAS *EVER* GOING TO TURN BACK INTO THE HULK AGAIN!
SO WHAT ARE YOU GOING TO DO?

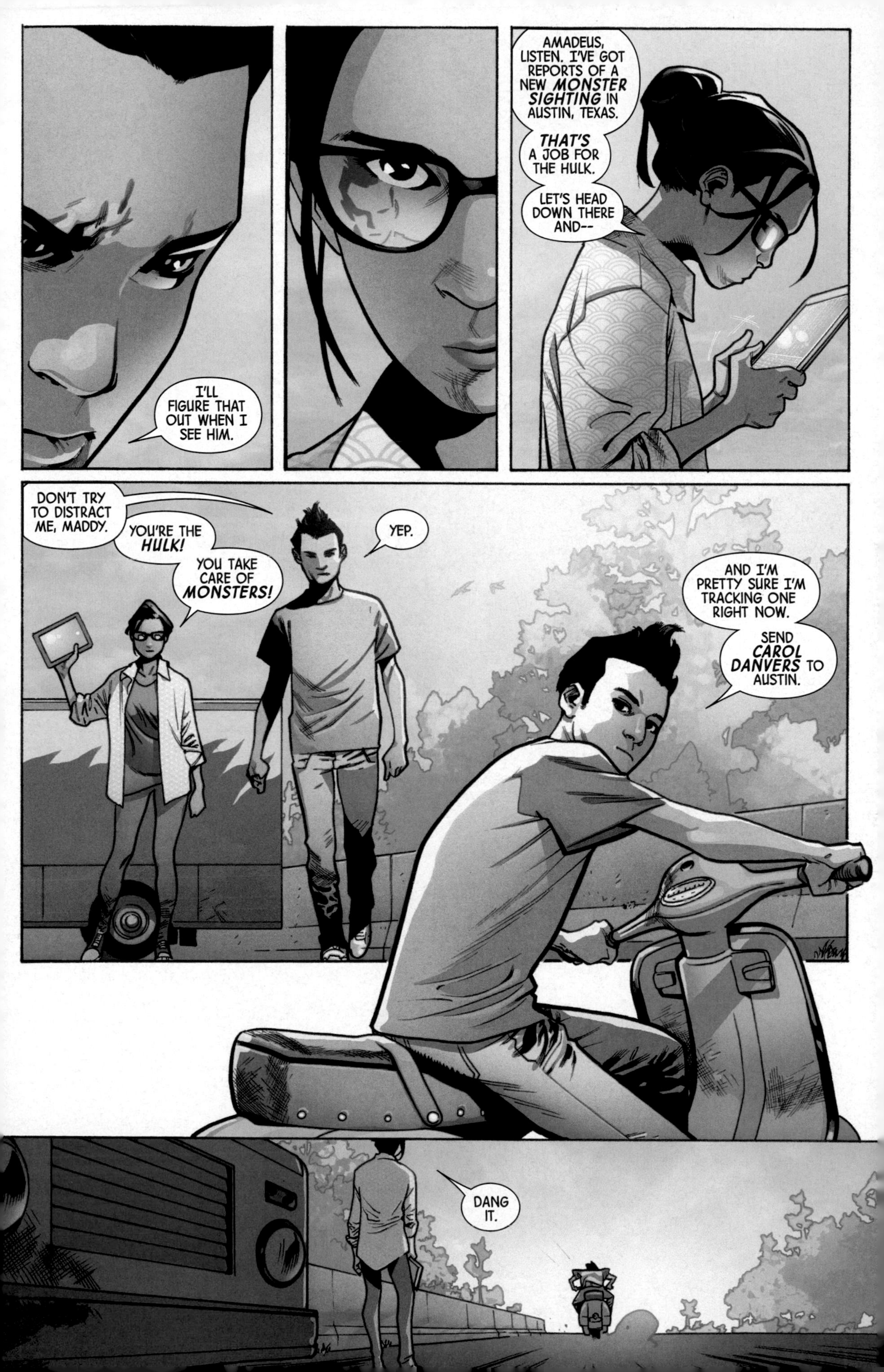
I'LL FIGURE THAT OUT WHEN I SEE HIM.
AMADEUS, LISTEN. I'VE GOT REPORTS OF A NEW MONSTER SIGHTING IN AUSTIN, TEXAS.
THAT'S A JOB FOR THE HULK.
LET'S HEAD DOWN THERE AND--
DON'T TRY TO DISTRACT ME, MADDY.
YOU'RE THE HULK!
YOU TAKE CARE OF MONSTERS!
YEP.
AND I'M PRETTY SURE I'M TRACKING ONE RIGHT NOW.
SEND CAROL DANVERS TO AUSTIN.
DANG IT.

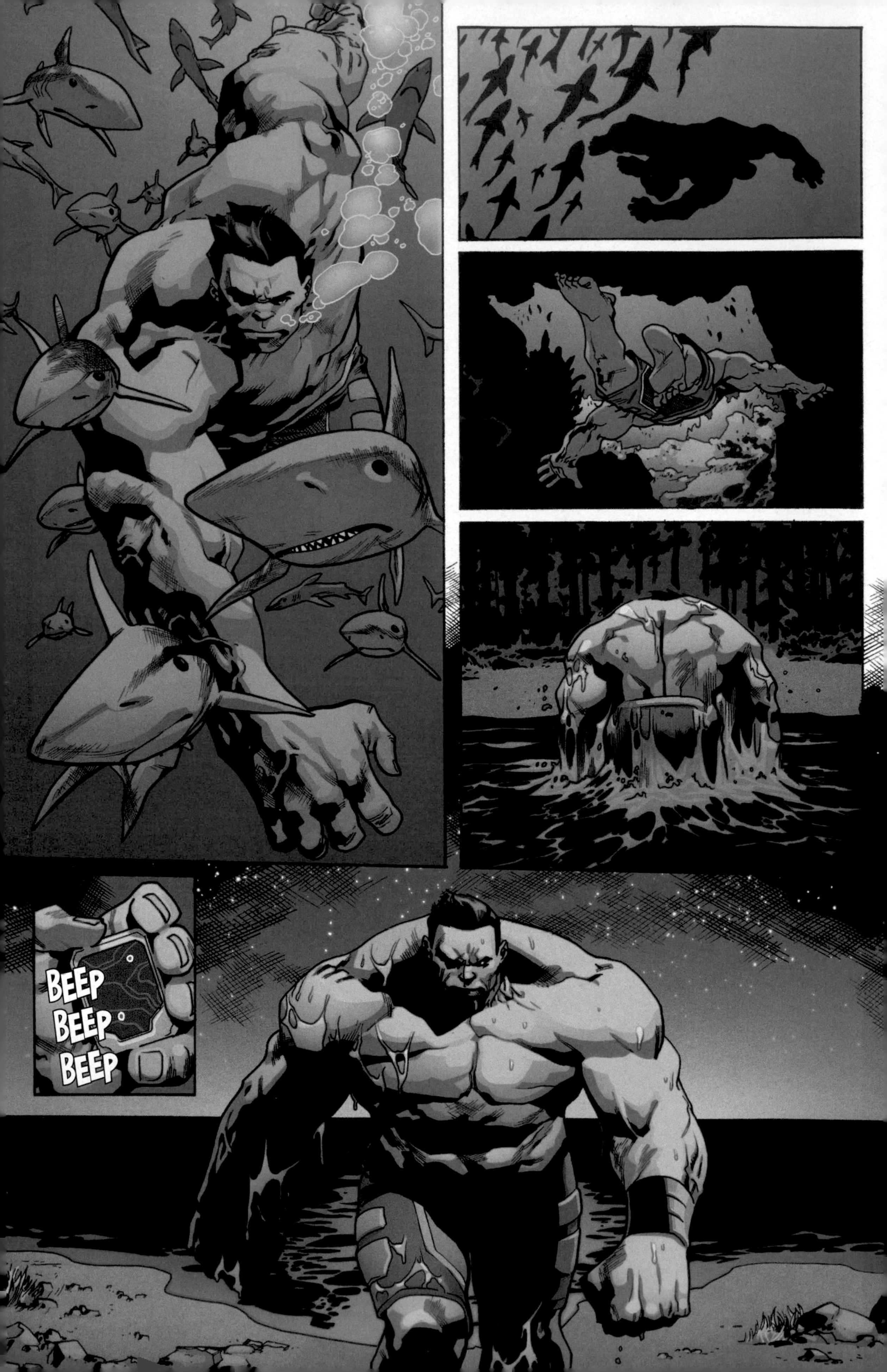
BEEP
BEEP
BEEP

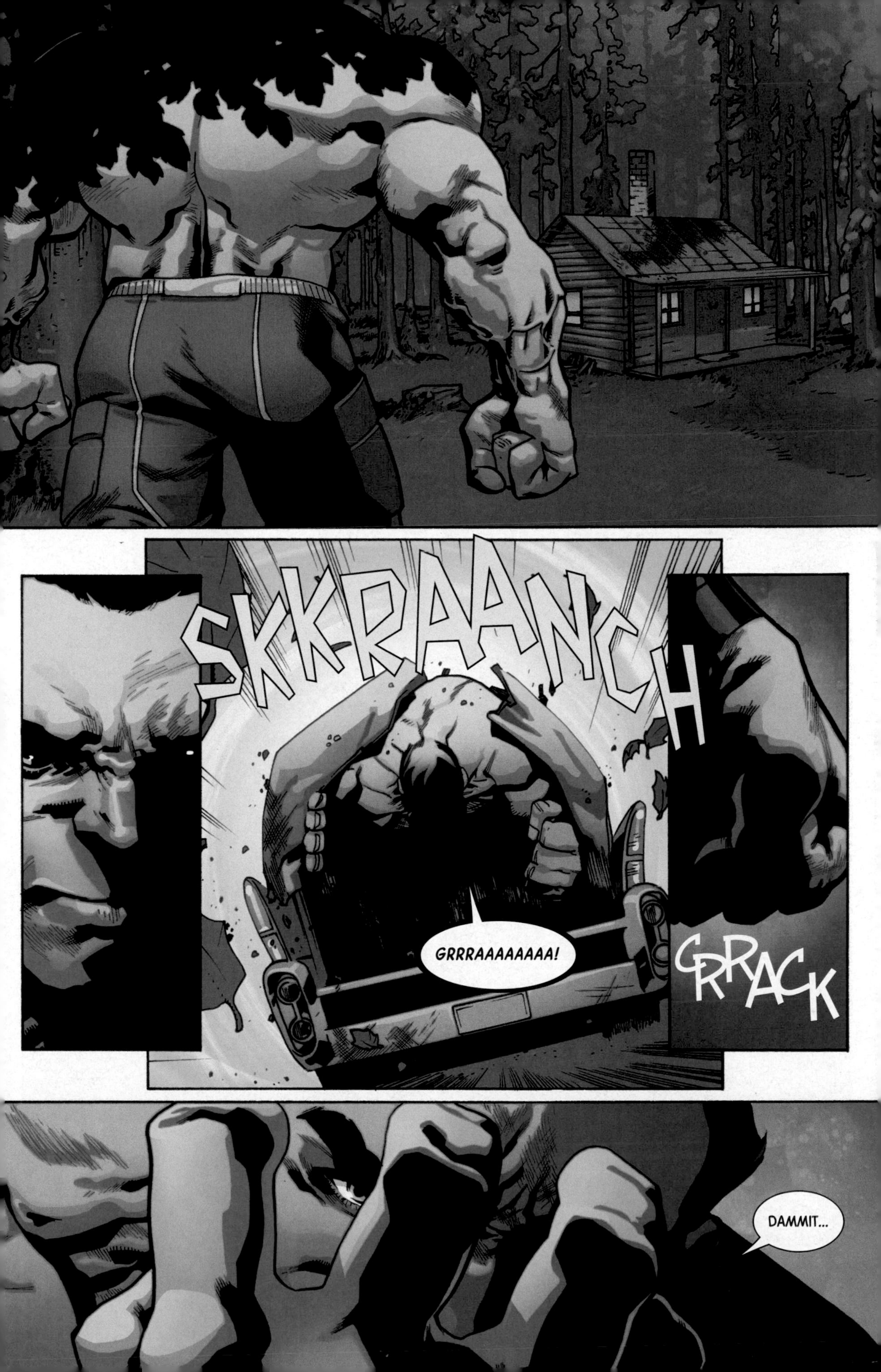
SKKRAANCH
GRRRAAAAAAAA!
CRRACK
DAMMIT...

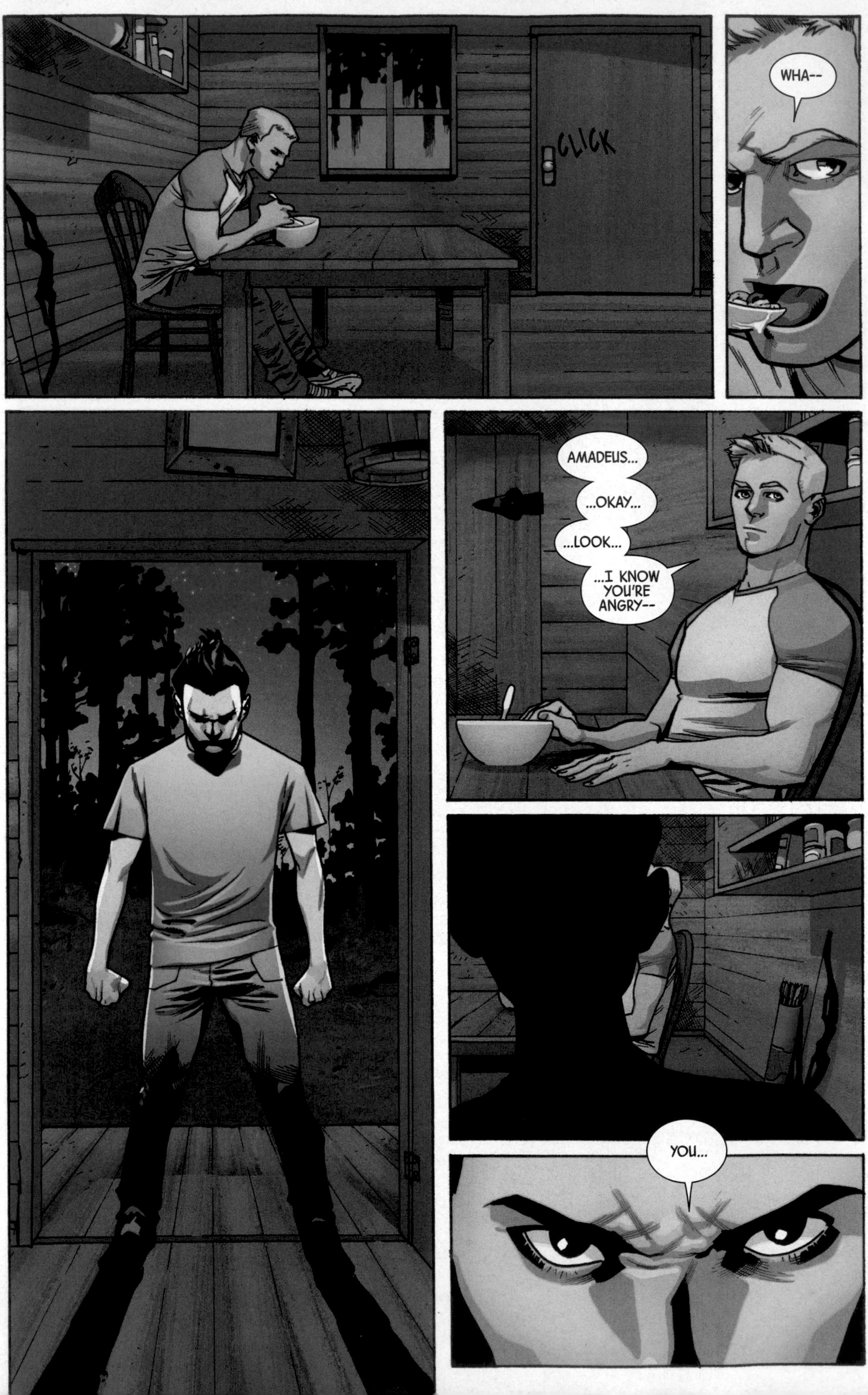
CLICK
WHA--
AMADEUS...
...OKAY...
...LOOK...
...I KNOW YOU'RE ANGRY--
YOU...

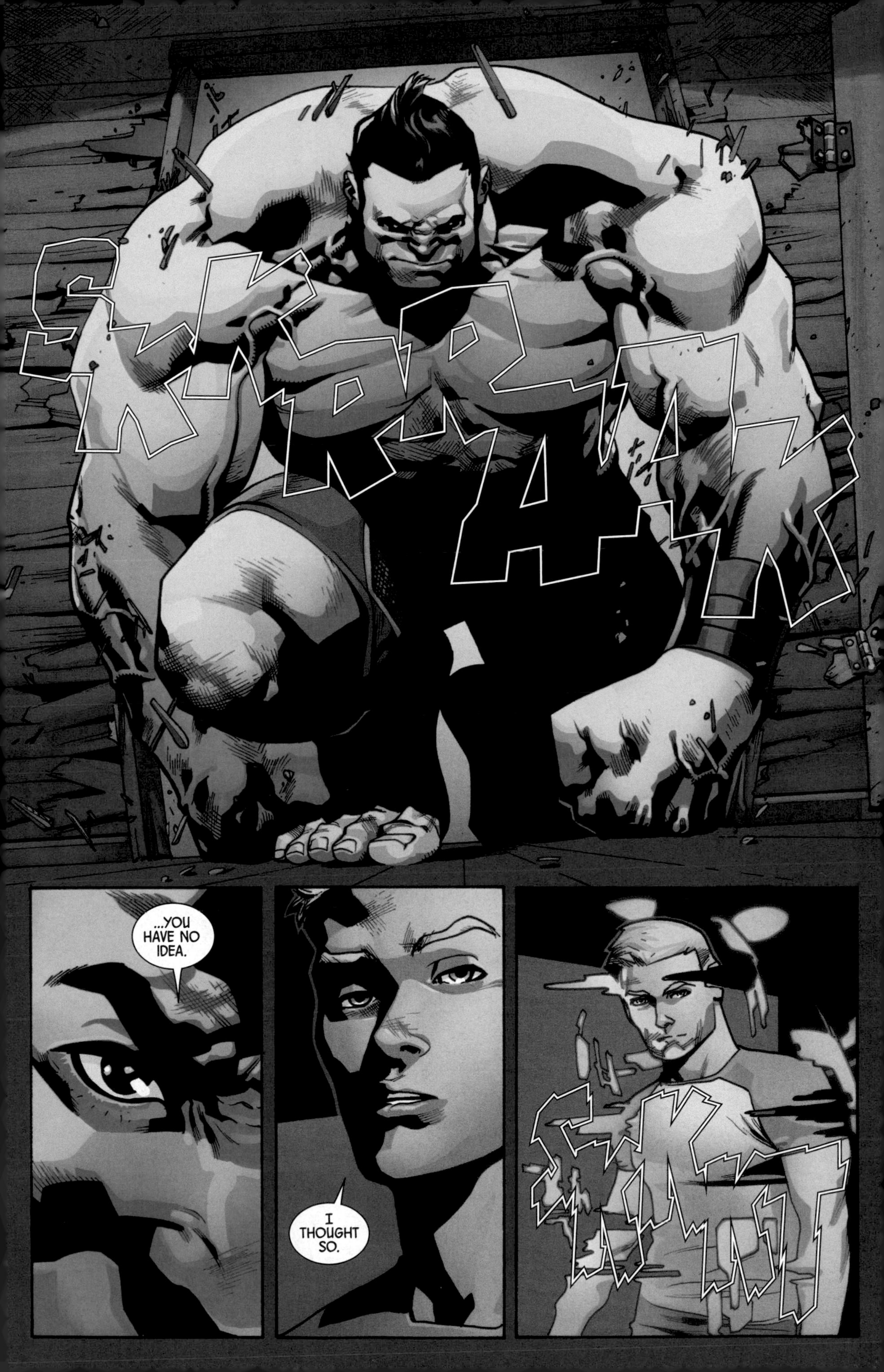
...YOU HAVE NO IDEA.
I THOUGHT SO.

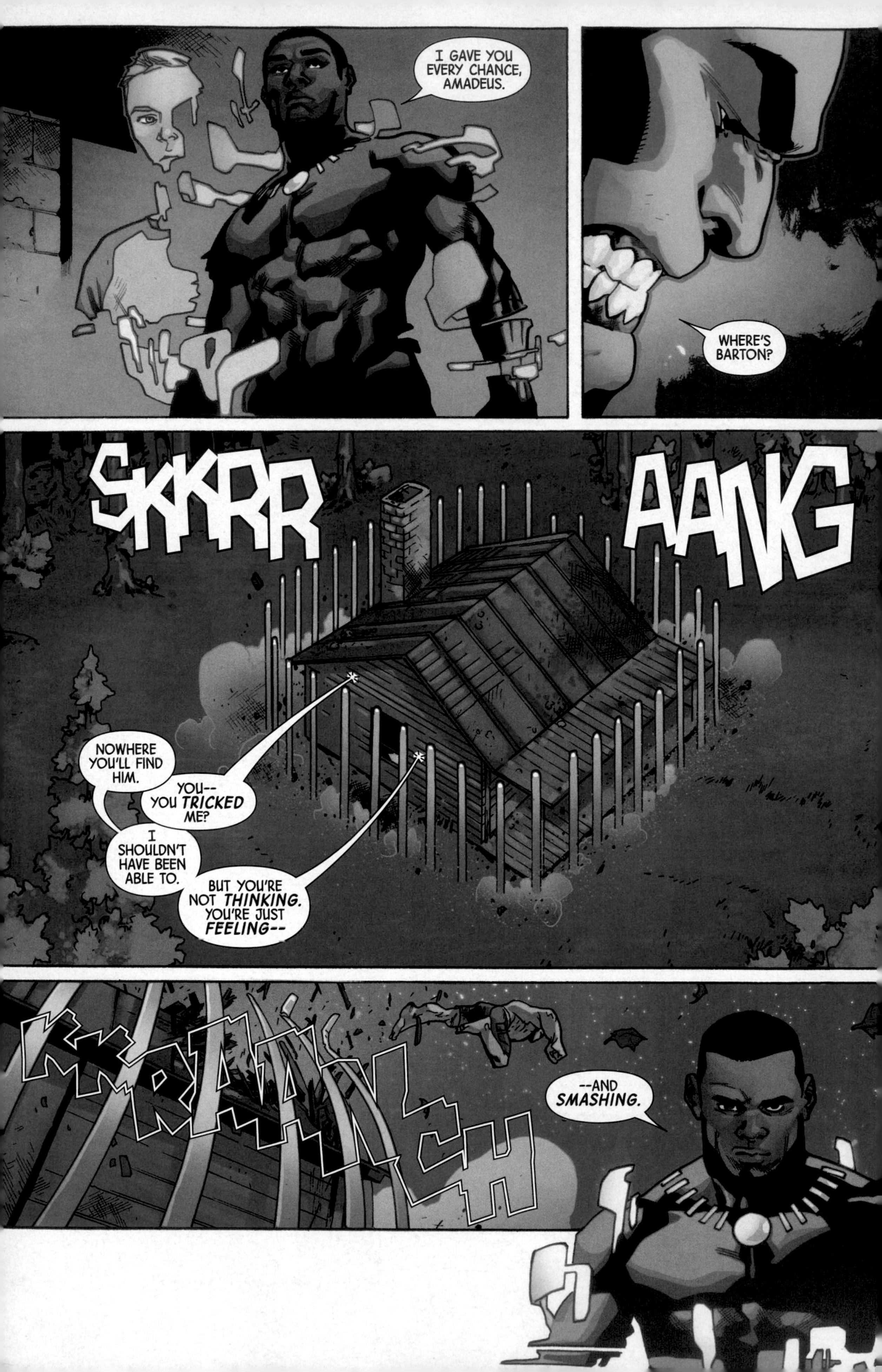
I GAVE YOU EVERY CHANCE, AMADEUS.
WHERE'S BARTON?
SKKRR
AANG
NOWHERE YOU'LL FIND HIM.
YOU-- YOU *TRICKED* ME?
I SHOULDN'T HAVE BEEN ABLE TO.
BUT YOU'RE NOT *THINKING.* YOU'RE JUST *FEELING--*
--AND *SMASHING.*

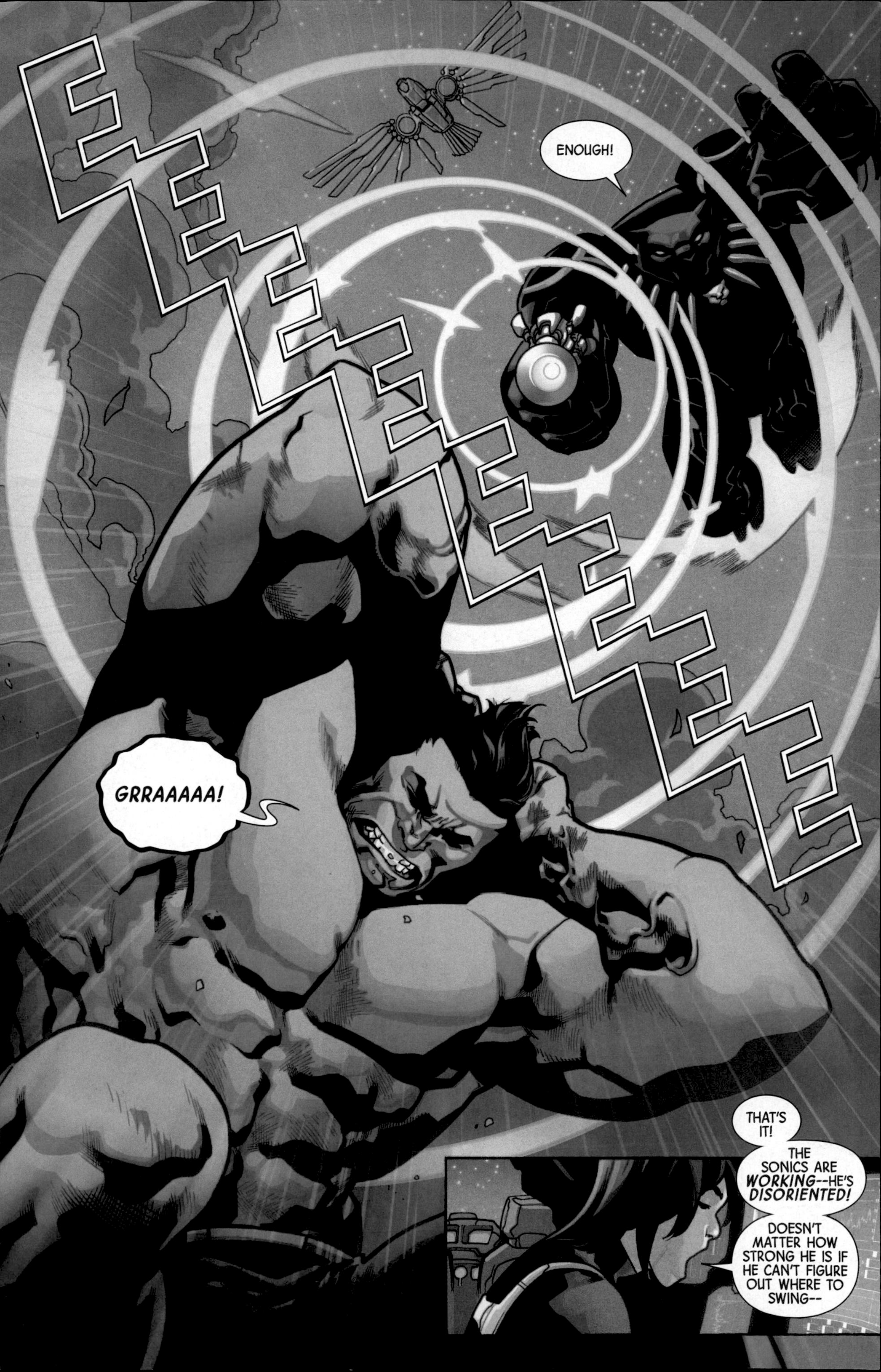
ENOUGH!
GRRAAAAA!
THAT'S IT!
THE SONICS ARE *WORKING*--HE'S *DISORIENTED!*
DOESN'T MATTER HOW STRONG HE IS IF HE CAN'T FIGURE OUT WHERE TO SWING--

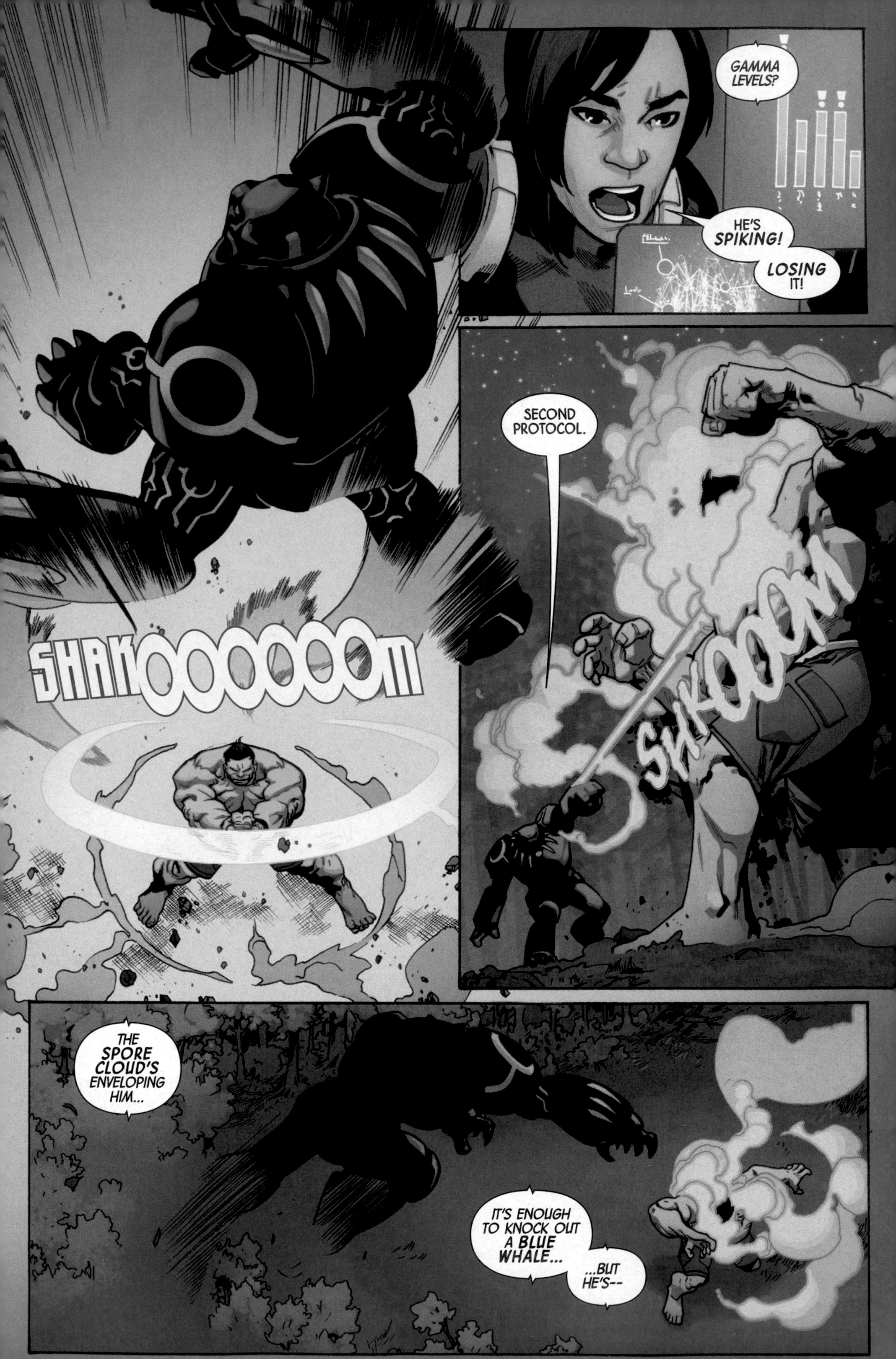
GAMMA LEVELS?
HE'S SPIKING!
LOSING IT!
SHAKOOOOOOOM
SECOND PROTOCOL.
SHKOOOOM
THE SPORE CLOUD'S ENVELOPING HIM...
IT'S ENOUGH TO KNOCK OUT A BLUE WHALE...
...BUT HE'S--

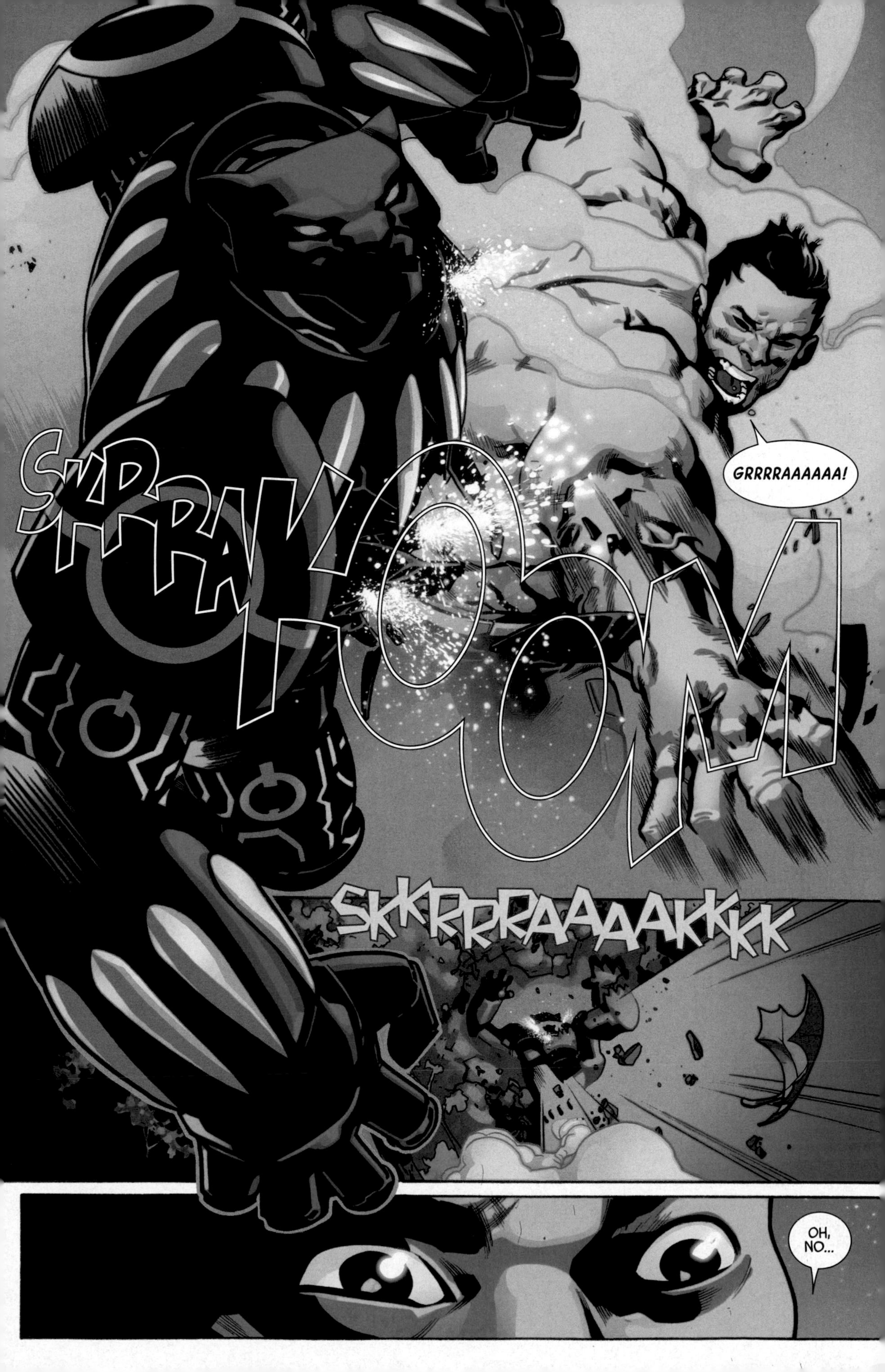
SKRRAKOOM
GRRRRAAAAAA!
SKKRRRRAAAAKKKK
OH, NO...

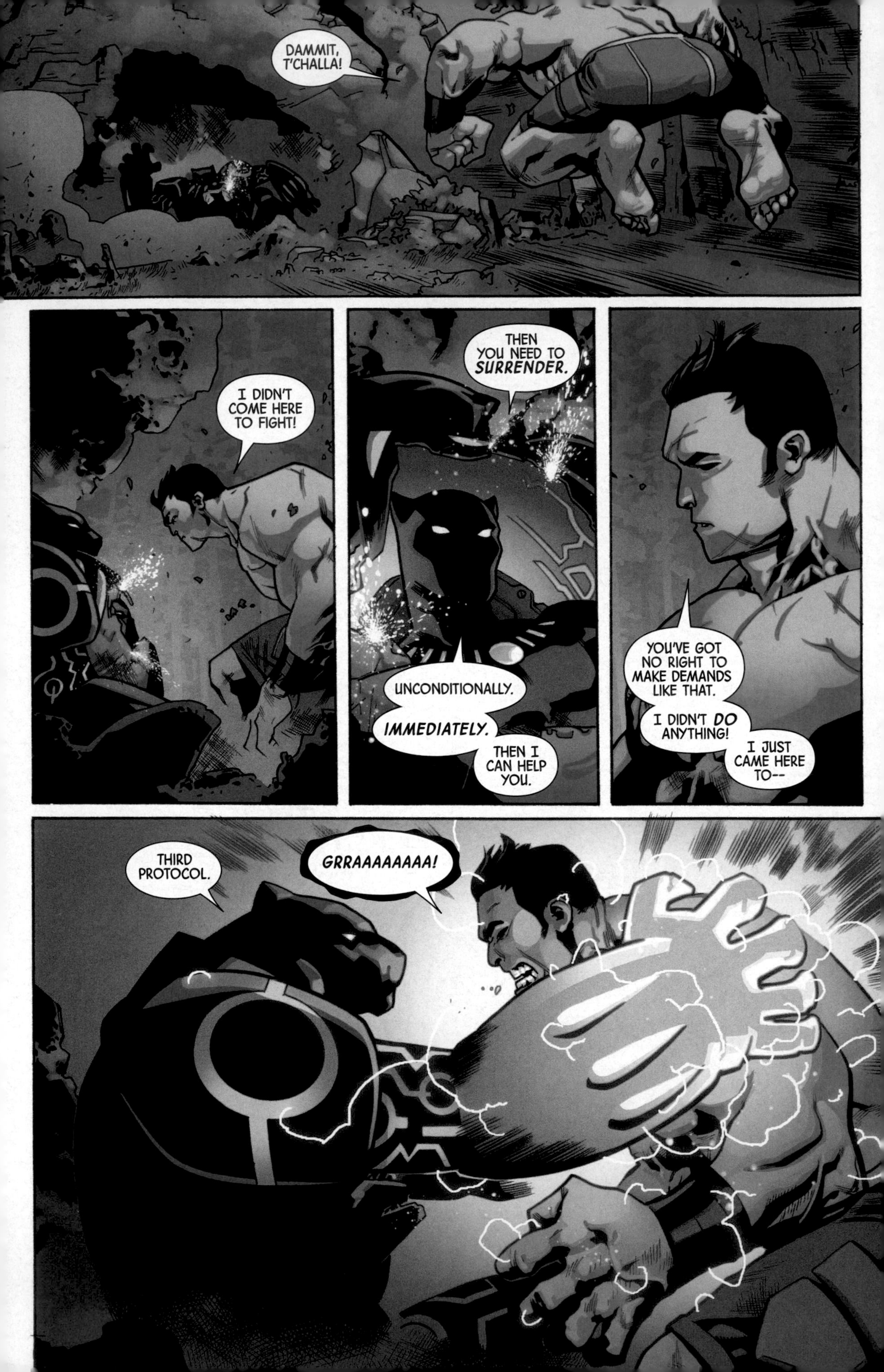
DAMMIT, T'CHALLA!
I DIDN'T COME HERE TO FIGHT!
THEN YOU NEED TO SURRENDER.
UNCONDITIONALLY.
IMMEDIATELY.
THEN I CAN HELP YOU.
YOU'VE GOT NO RIGHT TO MAKE DEMANDS LIKE THAT.
I DIDN'T DO ANYTHING!
I JUST CAME HERE TO--
THIRD PROTOCOL.
GRRAAAAAAAA!

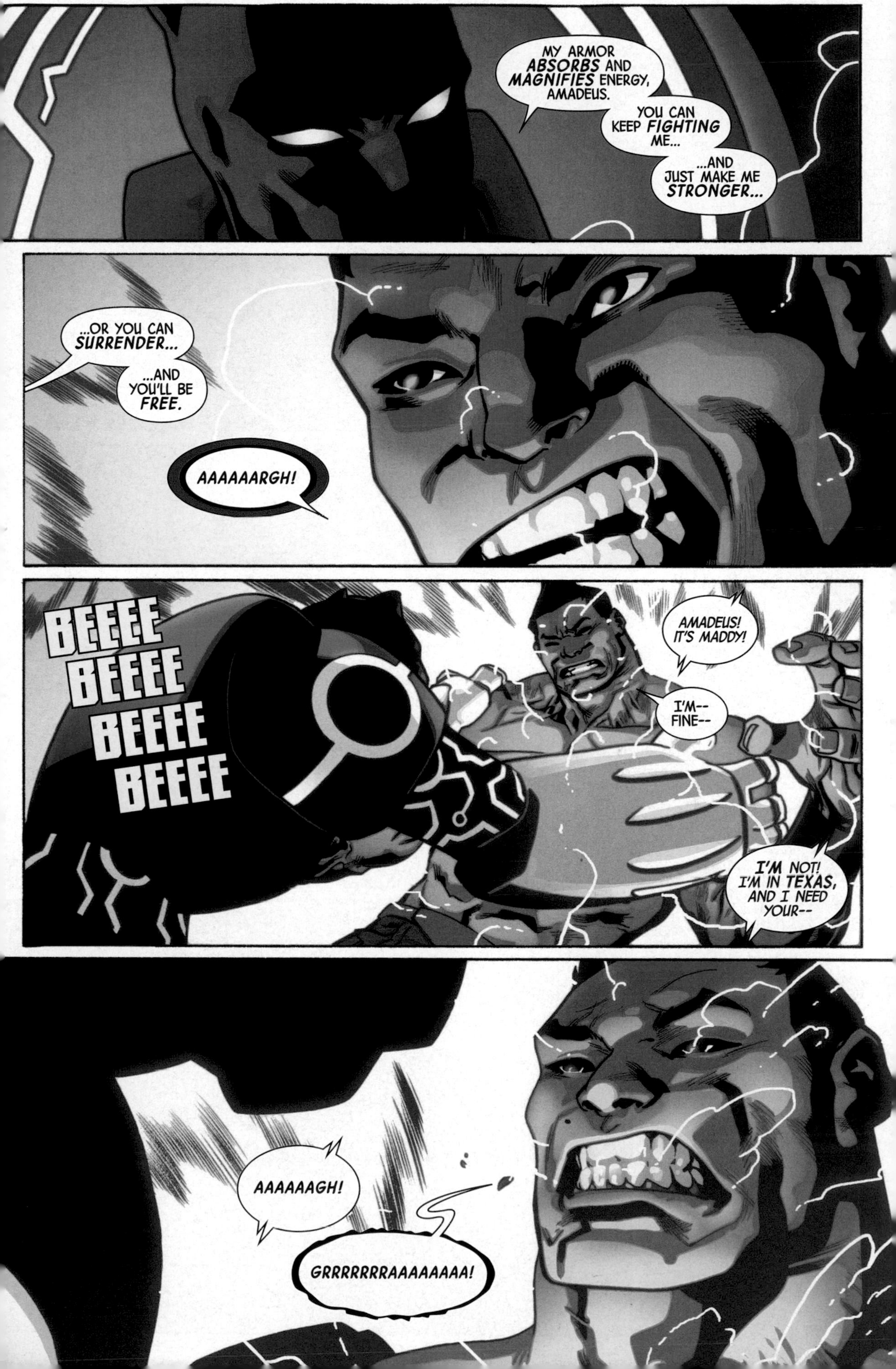
MY ARMOR ABSORBS AND MAGNIFIES ENERGY, AMADEUS.
YOU CAN KEEP FIGHTING ME...
...AND JUST MAKE ME STRONGER...
...OR YOU CAN SURRENDER...
...AND YOU'LL BE FREE.
AAAAAARGH!
BEEEE BEEEE BEEEE BEEEE
AMADEUS! IT'S MADDY!
I'M-- FINE--
I'M NOT! I'M IN TEXAS, AND I NEED YOUR--
AAAAAAGH!
GRRRRRRRAAAAAAAA!

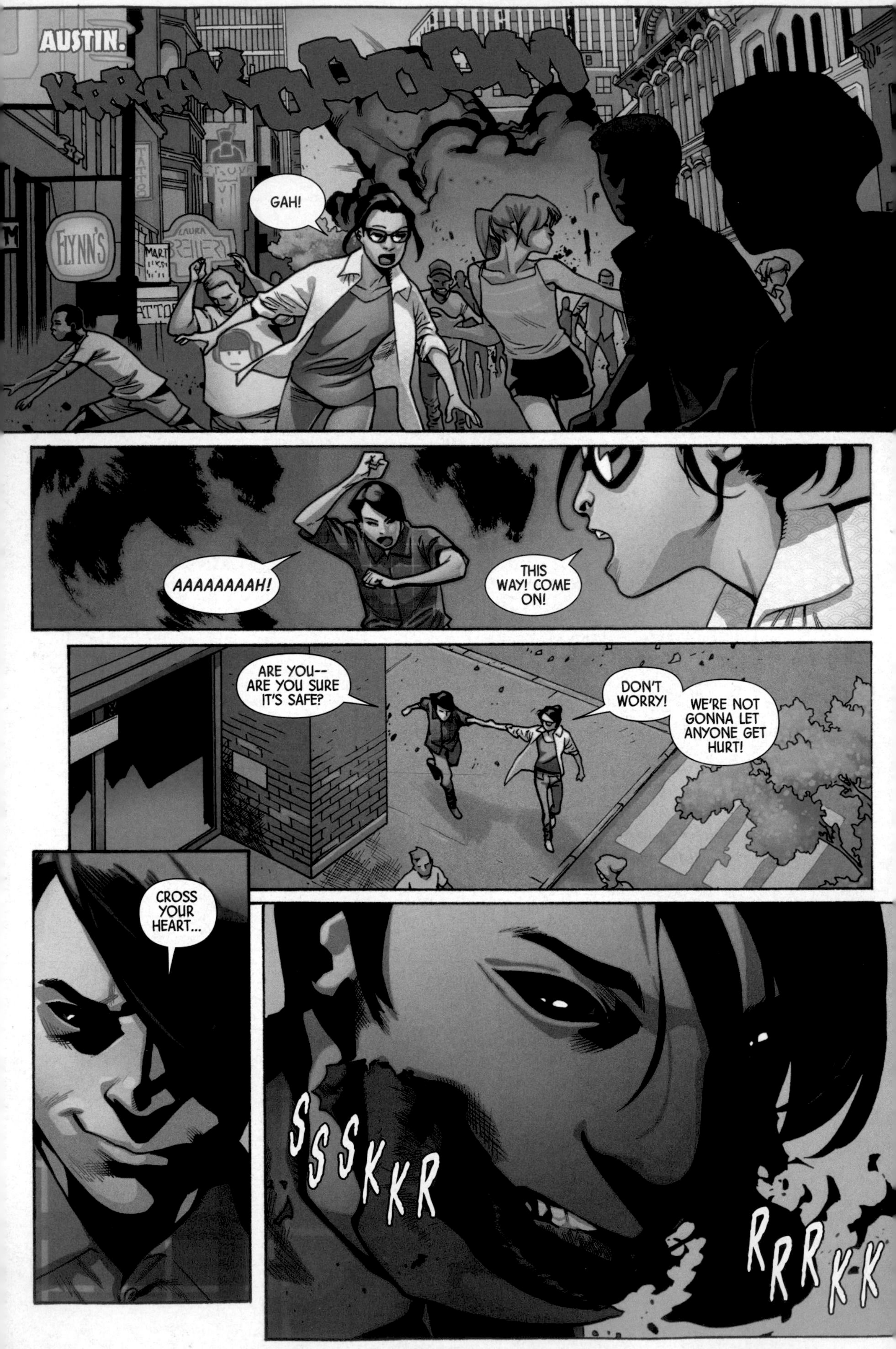
AUSTIN.
KRRAAKOOOOOM
GAH!
AAAAAAAAH!
THIS WAY! COME ON!
ARE YOU-- ARE YOU SURE IT'S SAFE?
DON'T WORRY!
WE'RE NOT GONNA LET ANYONE GET HURT!
CROSS YOUR HEART...
SSSKKR
RRRKK

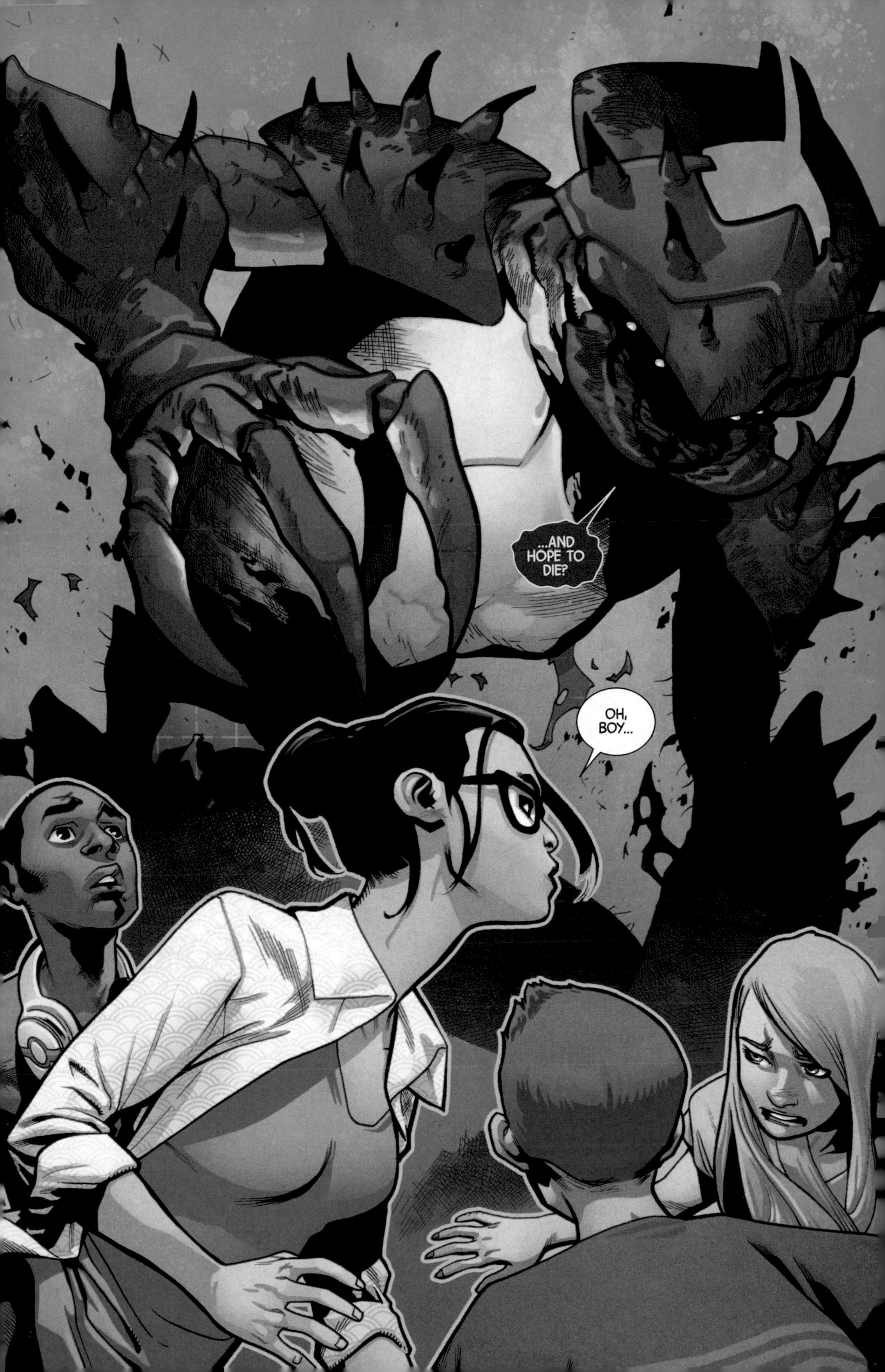
...AND HOPE TO DIE?
OH, BOY...

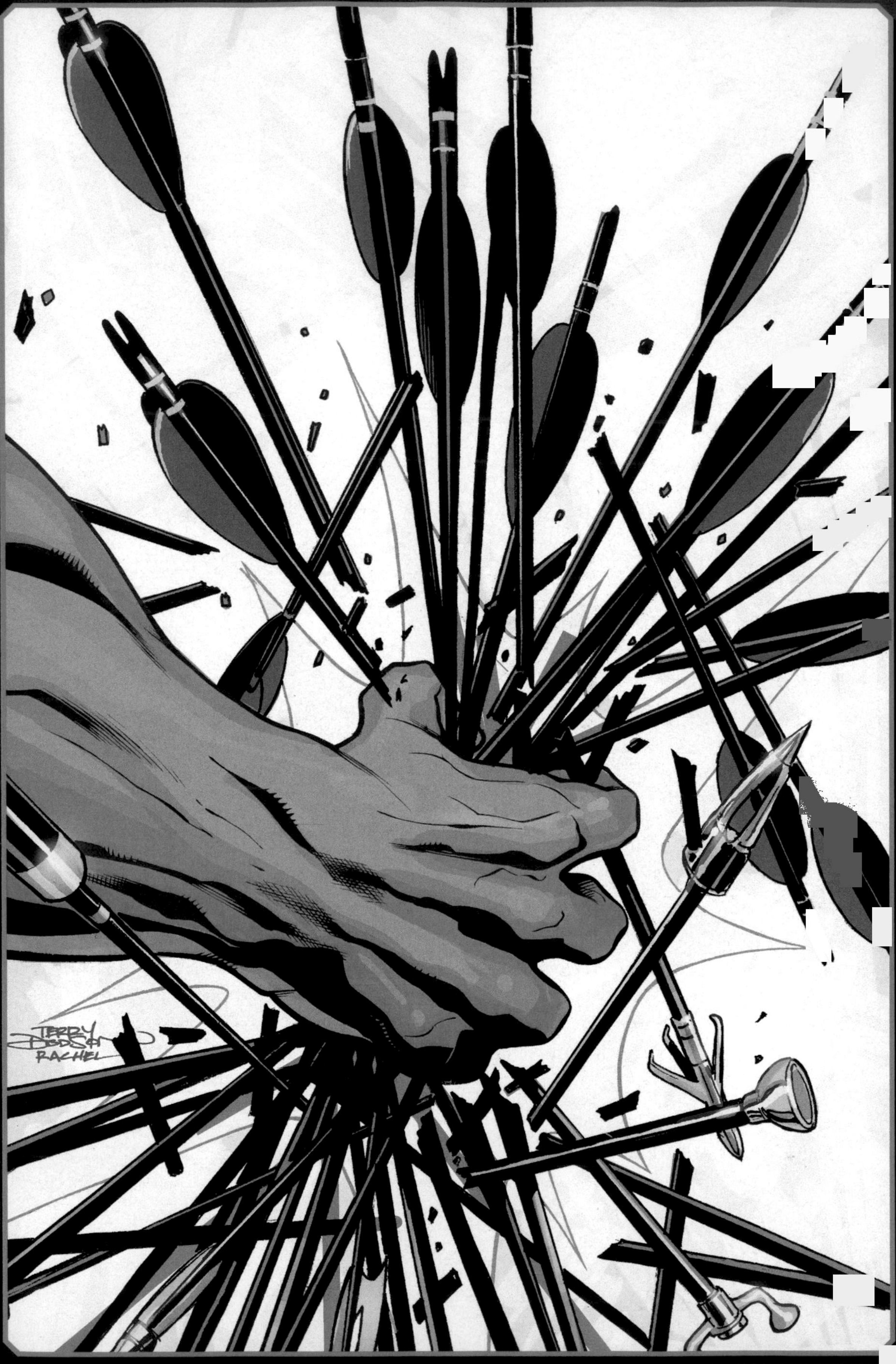
TERRY DODSON
RACHEL

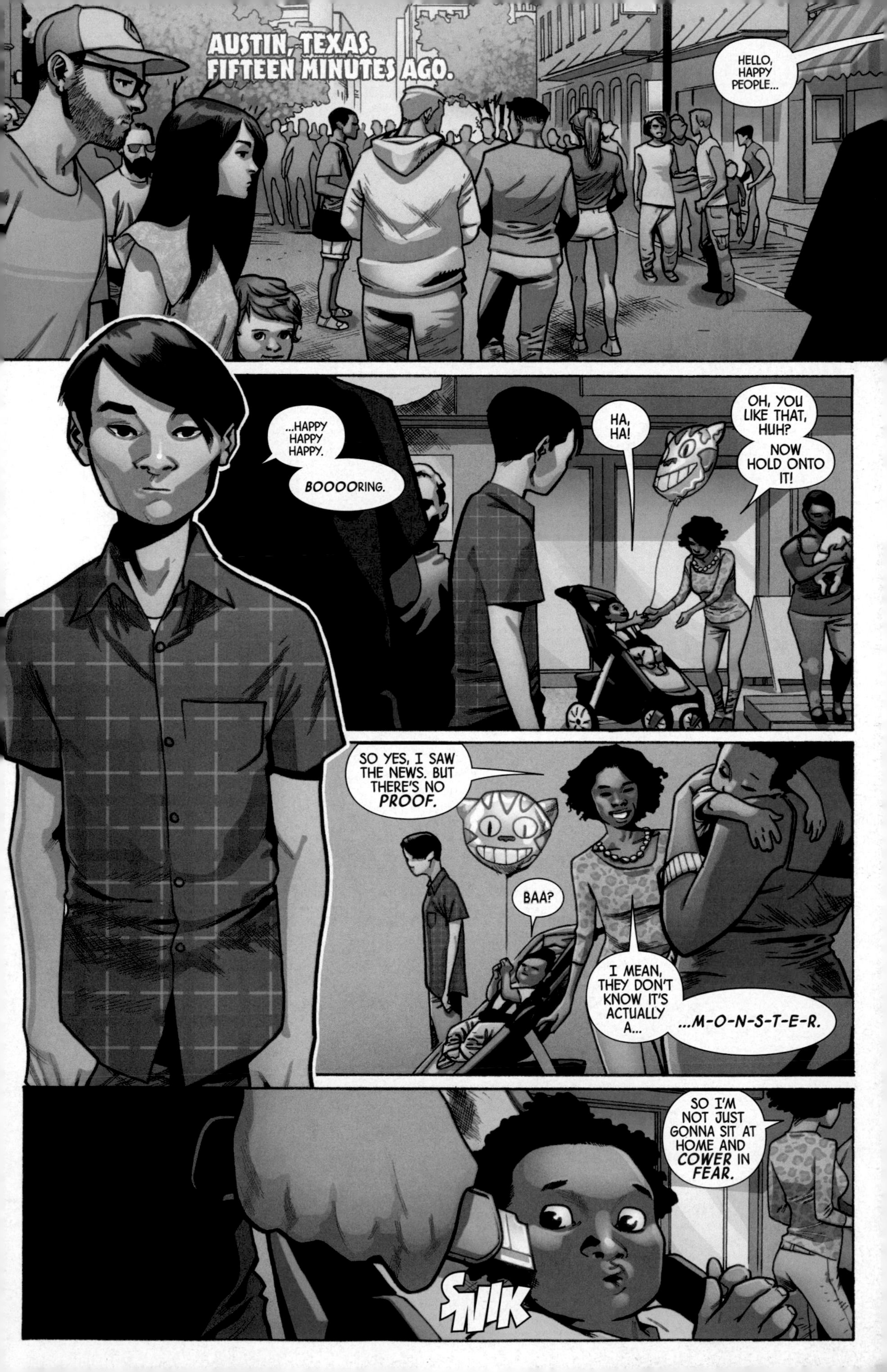

AUSTIN, TEXAS. FIFTEEN MINUTES AGO.
HELLO, HAPPY PEOPLE...
...HAPPY HAPPY HAPPY.
BOOOORING.
HA, HA!
OH, YOU LIKE THAT, HUH?
NOW HOLD ONTO IT!
SO YES, I SAW THE NEWS. BUT THERE'S NO PROOF.
BAA?
I MEAN, THEY DON'T KNOW IT'S ACTUALLY A...
...M-O-N-S-T-E-R.
SO I'M NOT JUST GONNA SIT AT HOME AND COWER IN FEAR.
SNIK

MAH BALLOOOOOOON!

AMADEUS, THIS IS *MADDY*.

I'M IN AUSTIN, EXTRAPOLATING THE LIKELY LOCATION OF THE NEXT *MONSTER ATTACK*.

MADAME CURIE "MADDY" CHO. SISTER AND MISSION CONTROL OF AMADEUS CHO, A.K.A. THE HULK.

NOTHING... *UNUSUAL* SO FAR.

OH, BABY! I TOLD YOU TO HOLD ONTO IT!

NOW PLAYING
OPE AND SWA

WWAAAAAA!

AAAAAAH!

HA.

NOT ENOUGH.

NOT ENOUGH, NOT ENOUGH, NOT ENOUGH.

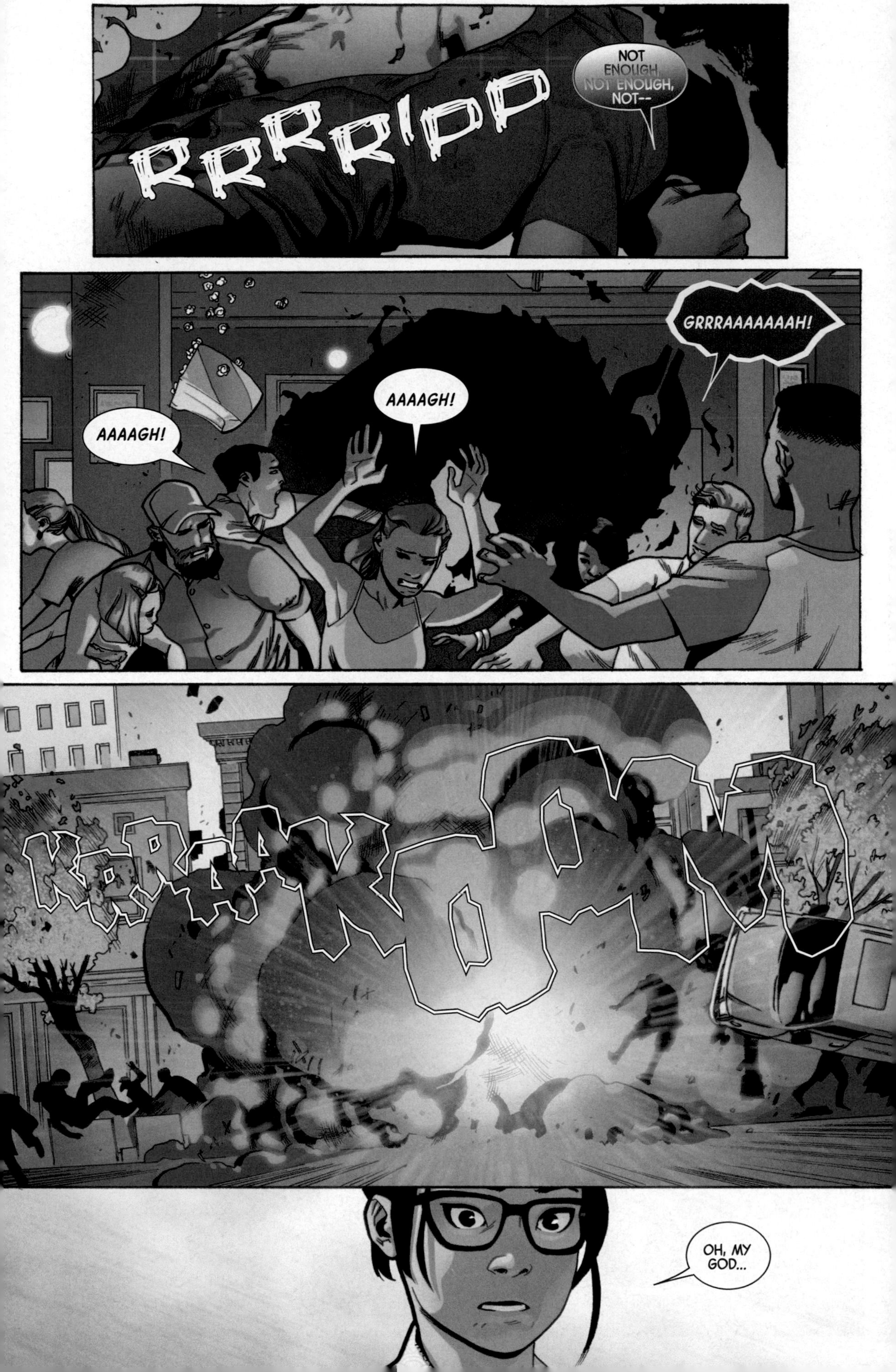
RRRRIPP
NOT ENOUGH, NOT ENOUGH, NOT--
AAAAGH!
AAAAGH!
GRRRAAAAAAAAH!
KARAKOOM
OH, MY GOD...

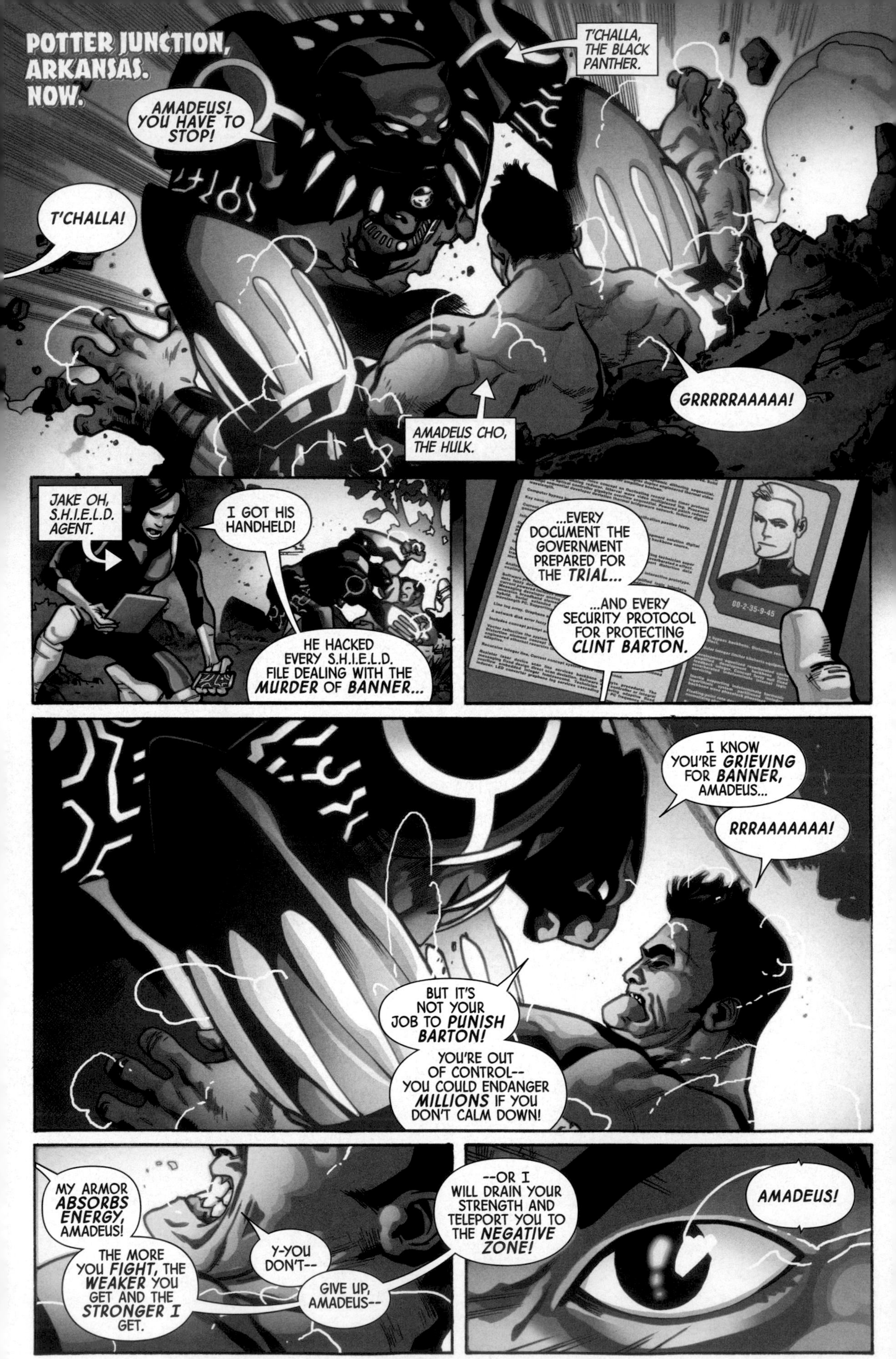
POTTER JUNCTION, ARKANSAS. NOW.
T'CHALLA, THE BLACK PANTHER.
AMADEUS! YOU HAVE TO STOP!
T'CHALLA!
GRRRRRAAAAA!
AMADEUS CHO, THE HULK.
JAKE OH, S.H.I.E.L.D. AGENT.
I GOT HIS HANDHELD!
HE HACKED EVERY S.H.I.E.L.D. FILE DEALING WITH THE MURDER OF BANNER...
...EVERY DOCUMENT THE GOVERNMENT PREPARED FOR THE TRIAL...
...AND EVERY SECURITY PROTOCOL FOR PROTECTING CLINT BARTON.
00-2-35-9-45
I KNOW YOU'RE GRIEVING FOR BANNER, AMADEUS...
RRRAAAAAAA!
BUT IT'S NOT YOUR JOB TO PUNISH BARTON!
YOU'RE OUT OF CONTROL-- YOU COULD ENDANGER MILLIONS IF YOU DON'T CALM DOWN!
MY ARMOR ABSORBS ENERGY, AMADEUS!
THE MORE YOU FIGHT, THE WEAKER YOU GET AND THE STRONGER I GET.
Y-YOU DON'T--
GIVE UP, AMADEUS--
--OR I WILL DRAIN YOUR STRENGTH AND TELEPORT YOU TO THE NEGATIVE ZONE!
AMADEUS!

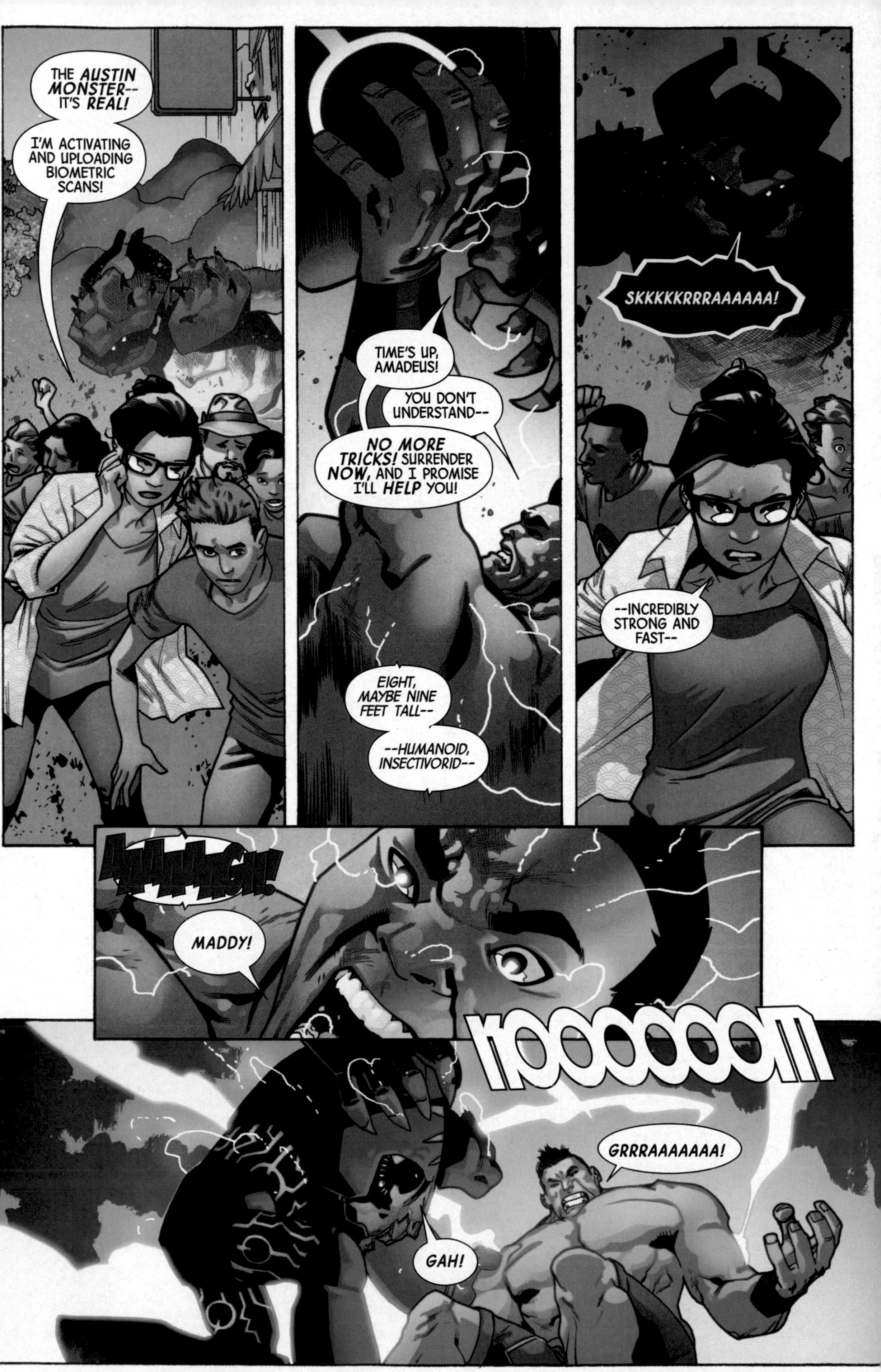
THE AUSTIN MONSTER-- IT'S REAL!
I'M ACTIVATING AND UPLOADING BIOMETRIC SCANS!
TIME'S UP, AMADEUS!
YOU DON'T UNDERSTAND--
NO MORE TRICKS! SURRENDER NOW, AND I PROMISE I'LL HELP YOU!
EIGHT, MAYBE NINE FEET TALL--
--HUMANOID, INSECTIVORID--
SKKKKKRRRAAAAAA!
--INCREDIBLY STRONG AND FAST--
MADDY!
rOOOOOOM
GRRRAAAAAAA!
GAH!

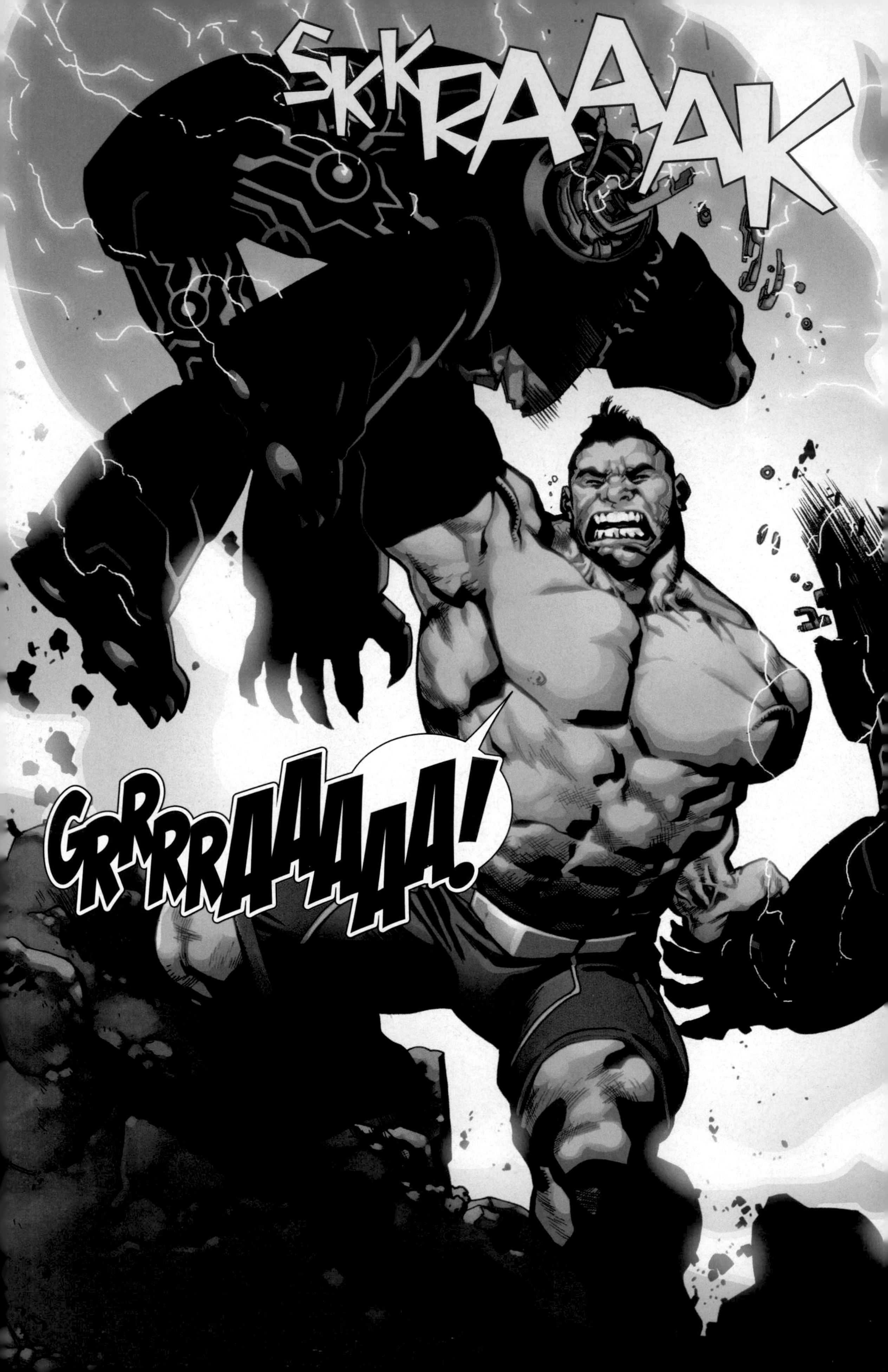
SKKRAAAAK
GRRRRAAAAAA!

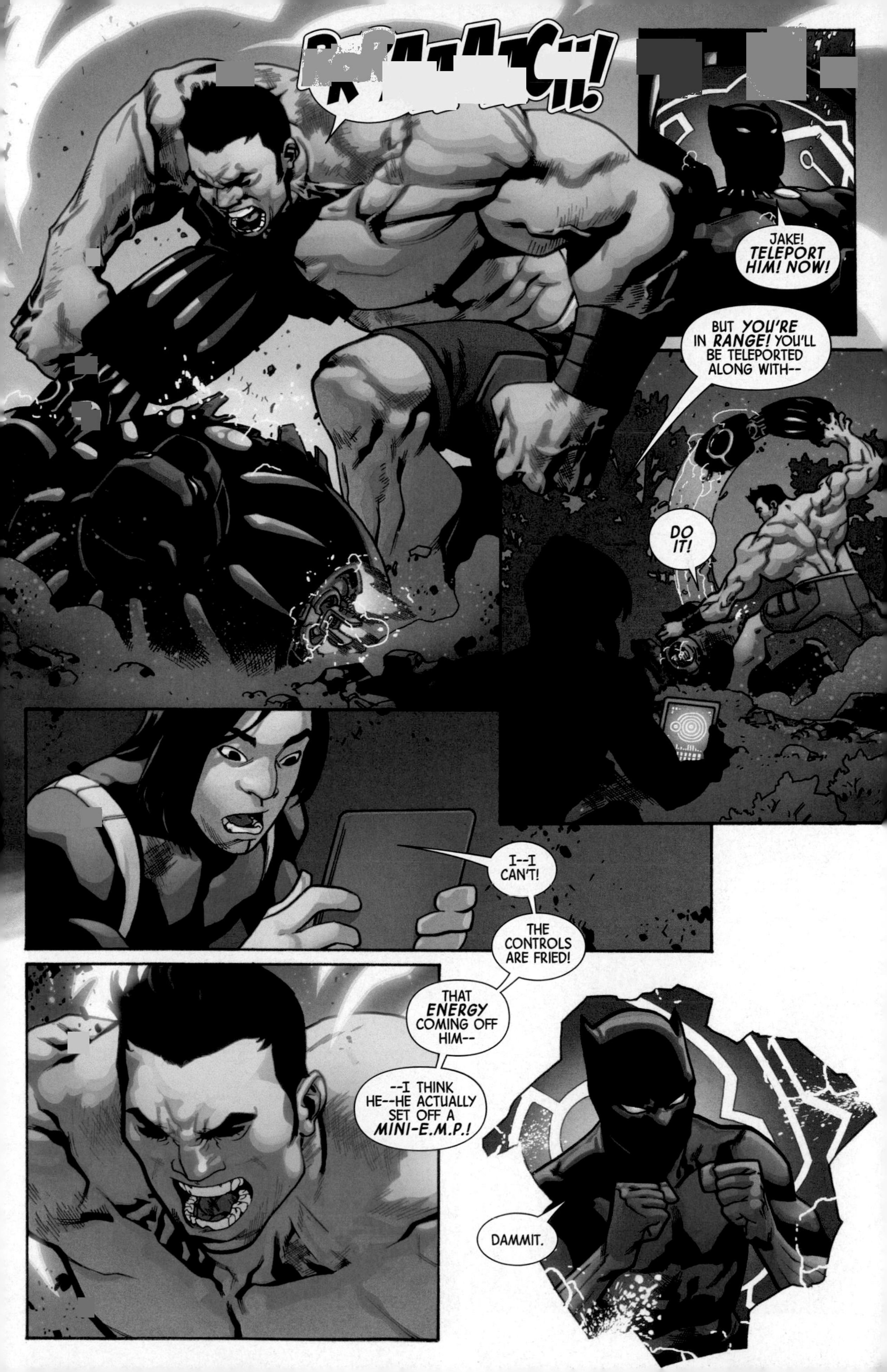
JAKE! TELEPORT HIM! NOW!
BUT YOU'RE IN RANGE! YOU'LL BE TELEPORTED ALONG WITH--
DO IT!
I--I CAN'T!
THE CONTROLS ARE FRIED!
THAT ENERGY COMING OFF HIM--
--I THINK HE--HE ACTUALLY SET OFF A MINI-E.M.P.!
DAMMIT.

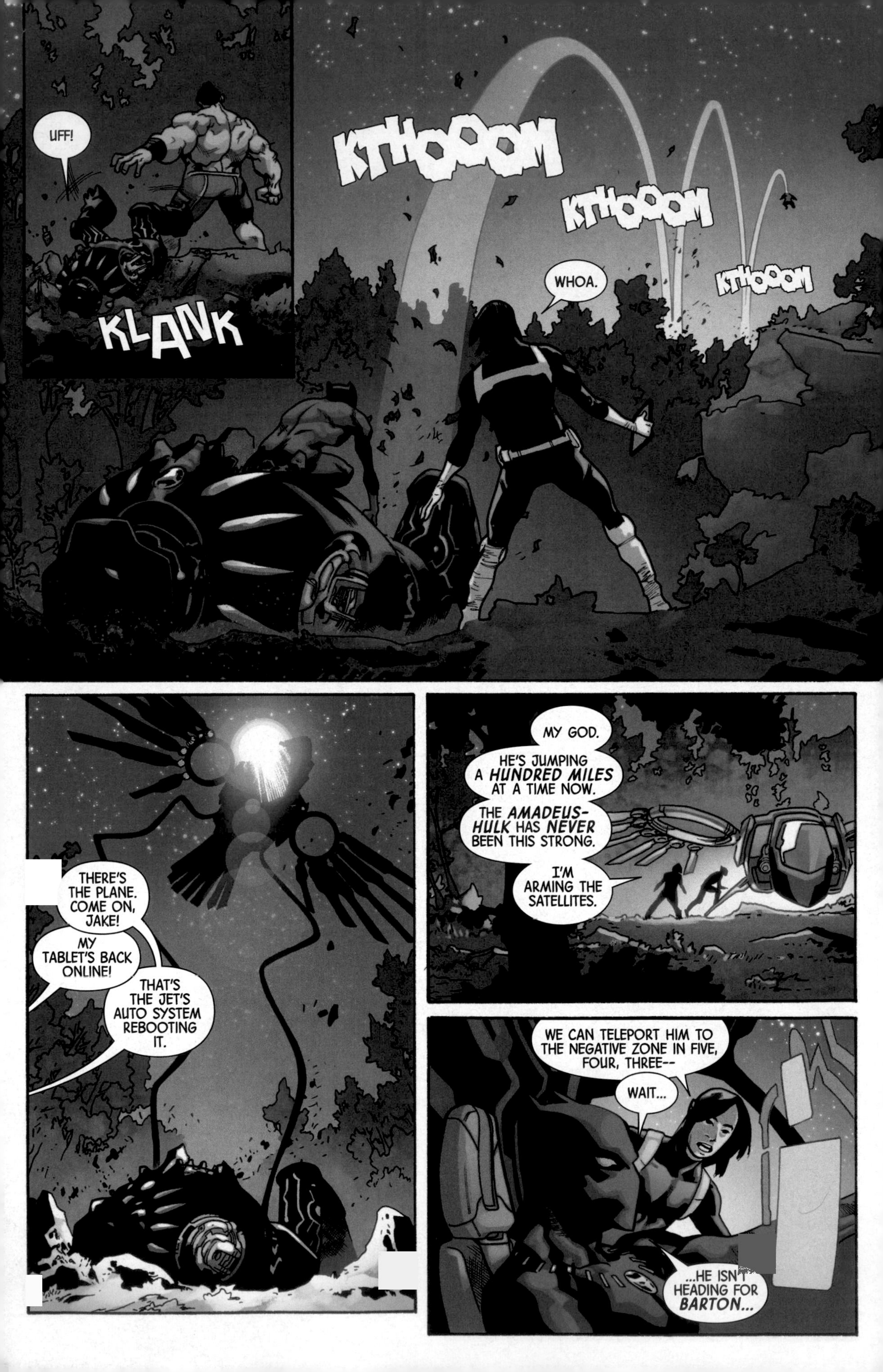
UFF!
KLANK
KTHOOOM
KTHOOOM
KTHOOOM
WHOA.
THERE'S THE PLANE. COME ON, JAKE!
MY TABLET'S BACK ONLINE!
THAT'S THE JET'S AUTO SYSTEM REBOOTING IT.
MY GOD.
HE'S JUMPING A *HUNDRED MILES* AT A TIME NOW.
THE *AMADEUS-HULK* HAS *NEVER* BEEN THIS STRONG.
I'M ARMING THE SATELLITES.
WE CAN TELEPORT HIM TO THE NEGATIVE ZONE IN FIVE, FOUR, THREE--
WAIT...
...HE ISN'T HEADING FOR *BARTON*...

"...AND HE YELLED *'MADDY.'*"

OKAY, VULNERABILITY TESTS...

CHARGING...

KRRRAAAAA!

...AND...

UOOOOOO

LASER.

KAPOW

FLAME.

RRROOOORRR

MOVE IT, MOVE IT, MOVE IT!

BOTH INEFFECTIVE.

DANG.

COME ON, YOU DIRTBAG! I'M RIGHT HERE!

KRRRRAAAAAA!

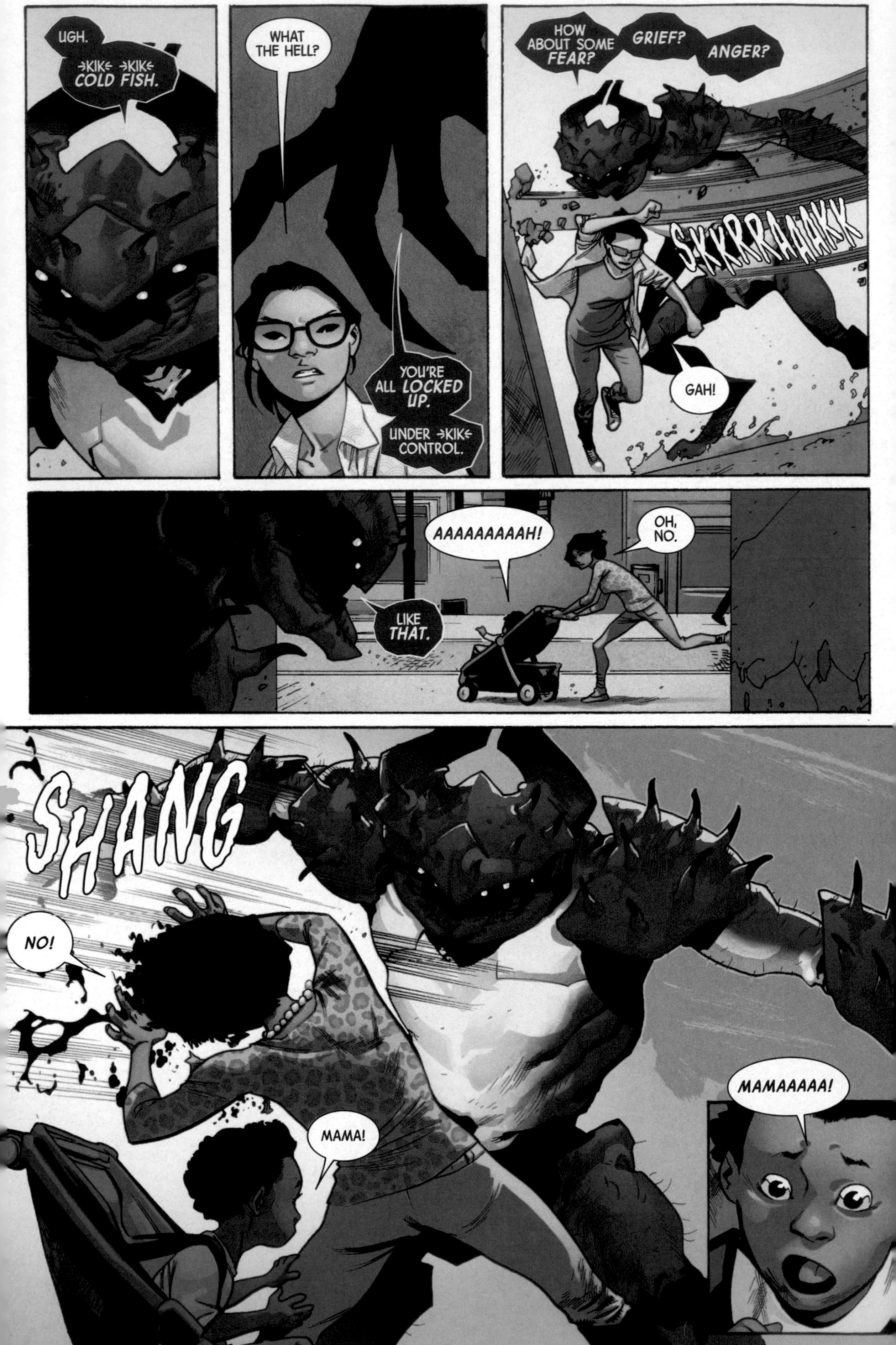
UGH.
⥽KIK⥼ ⥽KIK⥼ COLD FISH.
WHAT THE HELL?
YOU'RE ALL LOCKED UP.
UNDER ⥽KIK⥼ CONTROL.
HOW ABOUT SOME FEAR?
GRIEF?
ANGER?
SKKRRAAAKK
GAH!
AAAAAAAAAH!
OH, NO.
LIKE THAT.
SHANG
NO!
MAMA!
MAMAAAAAA!

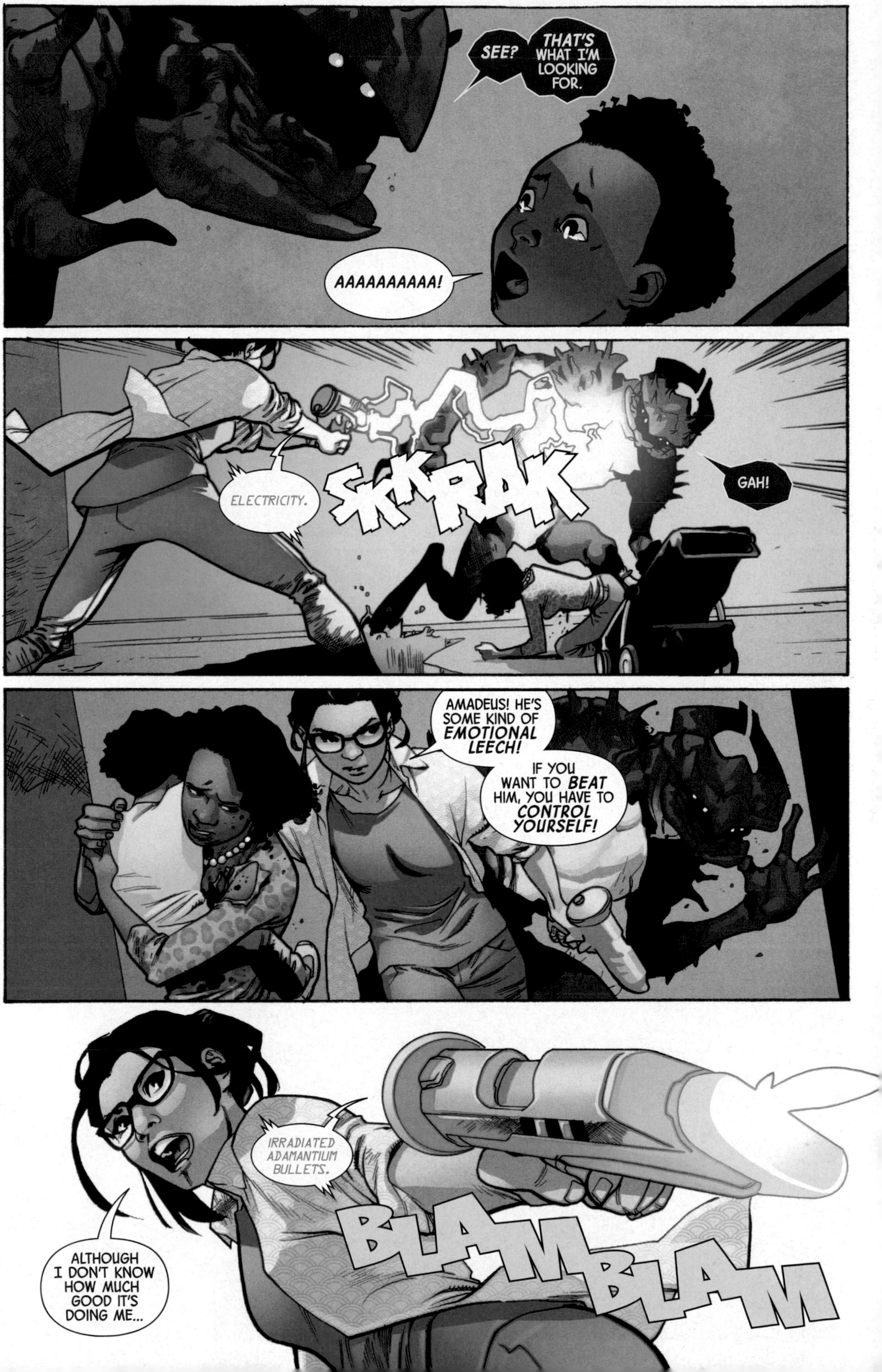

SEE?
THAT'S WHAT I'M LOOKING FOR.
AAAAAAAAAA!
ELECTRICITY.
SKKRAK
GAH!
AMADEUS! HE'S SOME KIND OF EMOTIONAL LEECH!
IF YOU WANT TO BEAT HIM, YOU HAVE TO CONTROL YOURSELF!
IRRADIATED ADAMANTIUM BULLETS.
ALTHOUGH I DON'T KNOW HOW MUCH GOOD IT'S DOING ME...
BLAM BLAM

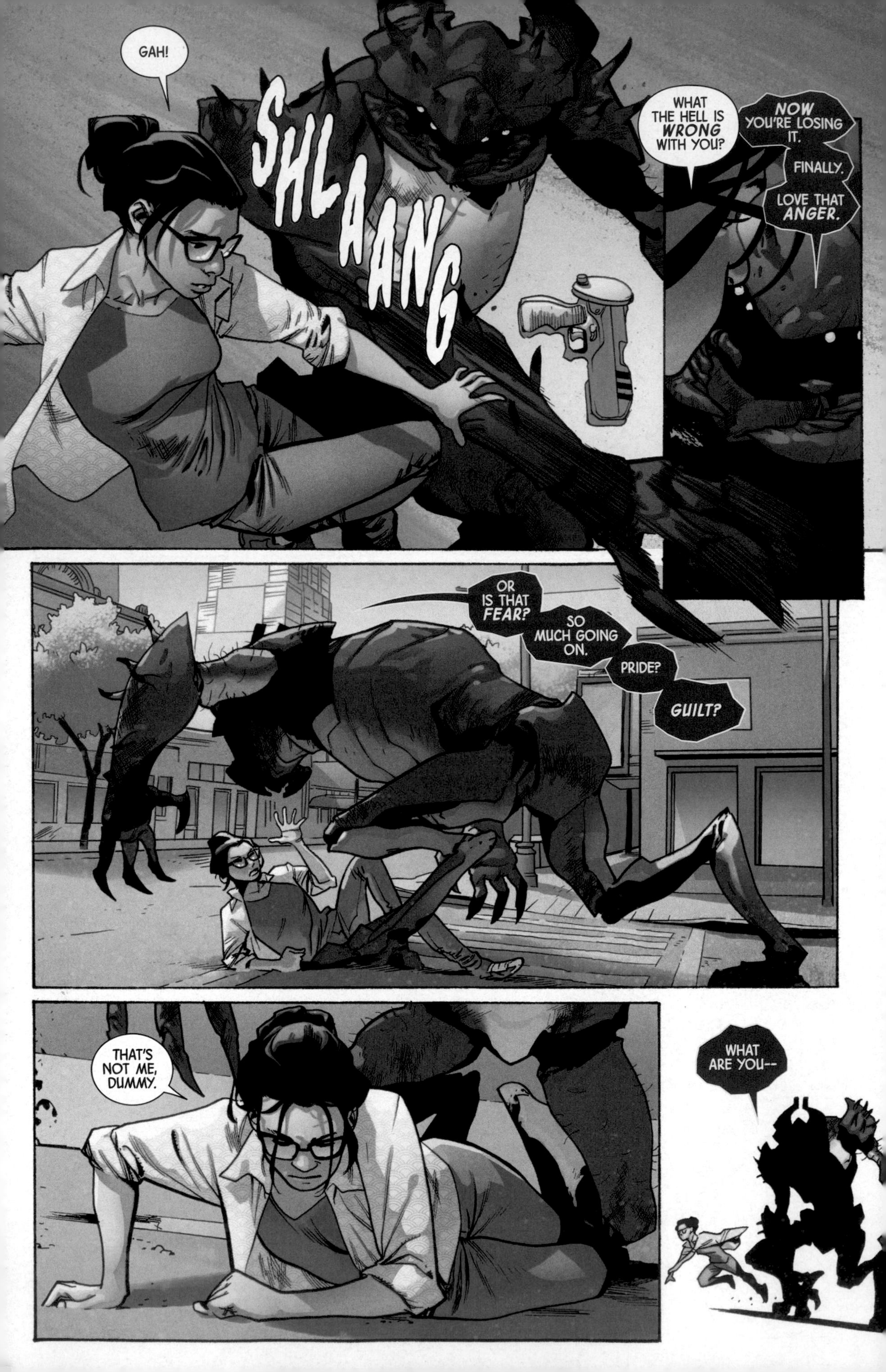
GAH!
SHLAANG
WHAT THE HELL IS WRONG WITH YOU?
NOW YOU'RE LOSING IT.
FINALLY.
LOVE THAT ANGER.
OR IS THAT FEAR?
SO MUCH GOING ON.
PRIDE?
GUILT?
THAT'S NOT ME, DUMMY.
WHAT ARE YOU--

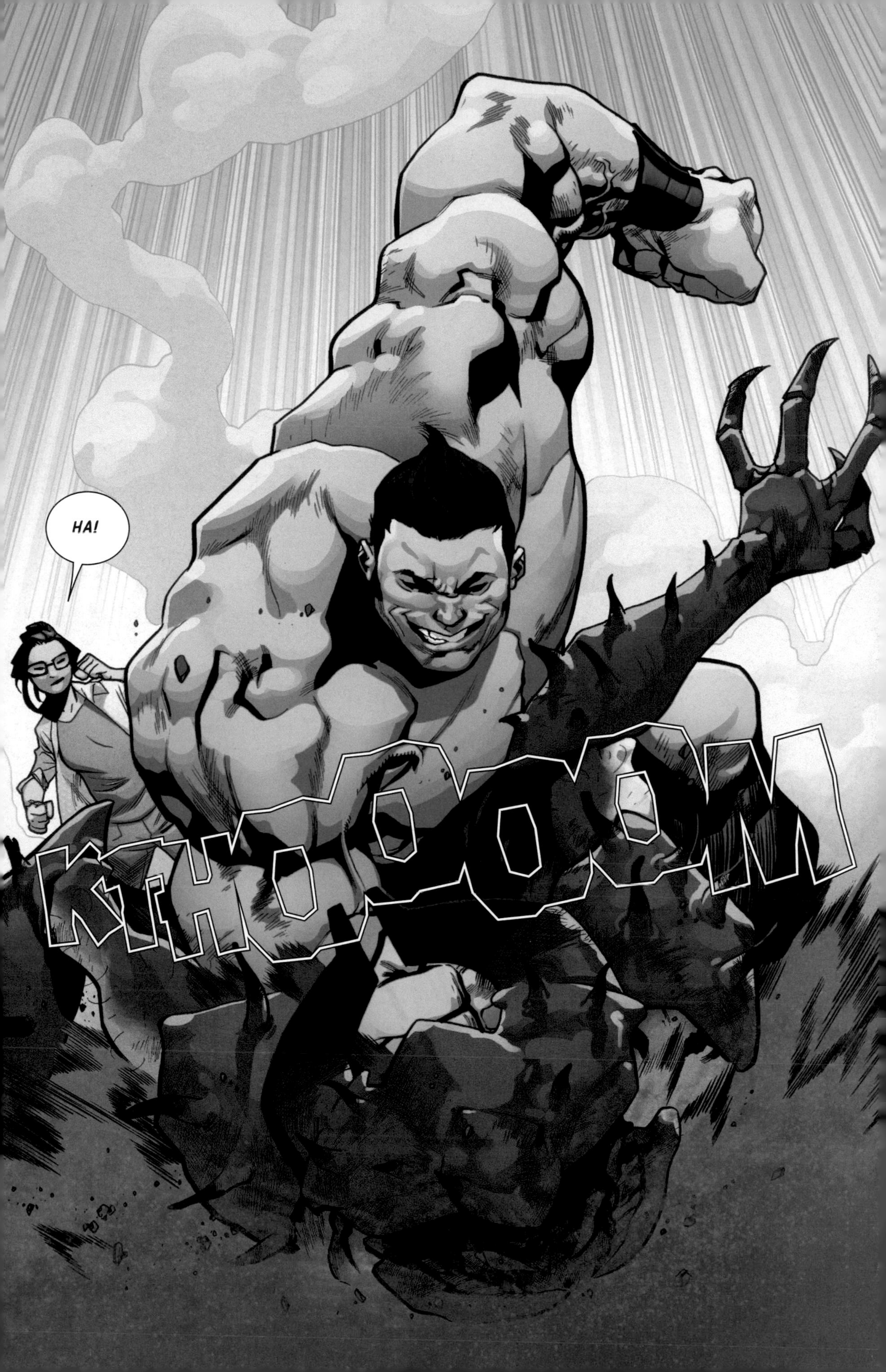
HA!
KTHOOOOOM

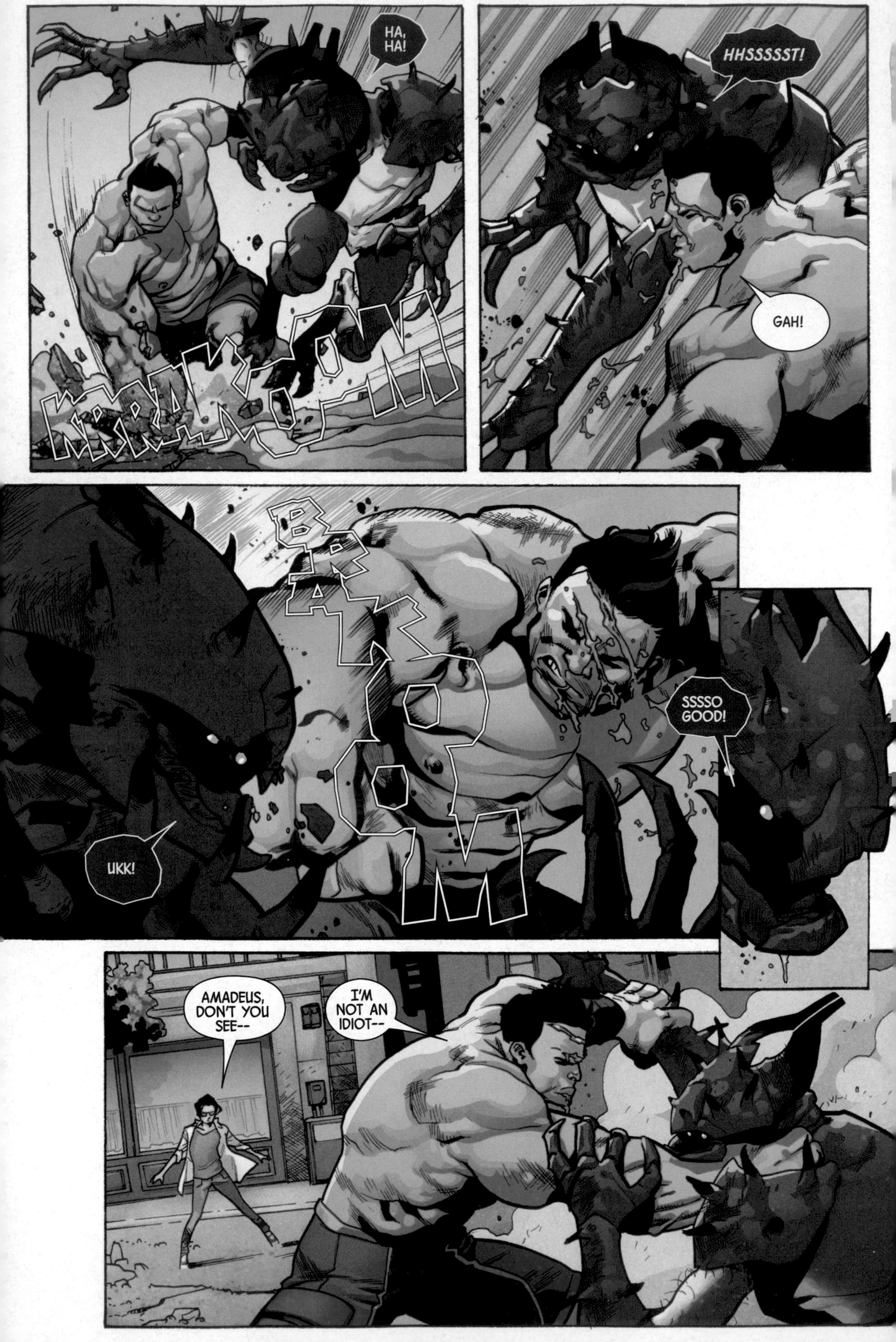
HA, HA!
KRRAKOOM
HHSSSSST!
GAH!
BRAKOOM
SSSSO GOOD!
UKK!
AMADEUS, DON'T YOU SEE--
I'M NOT AN IDIOT--

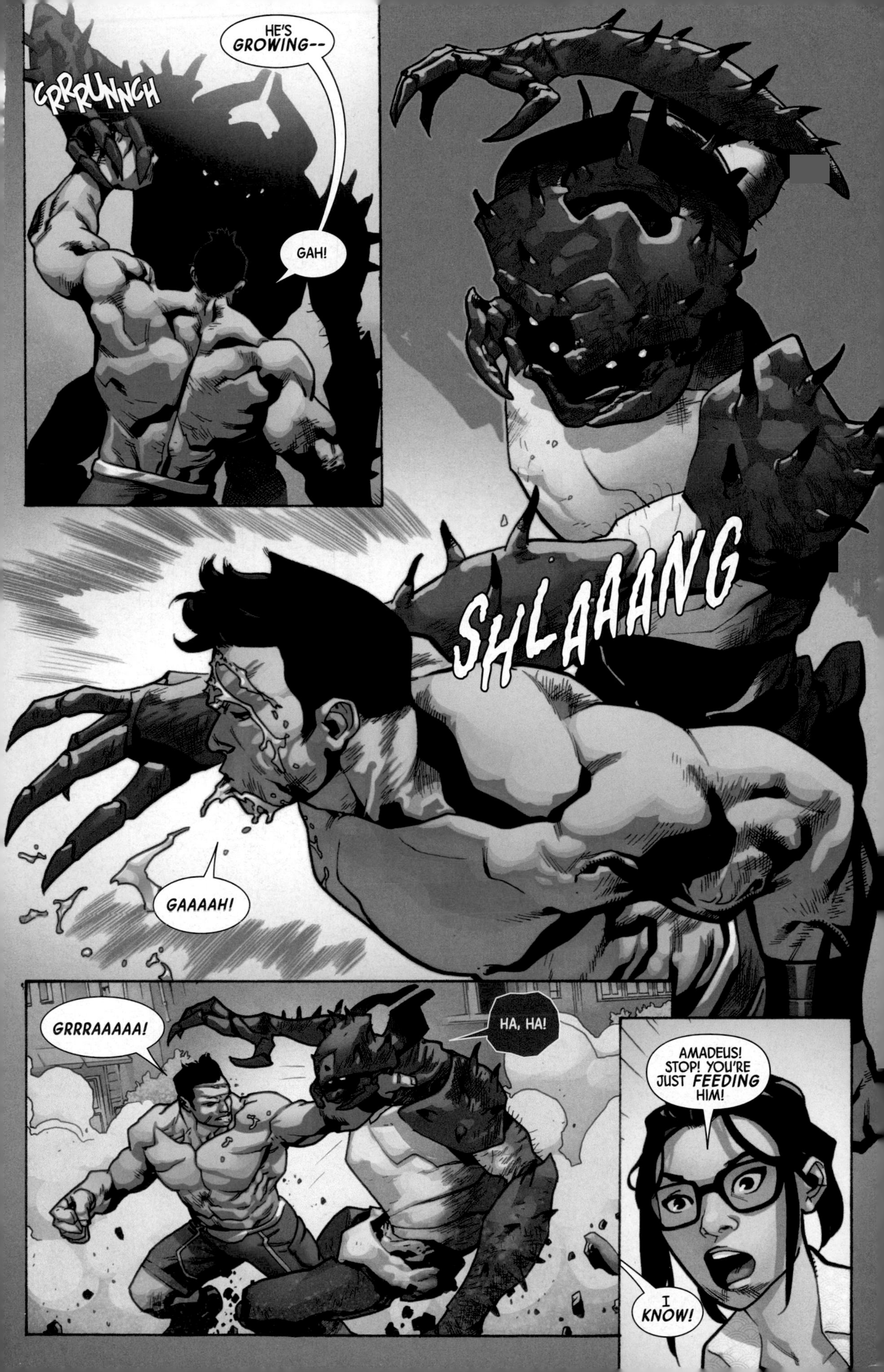
HE'S GROWING--
CRRRUNNCH
GAH!
SHLAAANG
GAAAAH!
GRRRAAAAAA!
HA, HA!
AMADEUS! STOP! YOU'RE JUST FEEDING HIM!
I KNOW!

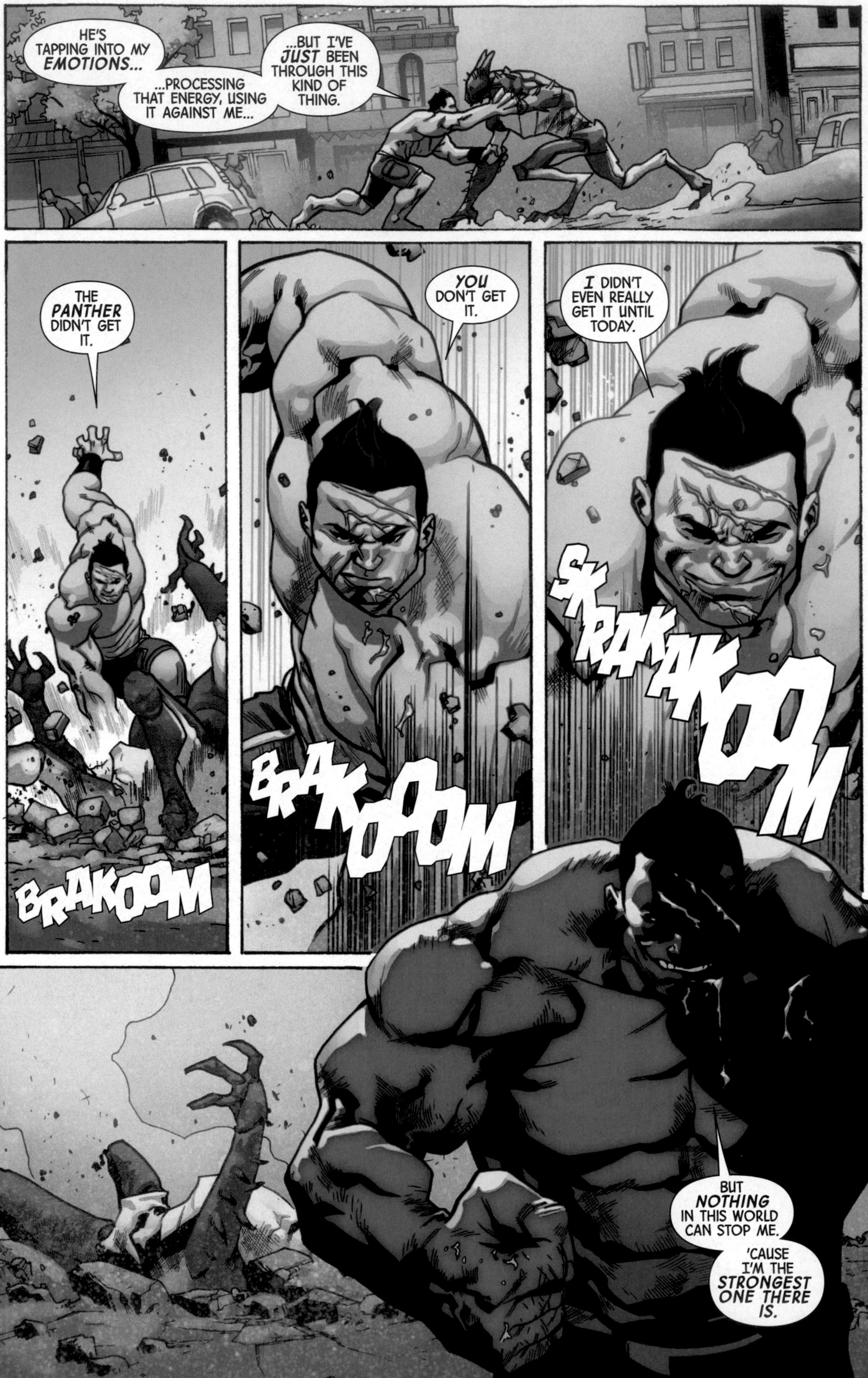
HE'S TAPPING INTO MY EMOTIONS...
...PROCESSING THAT ENERGY, USING IT AGAINST ME...
...BUT I'VE JUST BEEN THROUGH THIS KIND OF THING.
THE PANTHER DIDN'T GET IT.
BRAKOOM
YOU DON'T GET IT.
BRAKOOOM
I DIDN'T EVEN REALLY GET IT UNTIL TODAY.
SKRAKAKOOM
BUT NOTHING IN THIS WORLD CAN STOP ME.
'CAUSE I'M THE STRONGEST ONE THERE IS.

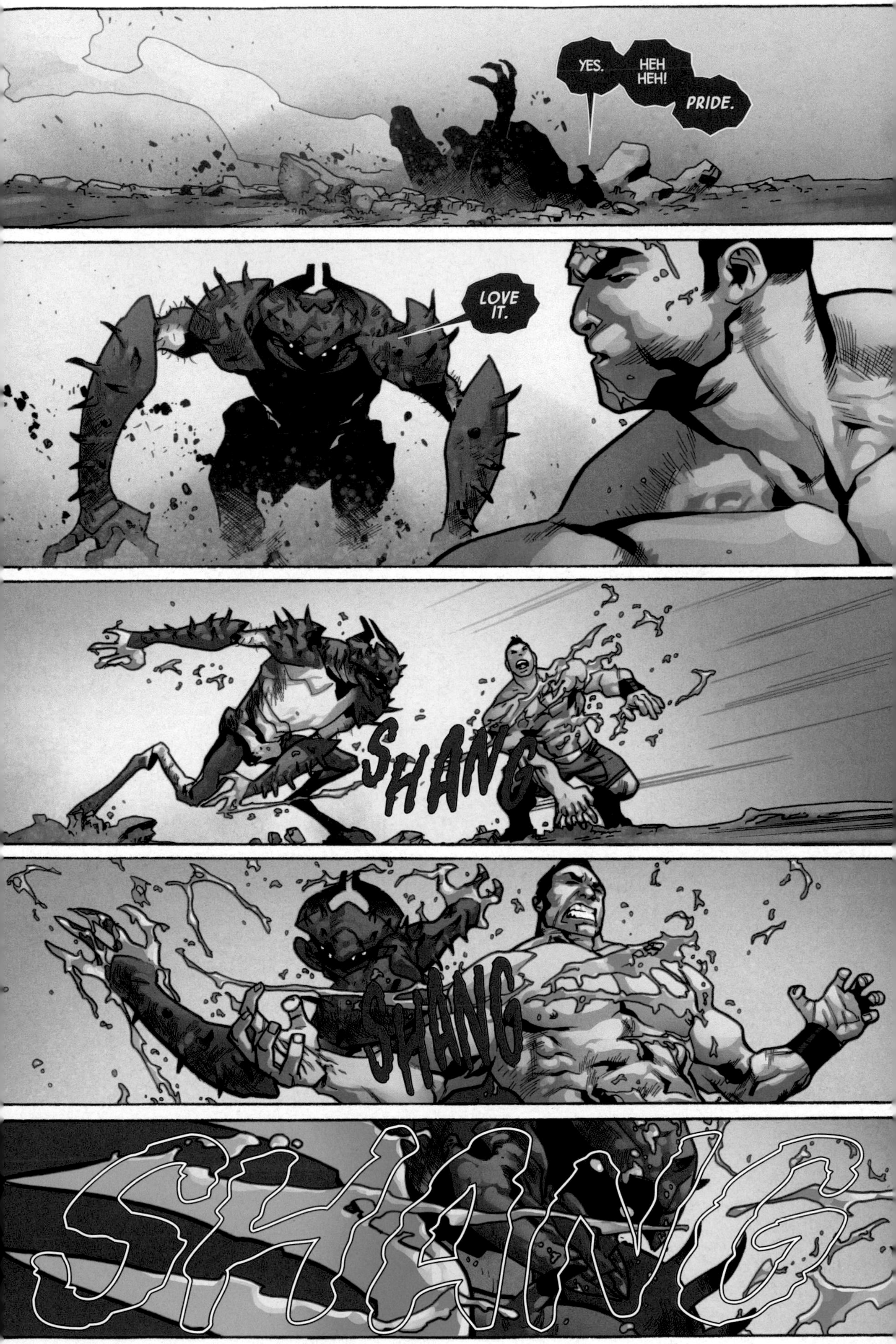
YES.
HEH HEH!
PRIDE.
LOVE IT.
SHANG
SHANG
SHANG

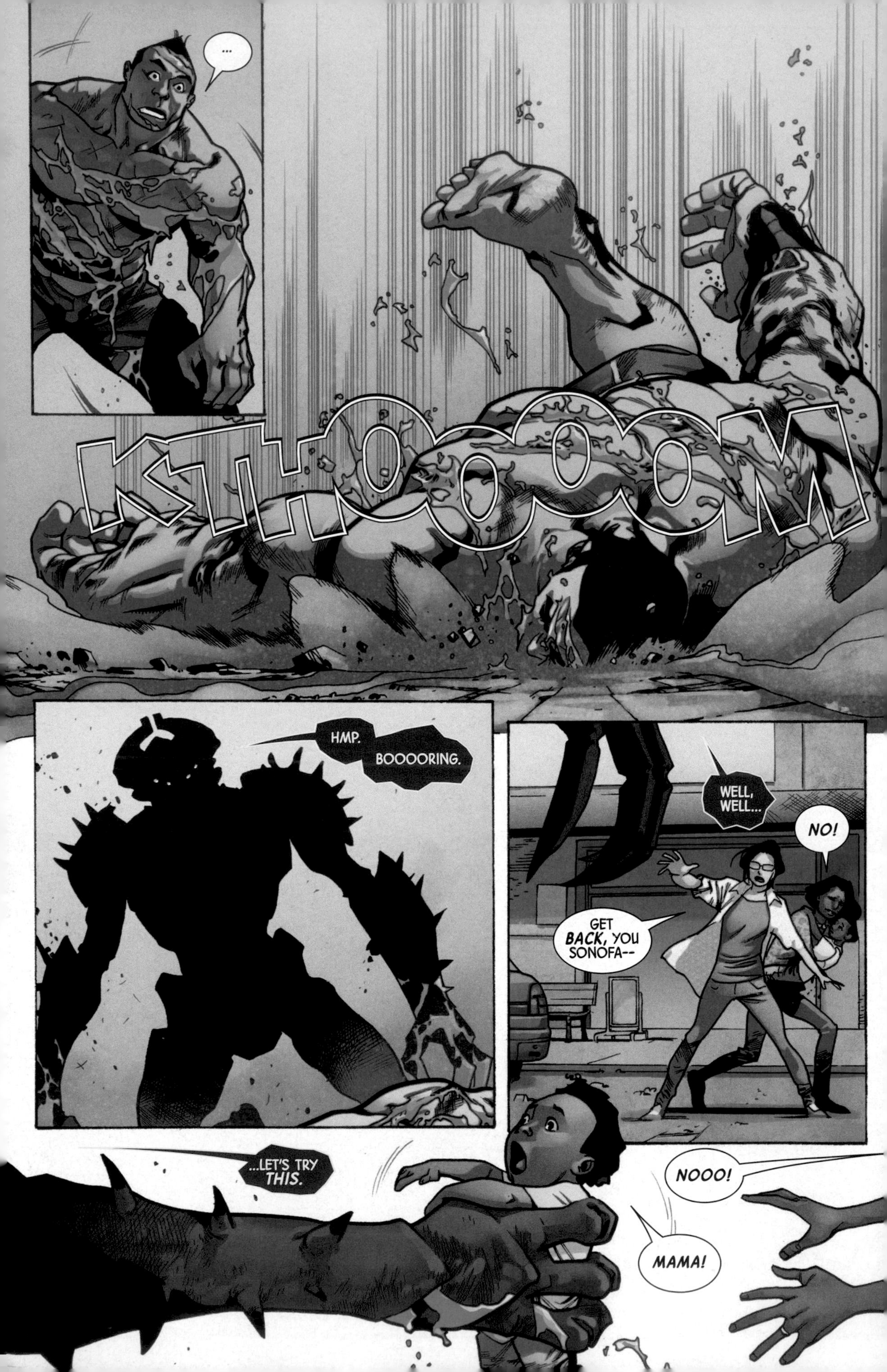
...
KTHOOOOM
HMP.
BOOOORING.
WELL, WELL...
NO!
GET BACK, YOU SONOFA--
...LET'S TRY THIS.
NOOO!
MAMA!

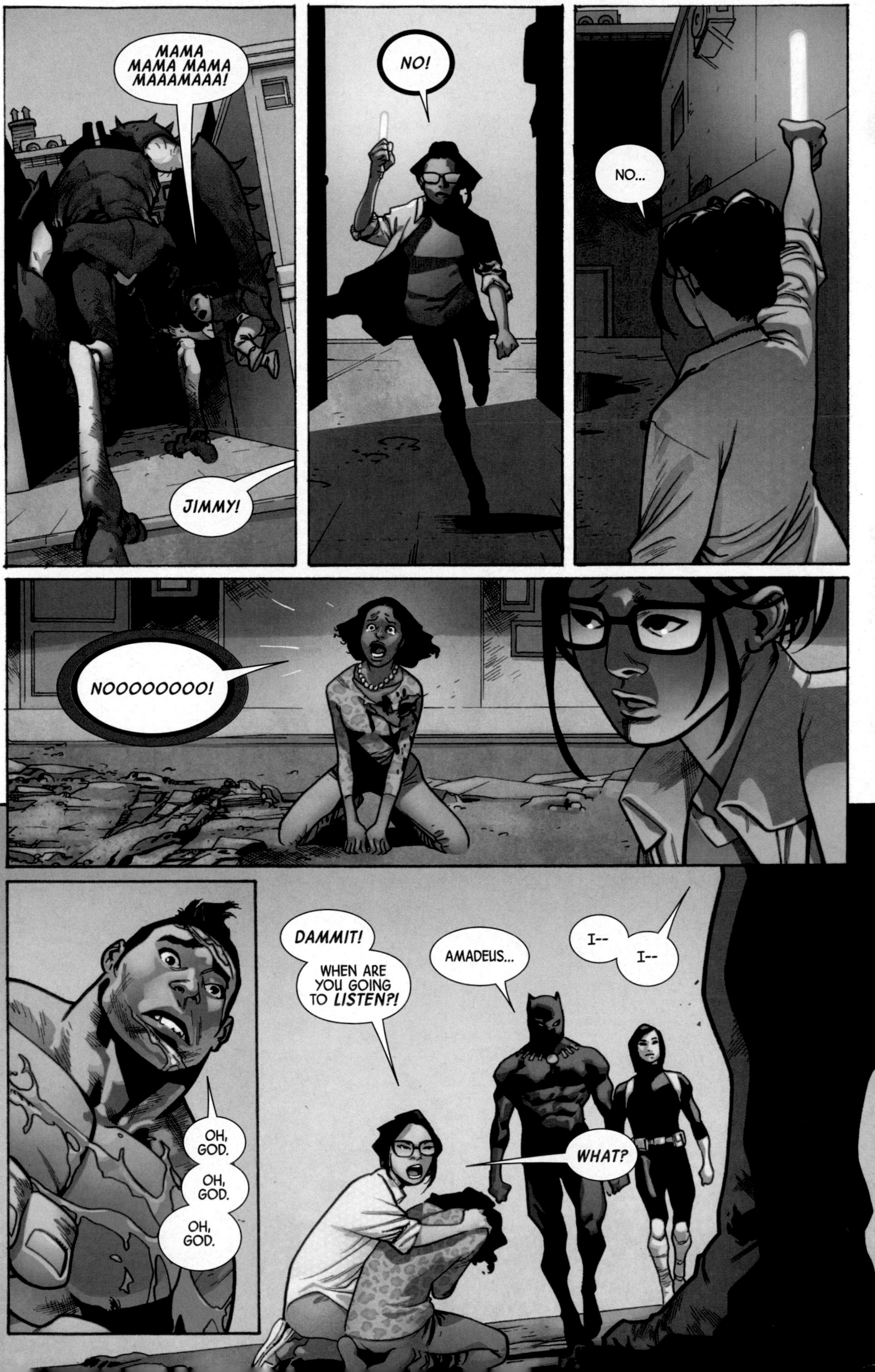
MAMA MAMA MAMA MAAAMAAA!
JIMMY!
NO!
NO...
NOOOOOOOO!
OH, GOD.
OH, GOD.
OH, GOD.
DAMMIT!
WHEN ARE YOU GOING TO LISTEN?!
AMADEUS...
I--
I--
WHAT?

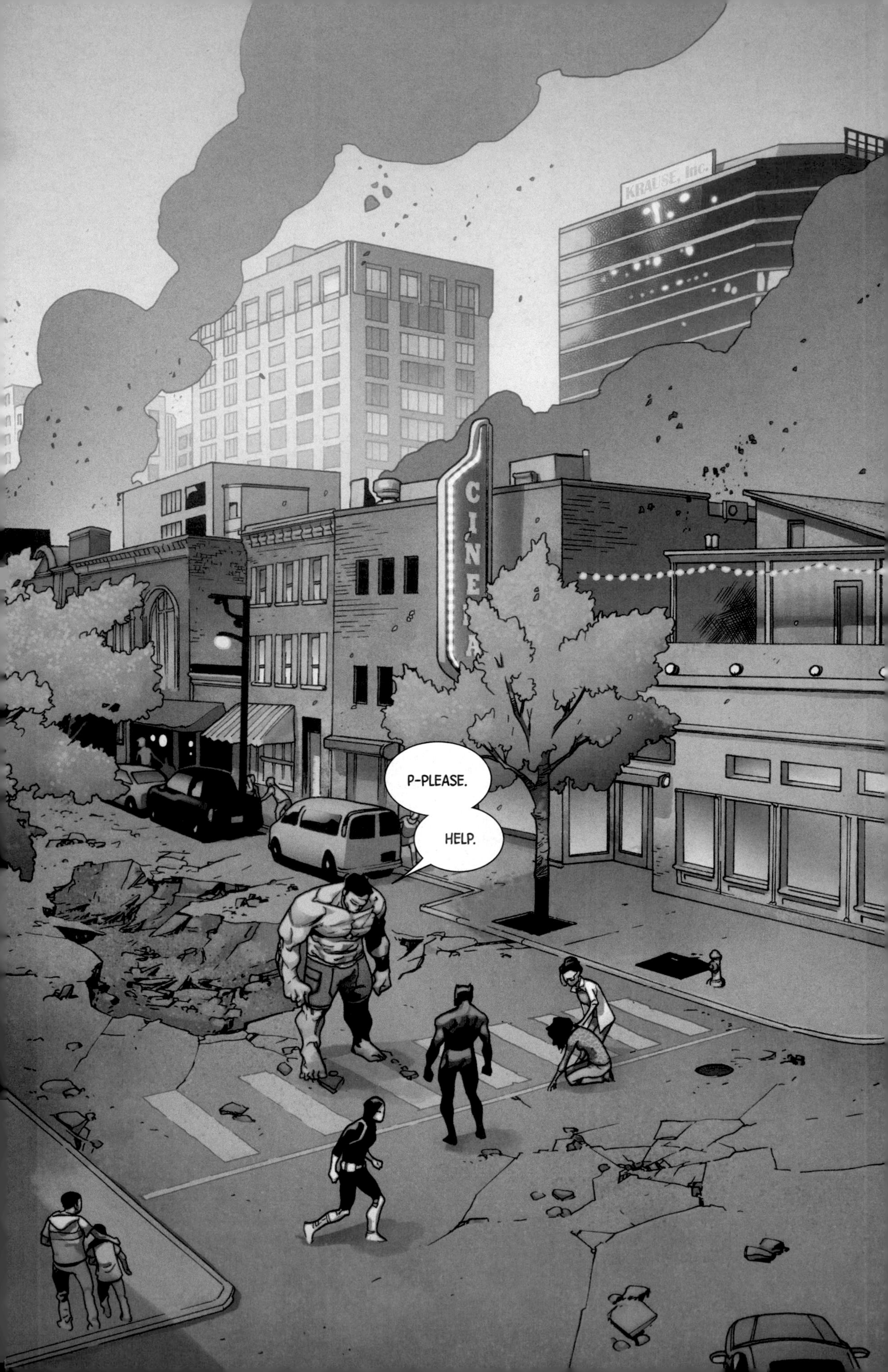
KRAUSE, Inc.
CINEMA
P-PLEASE.
HELP.

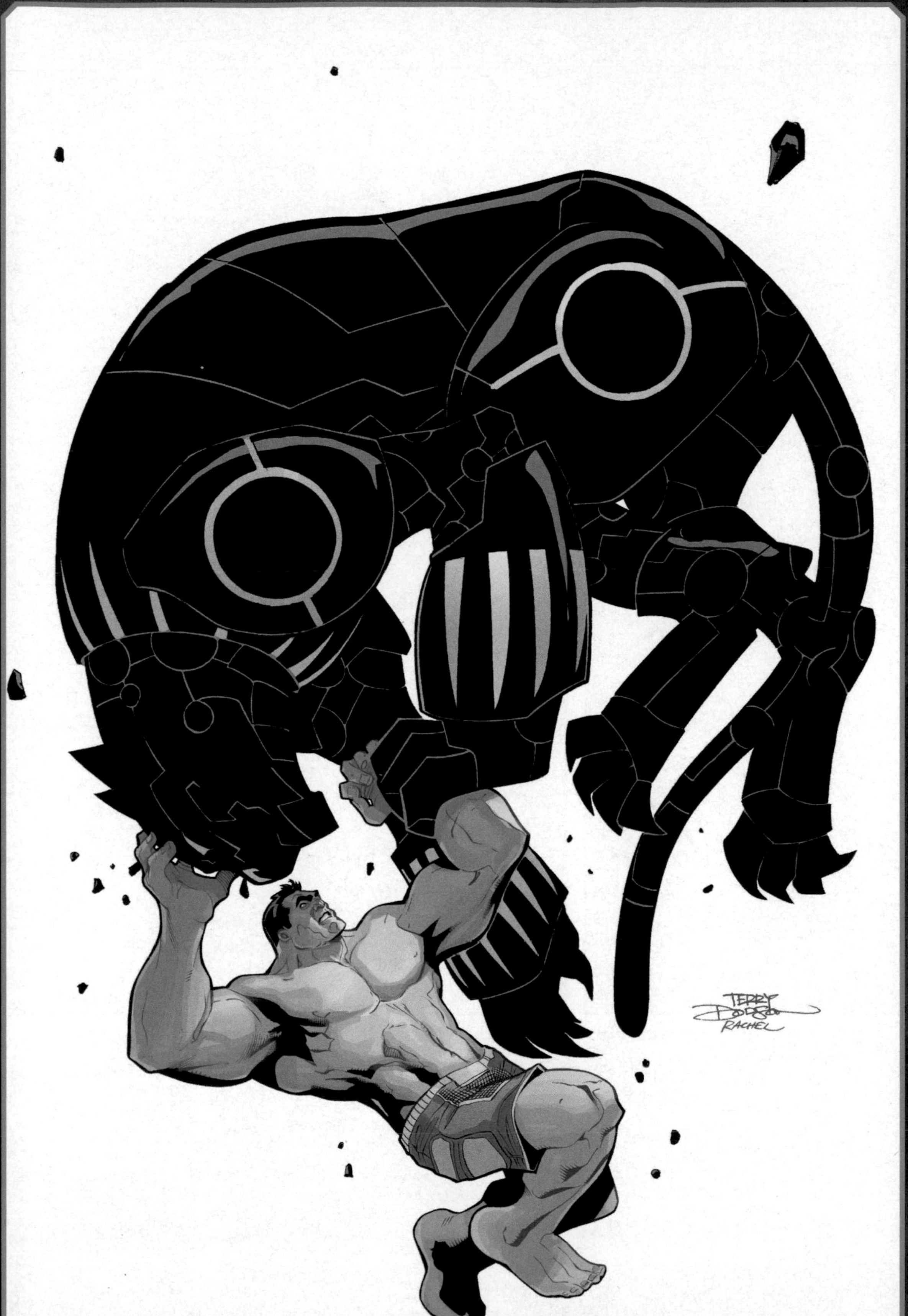
TERRY DODSON
RACHEL

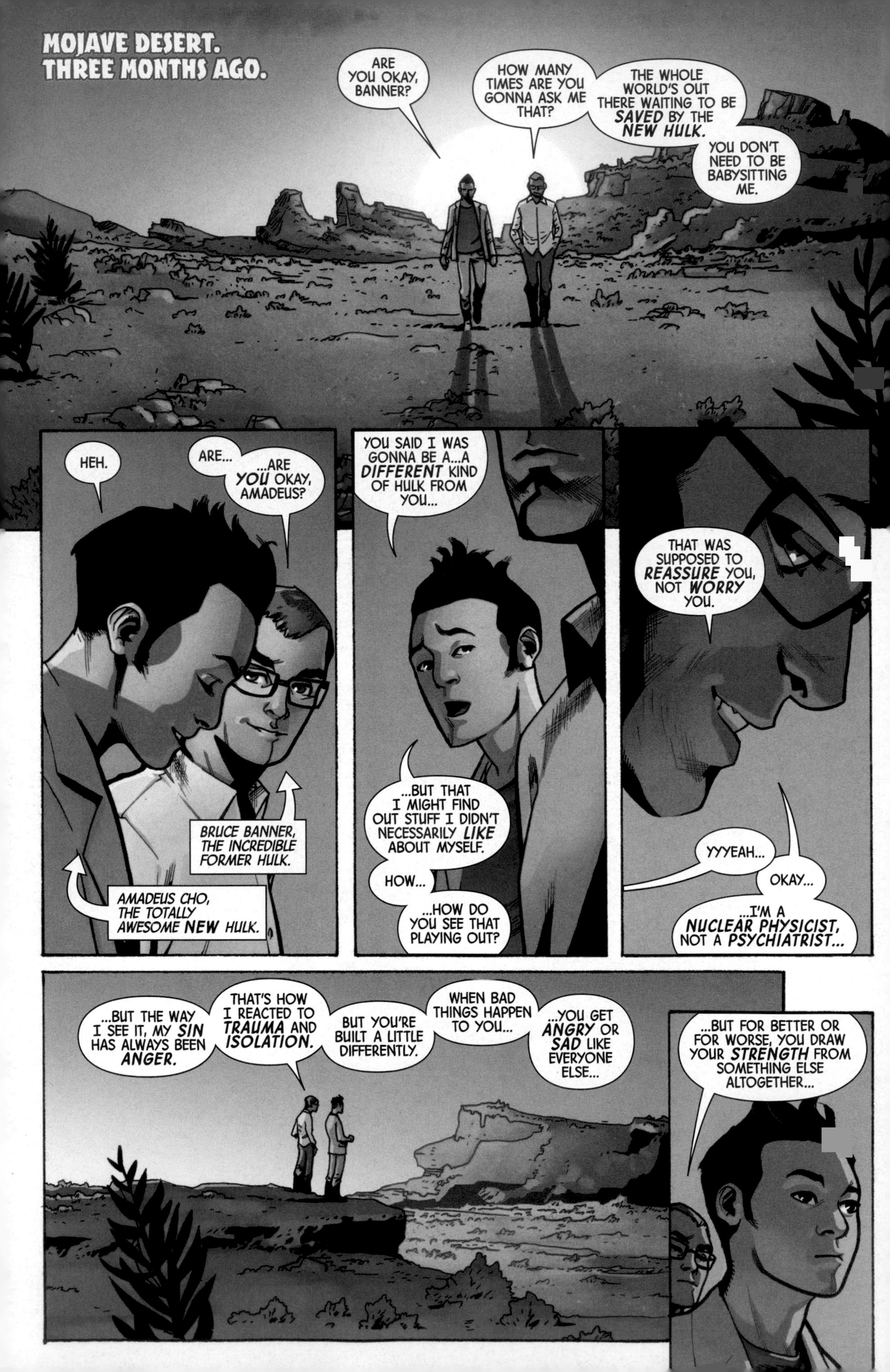
MOJAVE DESERT. THREE MONTHS AGO.
ARE YOU OKAY, BANNER?
HOW MANY TIMES ARE YOU GONNA ASK ME THAT?
THE WHOLE WORLD'S OUT THERE WAITING TO BE SAVED BY THE NEW HULK.
YOU DON'T NEED TO BE BABYSITTING ME.
HEH.
ARE...
...ARE YOU OKAY, AMADEUS?
BRUCE BANNER, THE INCREDIBLE FORMER HULK.
AMADEUS CHO, THE TOTALLY AWESOME NEW HULK.
YOU SAID I WAS GONNA BE A...A DIFFERENT KIND OF HULK FROM YOU...
...BUT THAT I MIGHT FIND OUT STUFF I DIDN'T NECESSARILY LIKE ABOUT MYSELF.
HOW...
...HOW DO YOU SEE THAT PLAYING OUT?
THAT WAS SUPPOSED TO REASSURE YOU, NOT WORRY YOU.
YYYEAH...
OKAY...
...I'M A NUCLEAR PHYSICIST, NOT A PSYCHIATRIST...
...BUT THE WAY I SEE IT, MY SIN HAS ALWAYS BEEN ANGER.
THAT'S HOW I REACTED TO TRAUMA AND ISOLATION.
BUT YOU'RE BUILT A LITTLE DIFFERENTLY.
WHEN BAD THINGS HAPPEN TO YOU...
...YOU GET ANGRY OR SAD LIKE EVERYONE ELSE...
...BUT FOR BETTER OR FOR WORSE, YOU DRAW YOUR STRENGTH FROM SOMETHING ELSE ALTOGETHER...

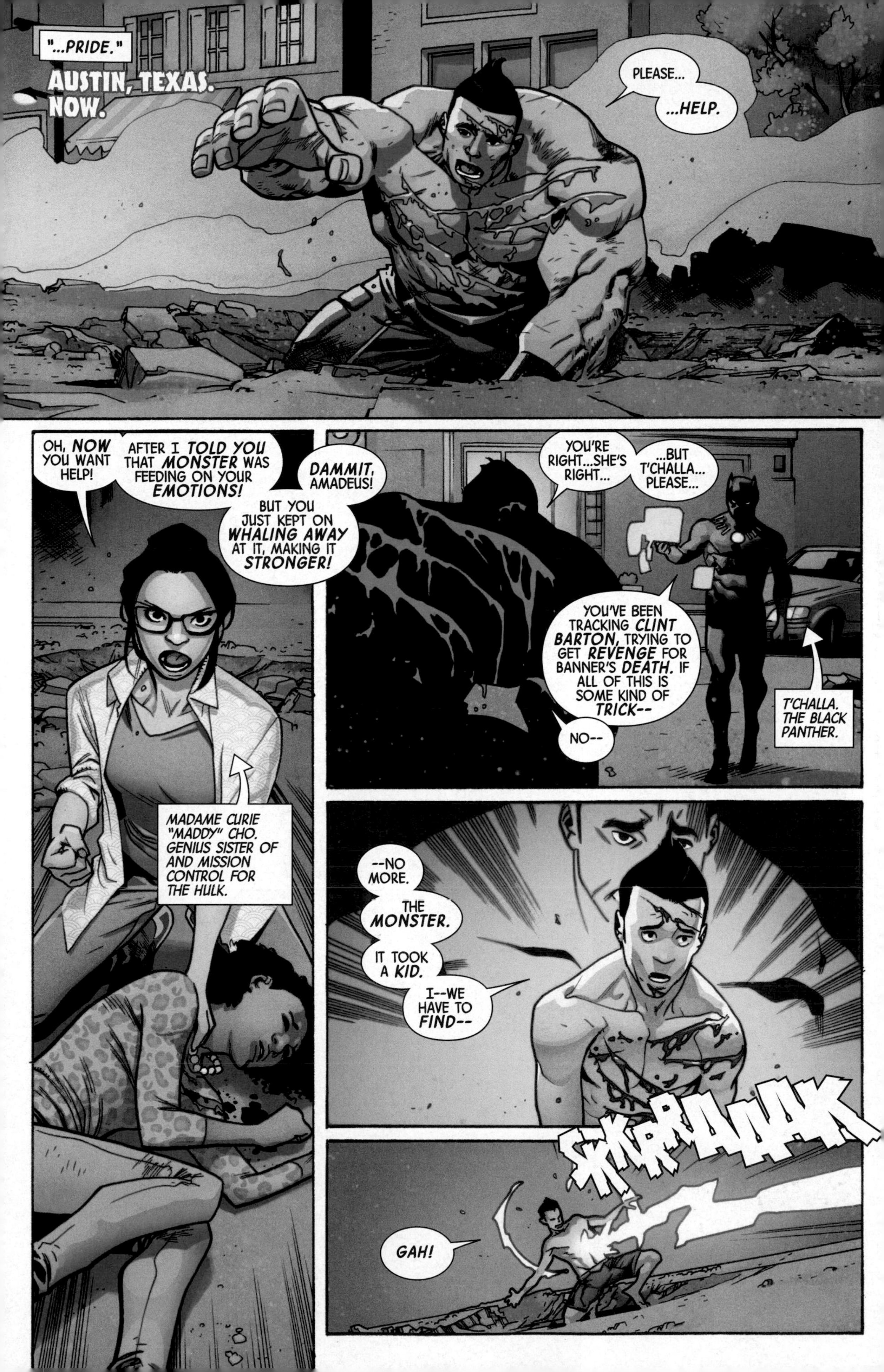
"...PRIDE."
AUSTIN, TEXAS. NOW.
PLEASE...
...HELP.
OH, NOW YOU WANT HELP!
AFTER I TOLD YOU THAT MONSTER WAS FEEDING ON YOUR EMOTIONS!
DAMMIT, AMADEUS!
BUT YOU JUST KEPT ON WHALING AWAY AT IT, MAKING IT STRONGER!
MADAME CURIE "MADDY" CHO. GENIUS SISTER OF AND MISSION CONTROL FOR THE HULK.
YOU'RE RIGHT...SHE'S RIGHT...
...BUT T'CHALLA... PLEASE...
YOU'VE BEEN TRACKING CLINT BARTON, TRYING TO GET REVENGE FOR BANNER'S DEATH. IF ALL OF THIS IS SOME KIND OF TRICK--
NO--
T'CHALLA. THE BLACK PANTHER.
--NO MORE.
THE MONSTER.
IT TOOK A KID.
I--WE HAVE TO FIND--
SKKRRAAAAK
GAH!

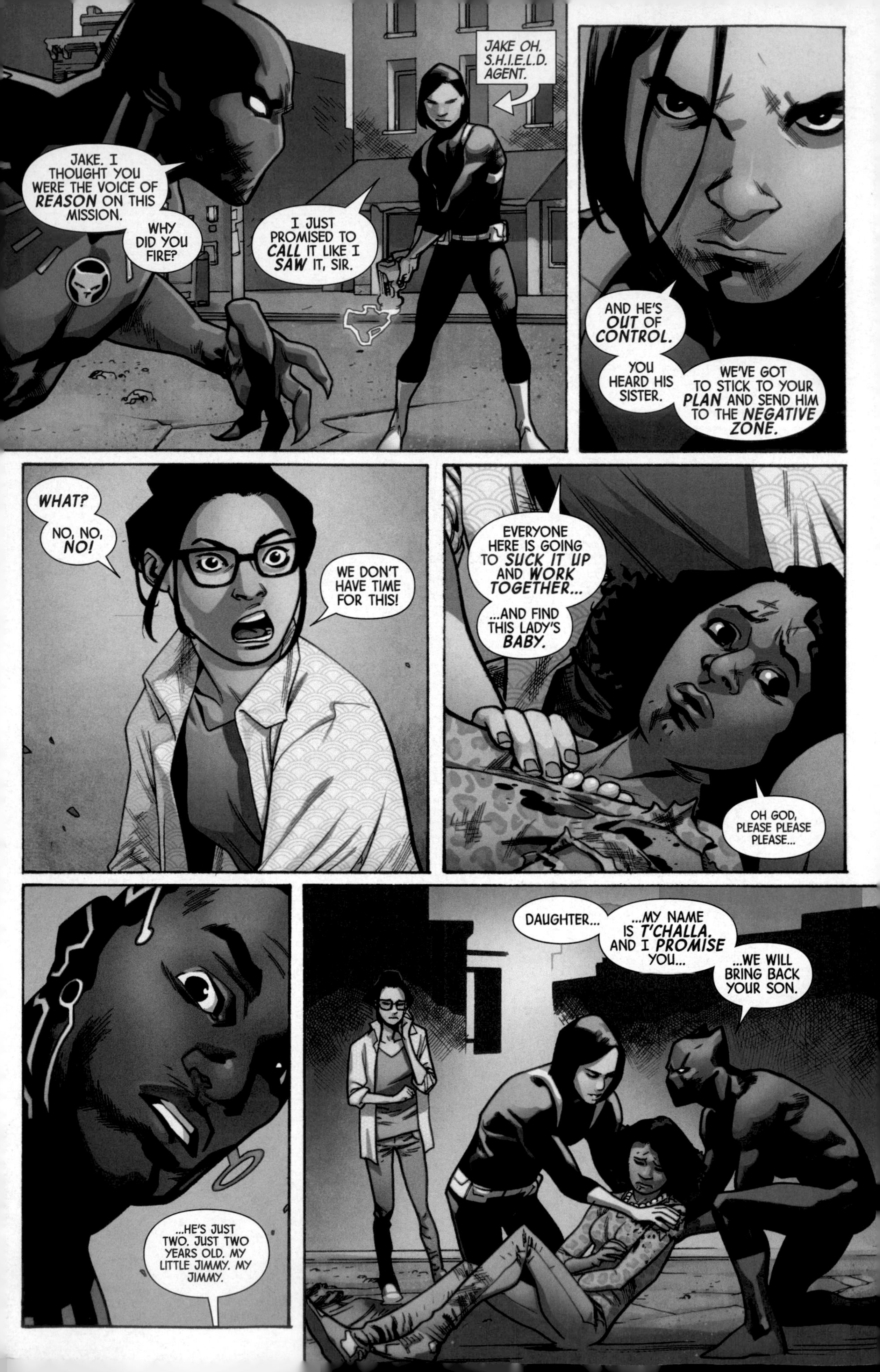
JAKE OH. S.H.I.E.L.D. AGENT.
JAKE. I THOUGHT YOU WERE THE VOICE OF REASON ON THIS MISSION.
WHY DID YOU FIRE?
I JUST PROMISED TO CALL IT LIKE I SAW IT, SIR.
AND HE'S OUT OF CONTROL.
YOU HEARD HIS SISTER.
WE'VE GOT TO STICK TO YOUR PLAN AND SEND HIM TO THE NEGATIVE ZONE.
WHAT?
NO, NO, NO!
WE DON'T HAVE TIME FOR THIS!
EVERYONE HERE IS GOING TO SUCK IT UP AND WORK TOGETHER...
...AND FIND THIS LADY'S BABY.
OH GOD, PLEASE PLEASE PLEASE...
...HE'S JUST TWO. JUST TWO YEARS OLD. MY LITTLE JIMMY. MY JIMMY.
DAUGHTER...
...MY NAME IS T'CHALLA. AND I PROMISE YOU...
...WE WILL BRING BACK YOUR SON.

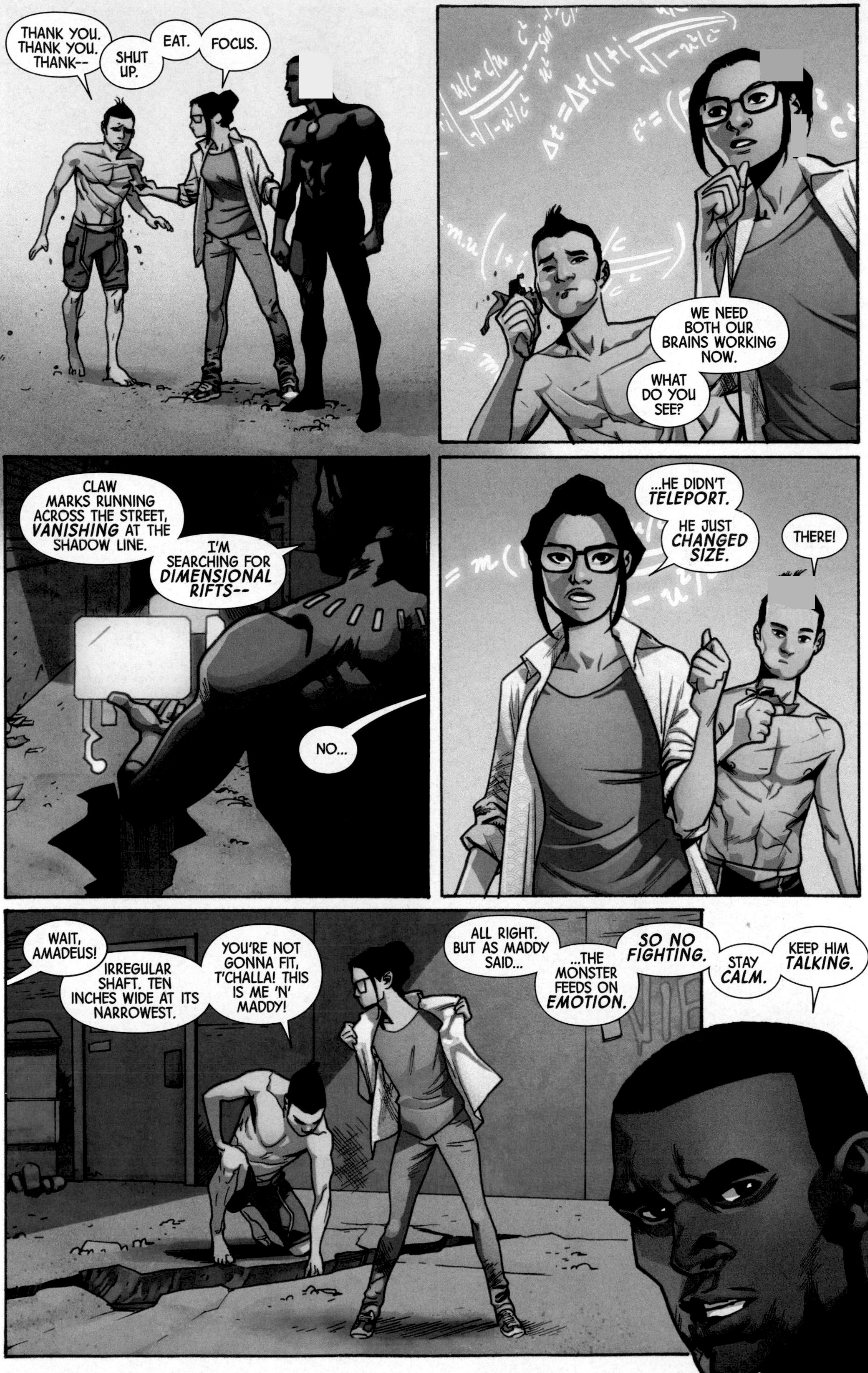
THANK YOU. THANK YOU. THANK--
SHUT UP.
EAT.
FOCUS.
WE NEED BOTH OUR BRAINS WORKING NOW.
WHAT DO YOU SEE?
CLAW MARKS RUNNING ACROSS THE STREET, VANISHING AT THE SHADOW LINE.
I'M SEARCHING FOR DIMENSIONAL RIFTS--
NO...
...HE DIDN'T TELEPORT.
HE JUST CHANGED SIZE.
THERE!
WAIT, AMADEUS!
IRREGULAR SHAFT. TEN INCHES WIDE AT ITS NARROWEST.
YOU'RE NOT GONNA FIT, T'CHALLA! THIS IS ME 'N' MADDY!
ALL RIGHT. BUT AS MADDY SAID...
...THE MONSTER FEEDS ON EMOTION.
SO NO FIGHTING.
STAY CALM.
KEEP HIM TALKING.

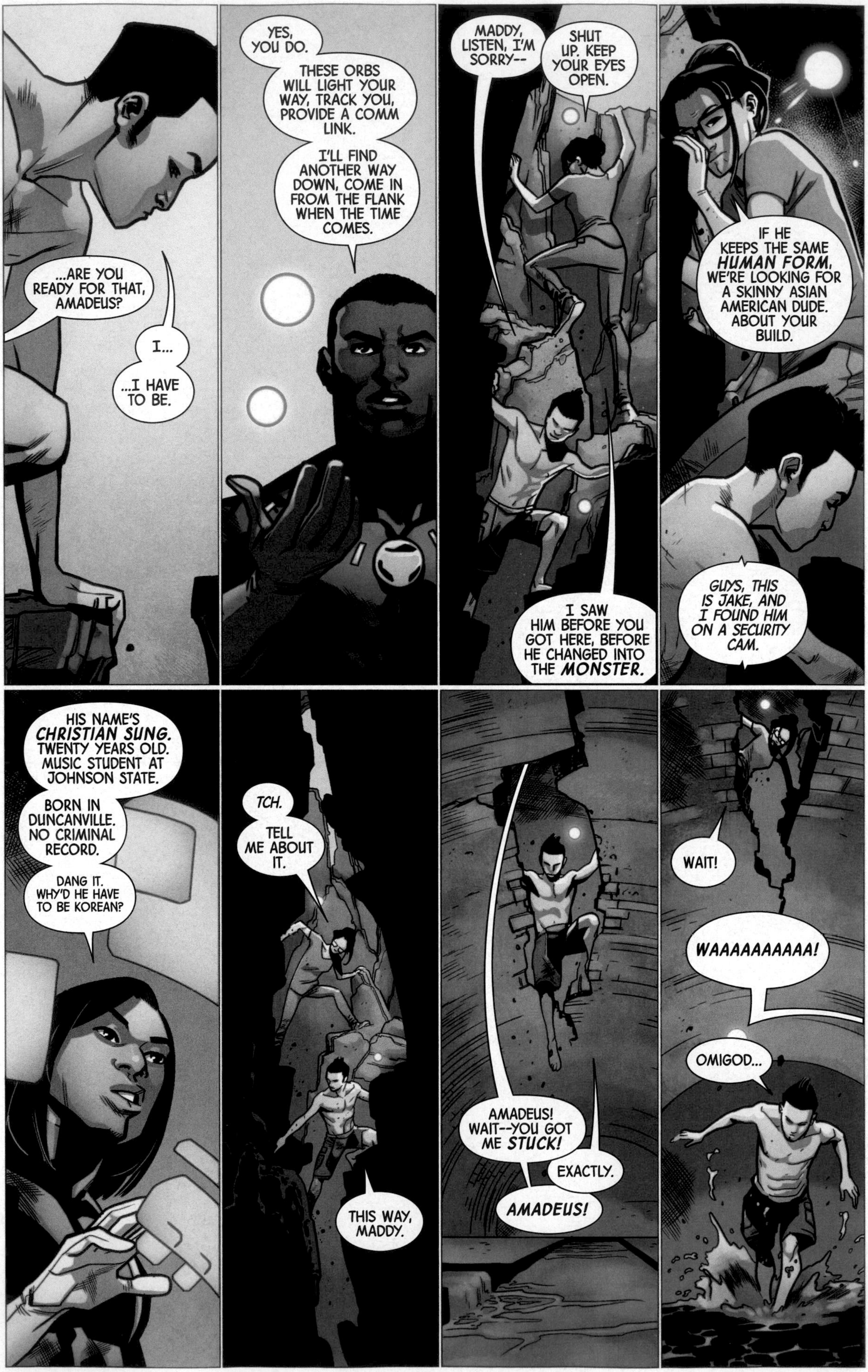
...ARE YOU READY FOR THAT, AMADEUS?
I...
...I HAVE TO BE.
YES, YOU DO.
THESE ORBS WILL LIGHT YOUR WAY, TRACK YOU, PROVIDE A COMM LINK.
I'LL FIND ANOTHER WAY DOWN, COME IN FROM THE FLANK WHEN THE TIME COMES.
MADDY, LISTEN, I'M SORRY--
SHUT UP. KEEP YOUR EYES OPEN.
I SAW HIM BEFORE YOU GOT HERE, BEFORE HE CHANGED INTO THE MONSTER.
IF HE KEEPS THE SAME HUMAN FORM, WE'RE LOOKING FOR A SKINNY ASIAN AMERICAN DUDE. ABOUT YOUR BUILD.
GUYS, THIS IS JAKE, AND I FOUND HIM ON A SECURITY CAM.
HIS NAME'S CHRISTIAN SUNG. TWENTY YEARS OLD. MUSIC STUDENT AT JOHNSON STATE.
BORN IN DUNCANVILLE. NO CRIMINAL RECORD.
DANG IT. WHY'D HE HAVE TO BE KOREAN?
TCH.
TELL ME ABOUT IT.
THIS WAY, MADDY.
AMADEUS! WAIT--YOU GOT ME STUCK!
EXACTLY.
AMADEUS!
WAIT!
WAAAAAAAAAA!
OMIGOD...

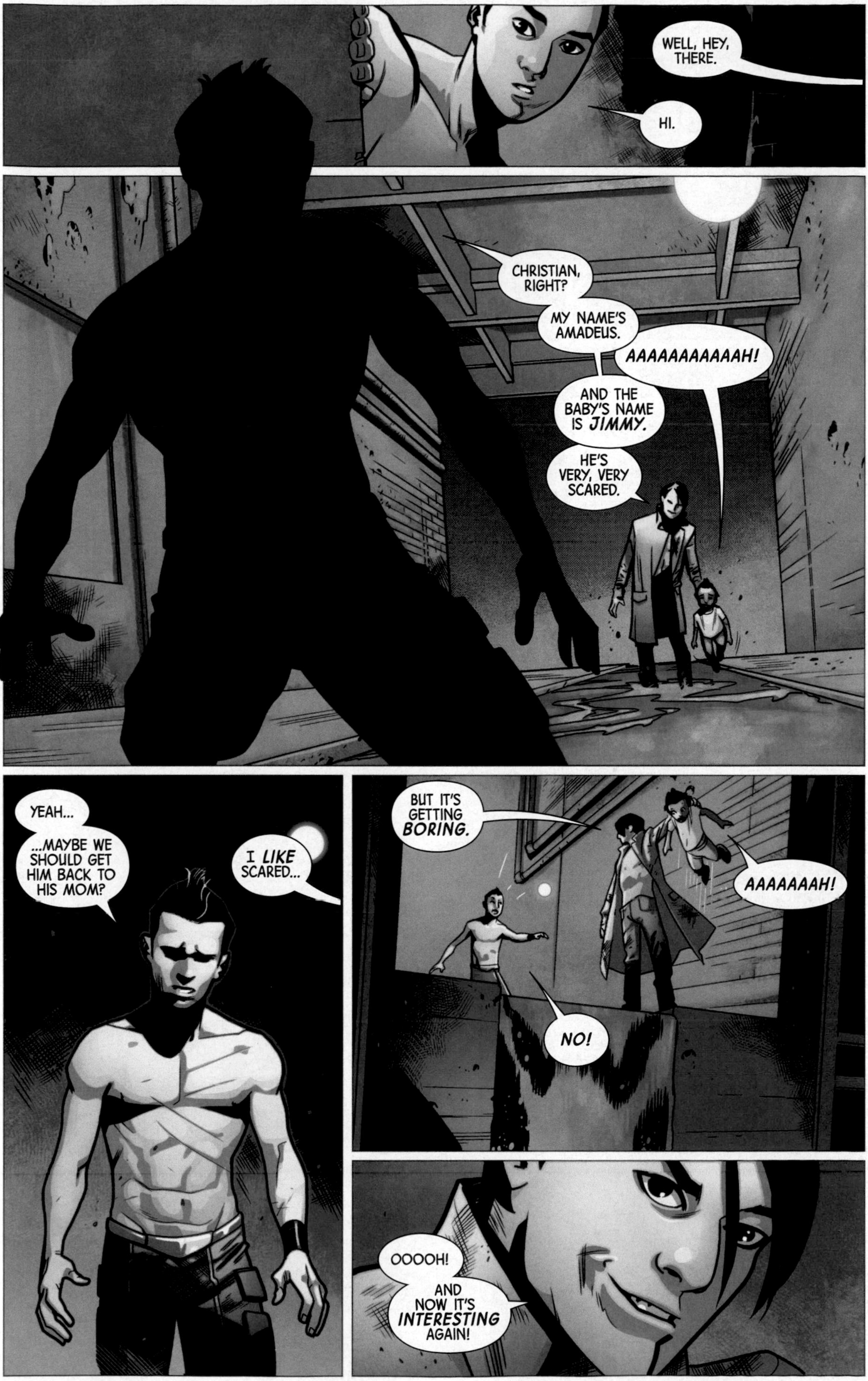
WELL, HEY, THERE.
HI.
CHRISTIAN, RIGHT?
MY NAME'S AMADEUS.
AAAAAAAAAAAH!
AND THE BABY'S NAME IS JIMMY.
HE'S VERY, VERY SCARED.
YEAH...
...MAYBE WE SHOULD GET HIM BACK TO HIS MOM?
I LIKE SCARED...
BUT IT'S GETTING BORING.
AAAAAAAH!
NO!
OOOOH!
AND NOW IT'S INTERESTING AGAIN!

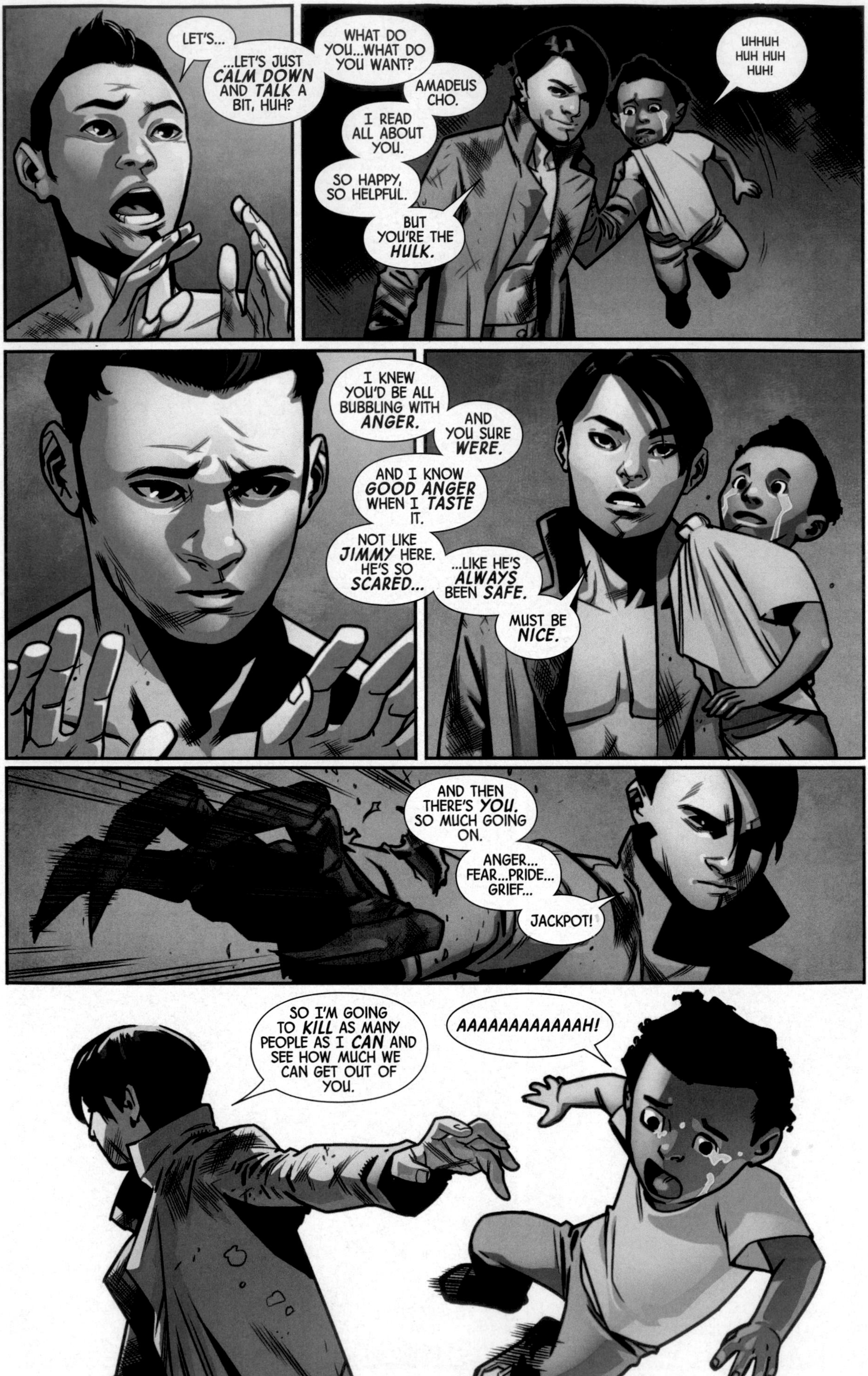
LET'S...
...LET'S JUST CALM DOWN AND TALK A BIT, HUH?
WHAT DO YOU...WHAT DO YOU WANT?
AMADEUS CHO.
I READ ALL ABOUT YOU.
SO HAPPY, SO HELPFUL.
BUT YOU'RE THE HULK.
UHHUH HUH HUH HUH!
I KNEW YOU'D BE ALL BUBBLING WITH ANGER.
AND YOU SURE WERE.
AND I KNOW GOOD ANGER WHEN I TASTE IT.
NOT LIKE JIMMY HERE. HE'S SO SCARED...
...LIKE HE'S ALWAYS BEEN SAFE.
MUST BE NICE.
AND THEN THERE'S YOU. SO MUCH GOING ON.
ANGER... FEAR...PRIDE... GRIEF...
JACKPOT!
SO I'M GOING TO KILL AS MANY PEOPLE AS I CAN AND SEE HOW MUCH WE CAN GET OUT OF YOU.
AAAAAAAAAAAAH!

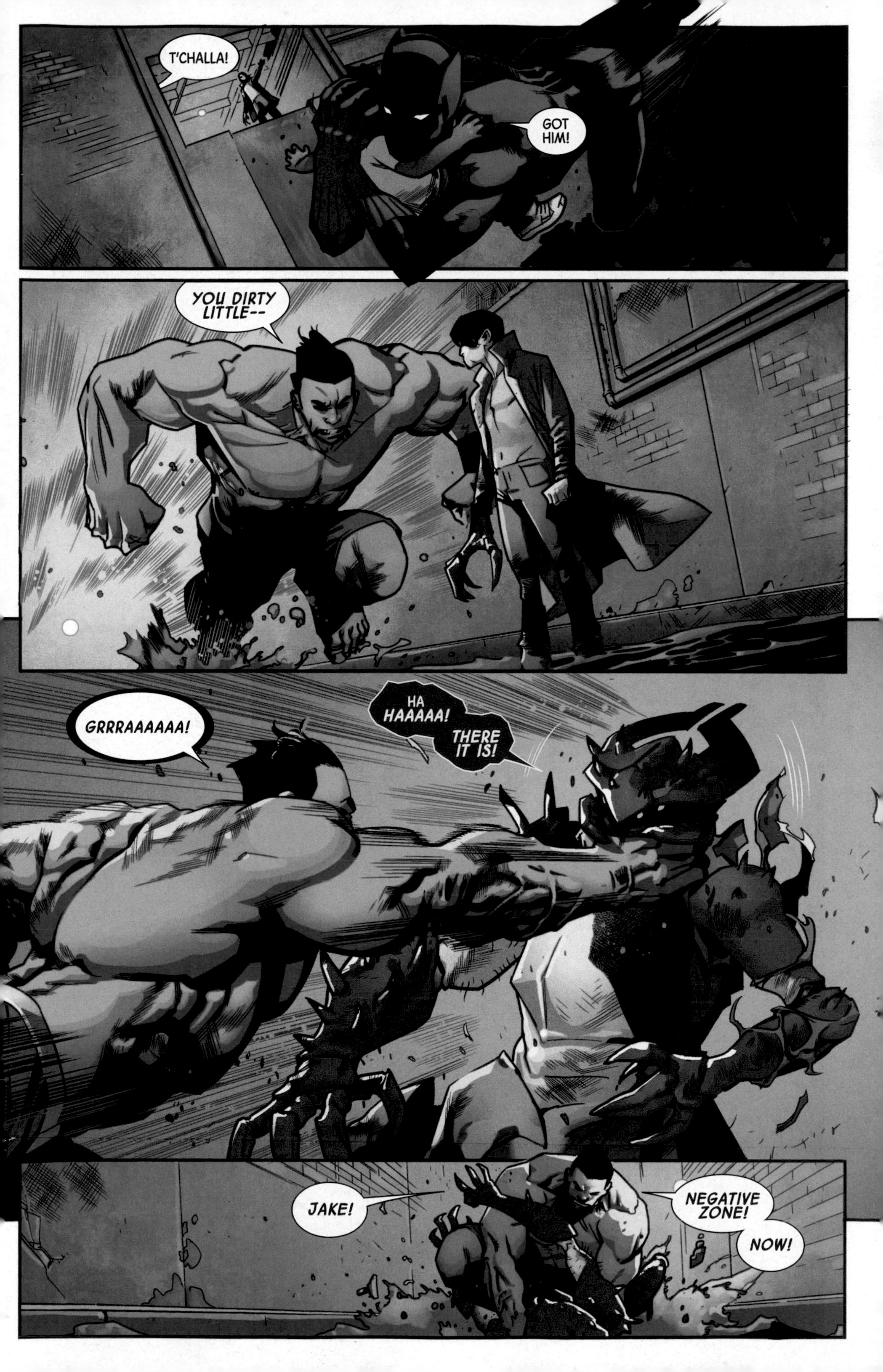
T'CHALLA!
GOT HIM!
YOU DIRTY LITTLE--
GRRRAAAAAAA!
HA HAAAAA! THERE IT IS!
JAKE!
NEGATIVE ZONE!
NOW!

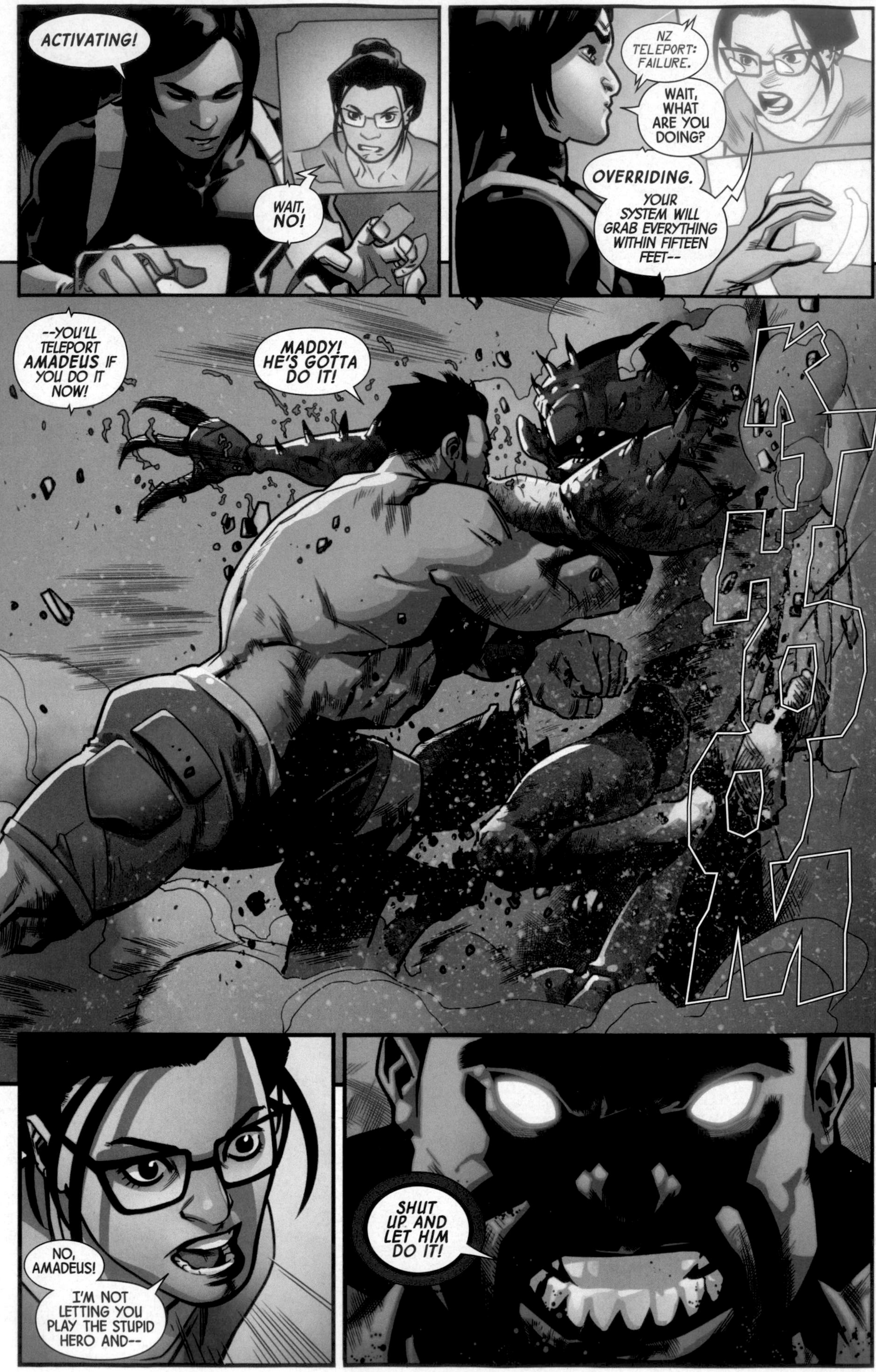
ACTIVATING!
WAIT, NO!
NZ TELEPORT: FAILURE.
WAIT, WHAT ARE YOU DOING?
OVERRIDING.
YOUR SYSTEM WILL GRAB EVERYTHING WITHIN FIFTEEN FEET--
--YOU'LL TELEPORT AMADEUS IF YOU DO IT NOW!
MADDY! HE'S GOTTA DO IT!
KTHOOM
NO, AMADEUS!
I'M NOT LETTING YOU PLAY THE STUPID HERO AND--
SHUT UP AND LET HIM DO IT!

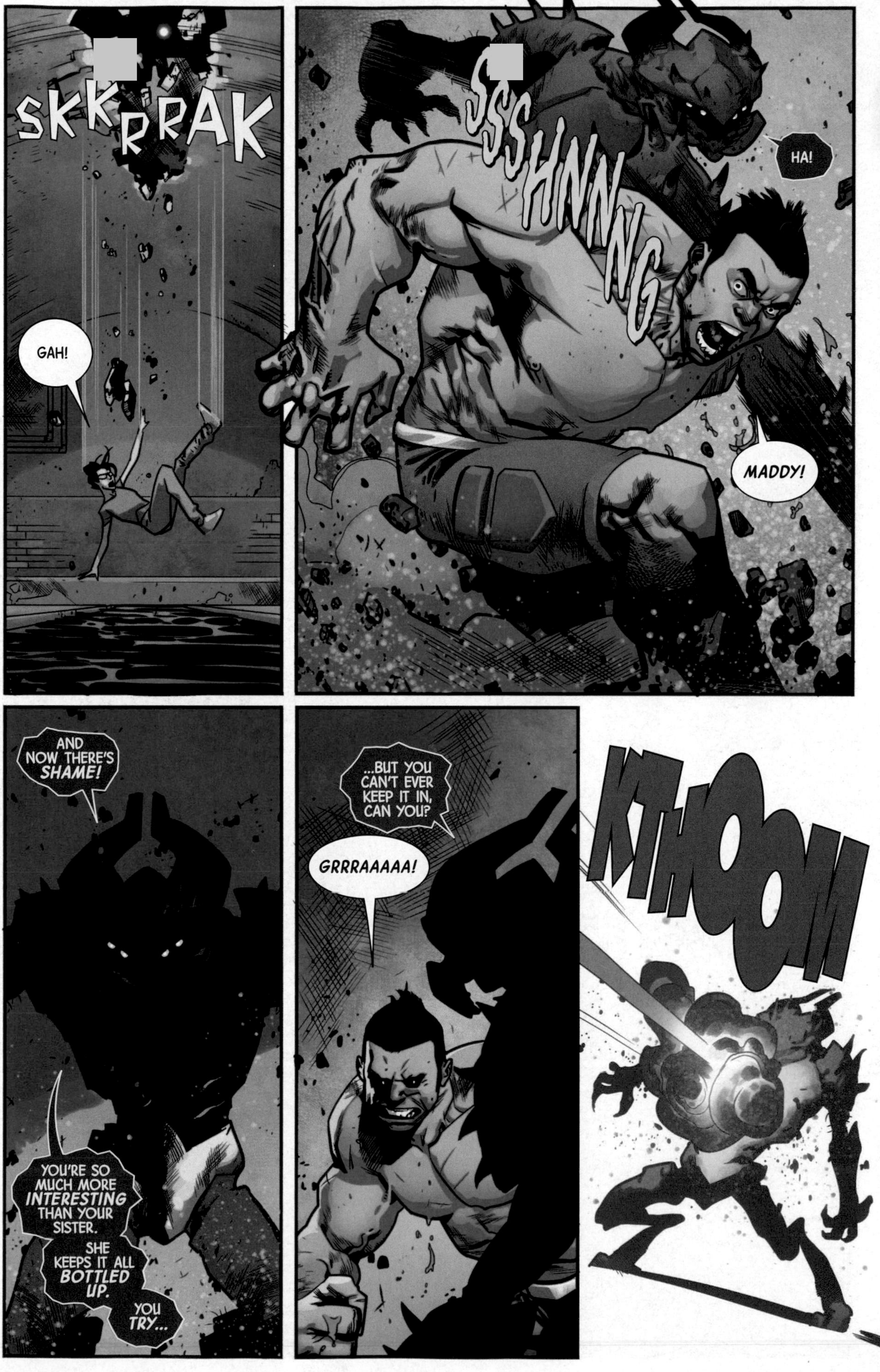
SKKRRAK
GAH!
SSSHINNNG
HA!
MADDY!
AND NOW THERE'S SHAME!
YOU'RE SO MUCH MORE INTERESTING THAN YOUR SISTER.
SHE KEEPS IT ALL BOTTLED UP.
YOU TRY...
...BUT YOU CAN'T EVER KEEP IT IN, CAN YOU?
GRRRAAAAA!
KTHOOM

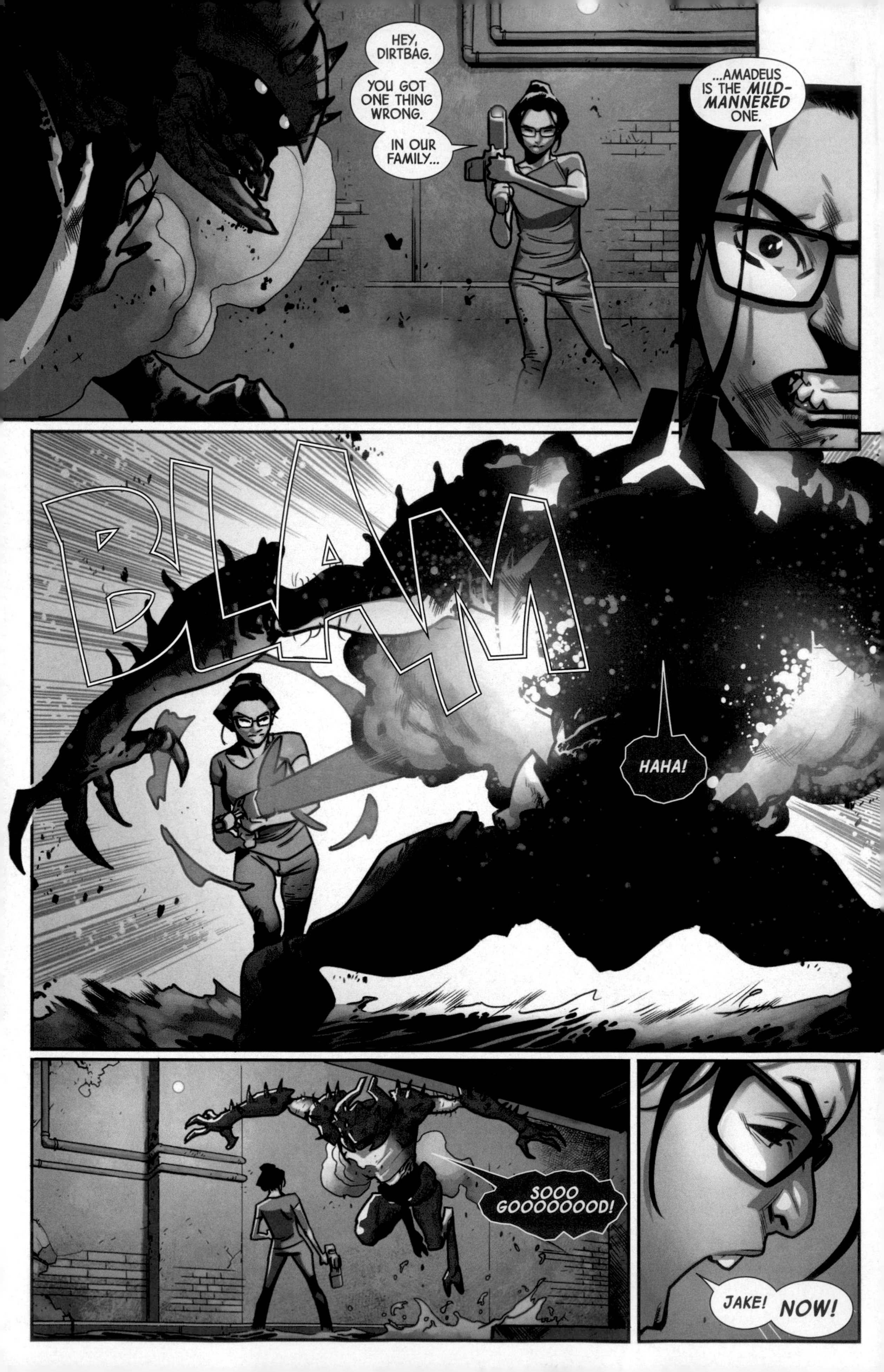
HEY, DIRTBAG.
YOU GOT ONE THING WRONG.
IN OUR FAMILY...
...AMADEUS IS THE MILD-MANNERED ONE.
BLAM
HAHA!
SOOO GOOOOOOOD!
JAKE! NOW!

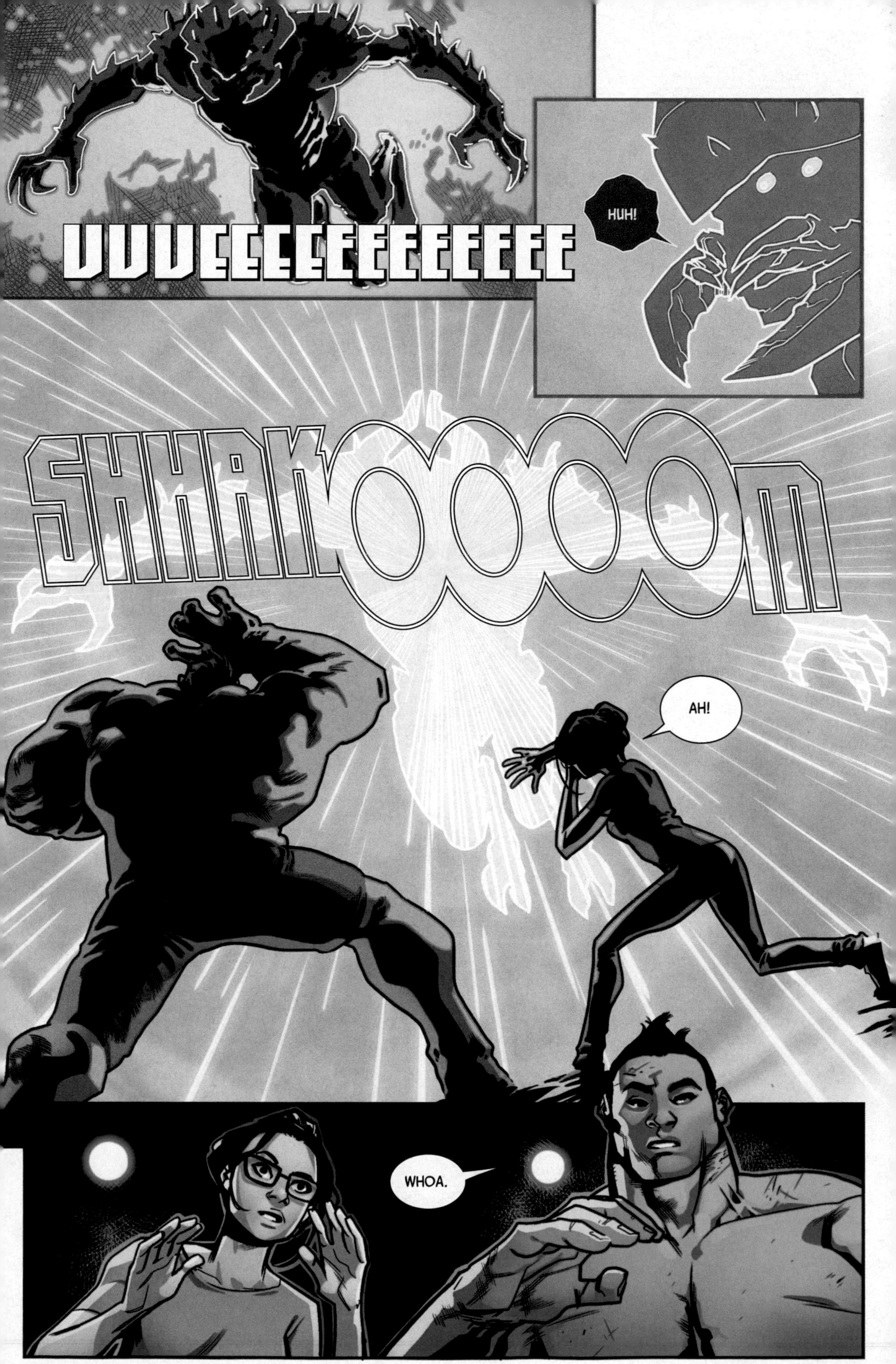
VVVEEEEEEEEEEEEE
HUH!
SHHAKOOOOOM
AH!
WHOA.

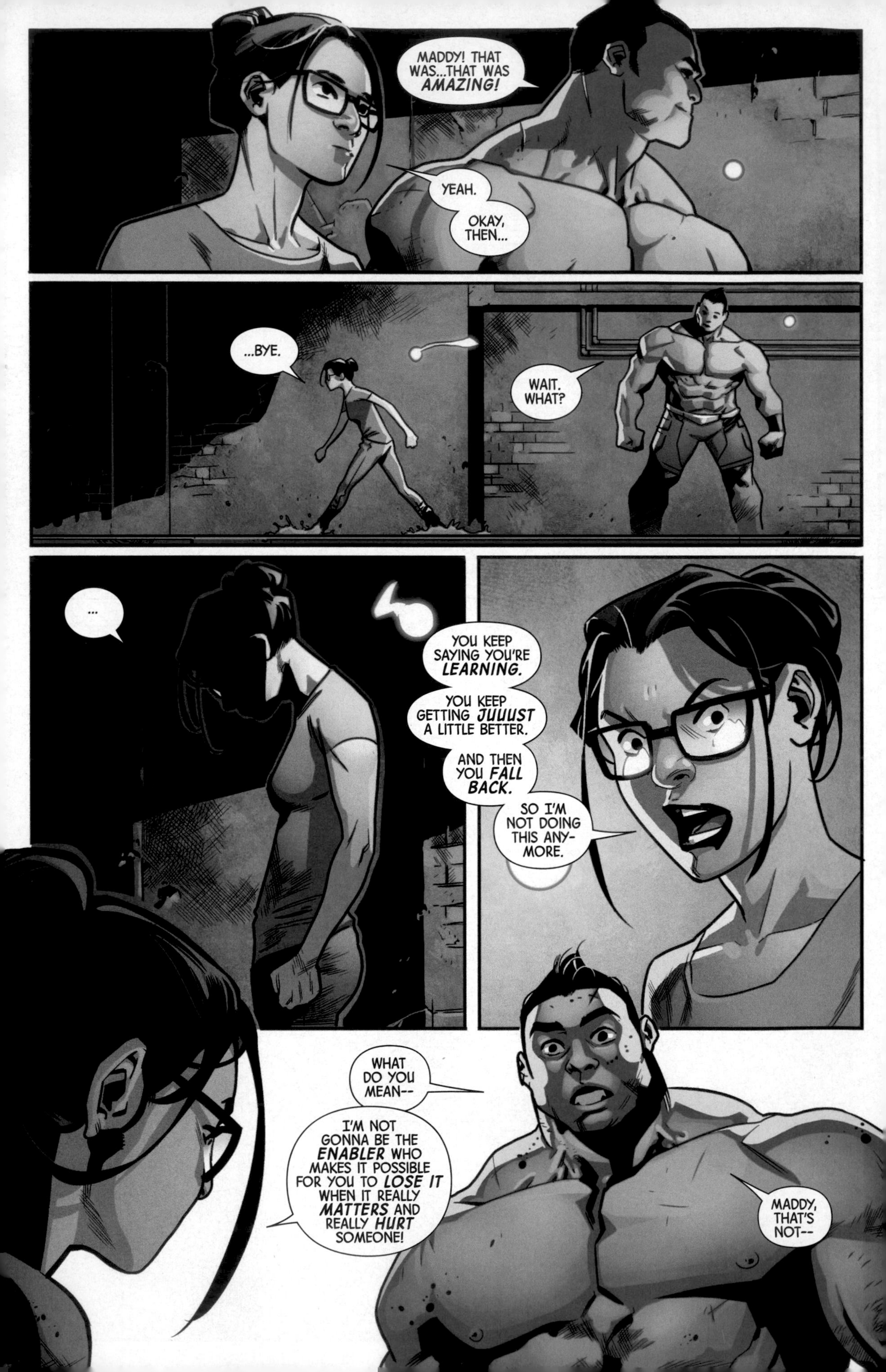
MADDY! THAT WAS...THAT WAS AMAZING!
YEAH.
OKAY, THEN...
...BYE.
WAIT. WHAT?
...
YOU KEEP SAYING YOU'RE LEARNING.
YOU KEEP GETTING JUUUST A LITTLE BETTER.
AND THEN YOU FALL BACK.
SO I'M NOT DOING THIS ANY-MORE.
WHAT DO YOU MEAN--
I'M NOT GONNA BE THE ENABLER WHO MAKES IT POSSIBLE FOR YOU TO LOSE IT WHEN IT REALLY MATTERS AND REALLY HURT SOMEONE!
MADDY, THAT'S NOT--

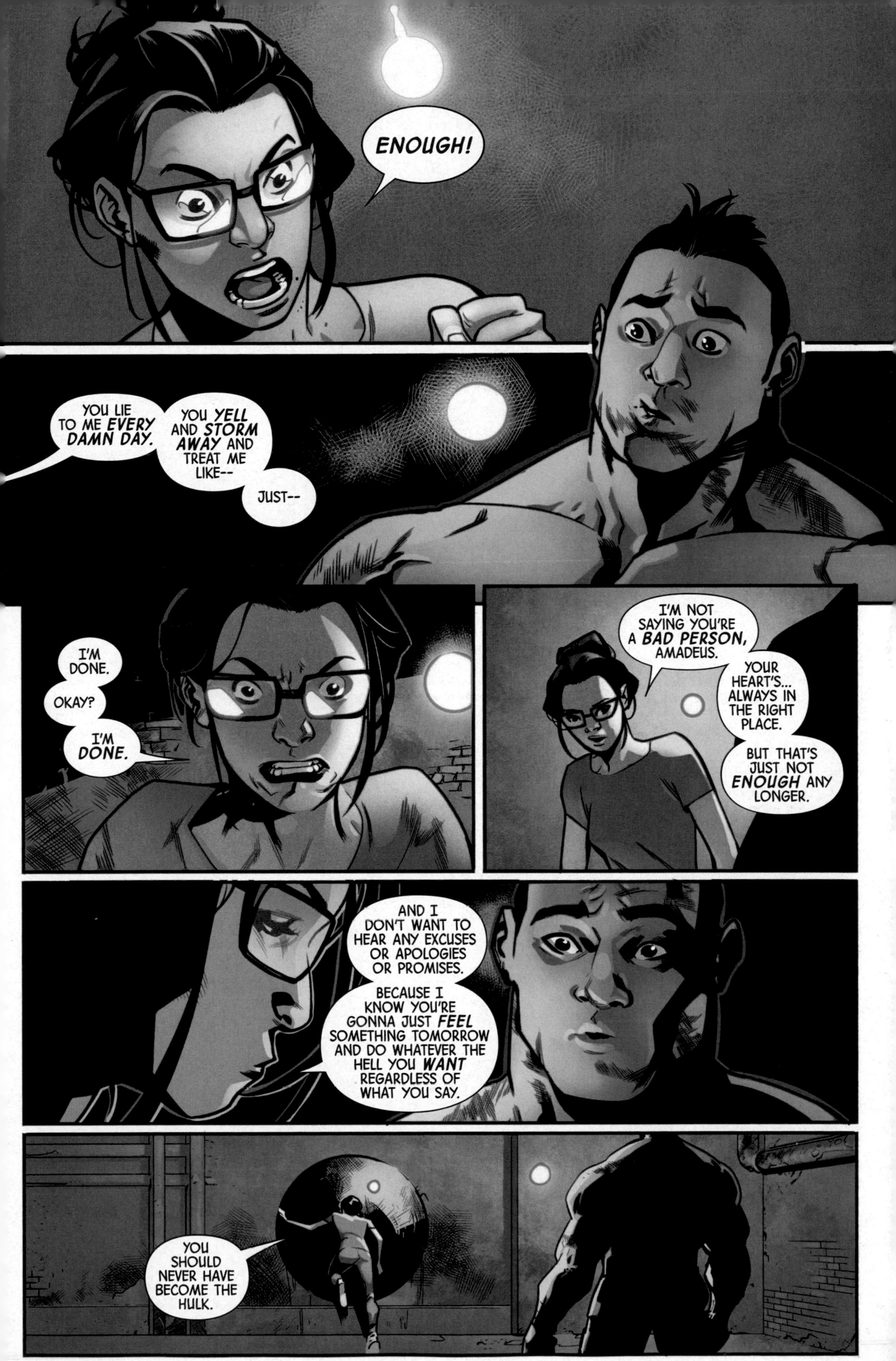
ENOUGH!
YOU LIE TO ME EVERY DAMN DAY.
YOU YELL AND STORM AWAY AND TREAT ME LIKE--
JUST--
I'M DONE.
OKAY?
I'M DONE.
I'M NOT SAYING YOU'RE A BAD PERSON, AMADEUS.
YOUR HEART'S... ALWAYS IN THE RIGHT PLACE.
BUT THAT'S JUST NOT ENOUGH ANY LONGER.
AND I DON'T WANT TO HEAR ANY EXCUSES OR APOLOGIES OR PROMISES.
BECAUSE I KNOW YOU'RE GONNA JUST FEEL SOMETHING TOMORROW AND DO WHATEVER THE HELL YOU WANT REGARDLESS OF WHAT YOU SAY.
YOU SHOULD NEVER HAVE BECOME THE HULK.

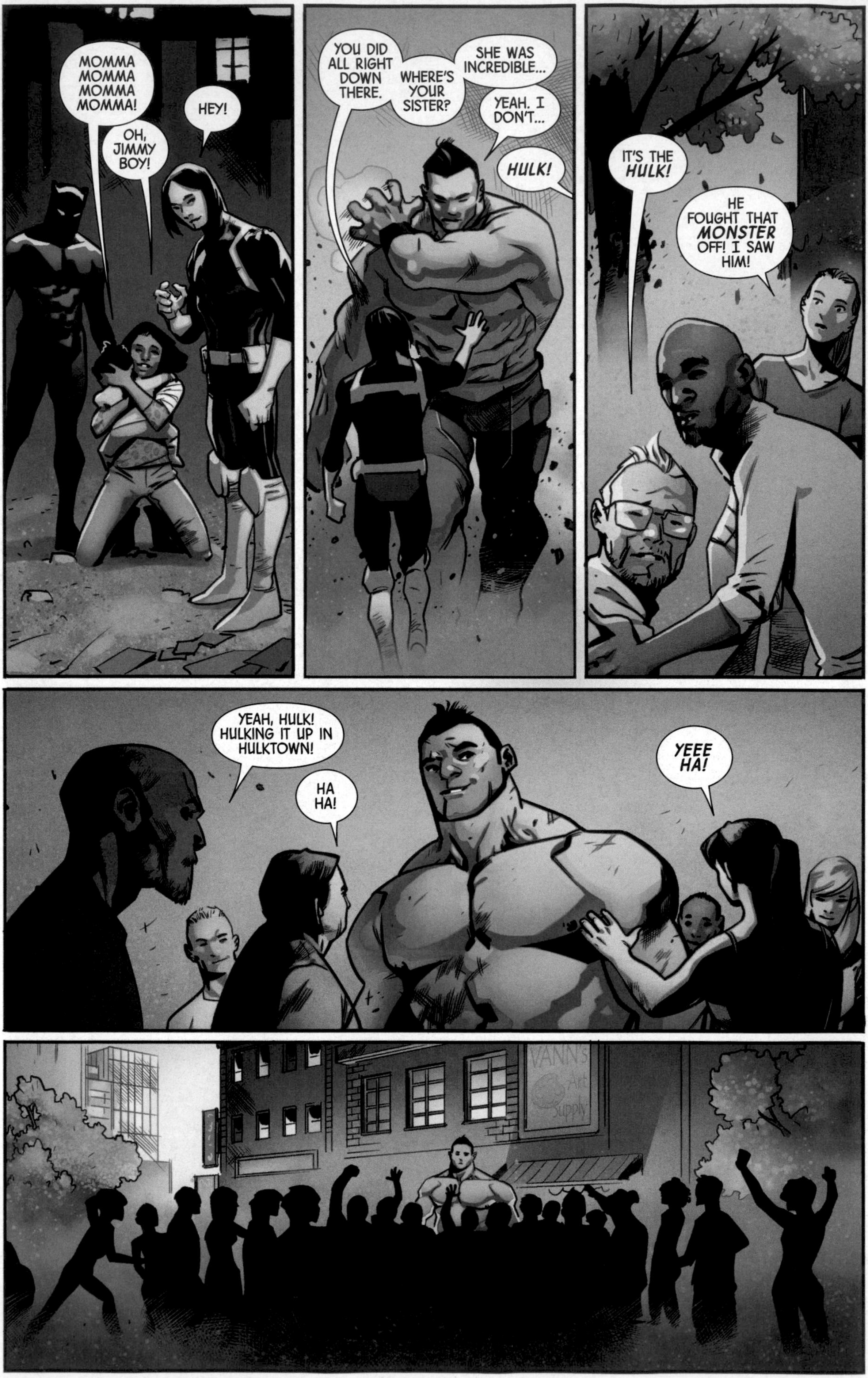
MOMMA MOMMA MOMMA MOMMA!
OH, JIMMY BOY!
HEY!
YOU DID ALL RIGHT DOWN THERE.
WHERE'S YOUR SISTER?
SHE WAS INCREDIBLE...
YEAH. I DON'T...
HULK!
IT'S THE HULK!
HE FOUGHT THAT MONSTER OFF! I SAW HIM!
YEAH, HULK! HULKING IT UP IN HULKTOWN!
HA HA!
YEEE HA!
VANN'S Art Supply

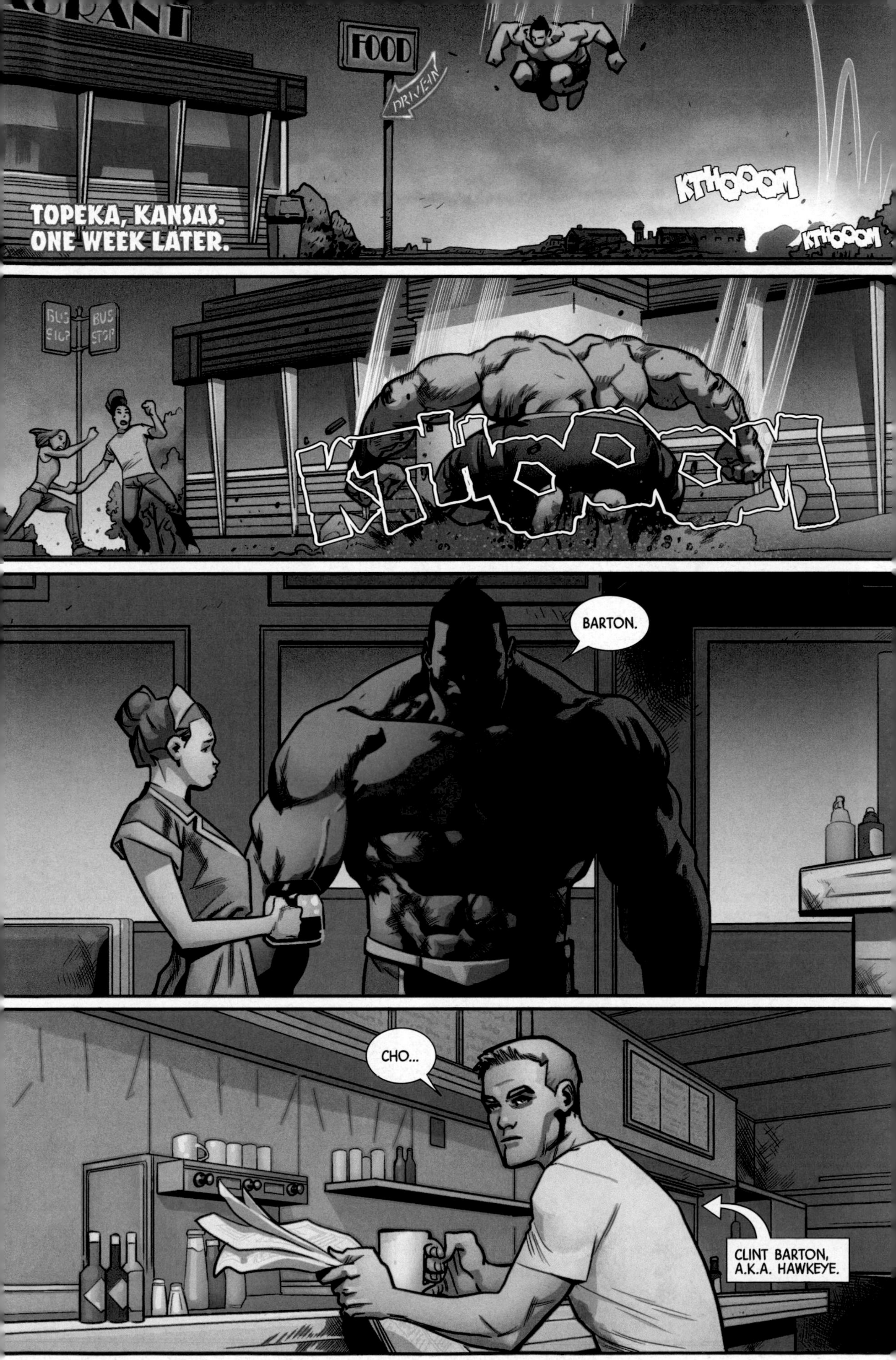

TOPEKA, KANSAS. ONE WEEK LATER.
FOOD
DRIVE-IN
KTHOOOM
KTHOOOM
BUS STOP
BUS STOP
KTHOOOM
BARTON.
CHO...
CLINT BARTON, A.K.A. HAWKEYE.

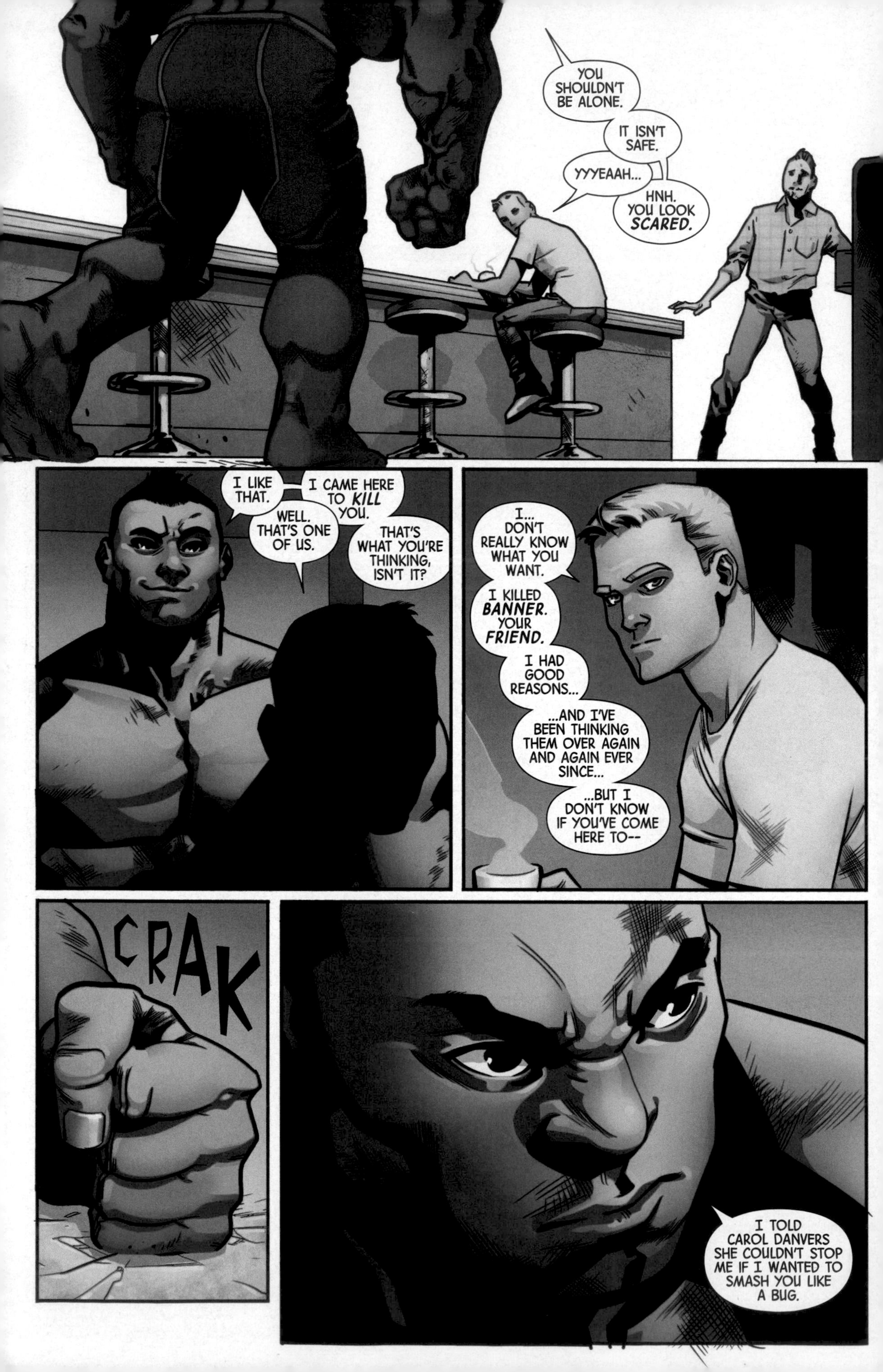

YOU SHOULDN'T BE ALONE.
IT ISN'T SAFE.
YYYEAAH...
HNH. YOU LOOK SCARED.
I LIKE THAT.
I CAME HERE TO KILL YOU.
WELL. THAT'S ONE OF US.
THAT'S WHAT YOU'RE THINKING, ISN'T IT?
I... DON'T REALLY KNOW WHAT YOU WANT.
I KILLED BANNER. YOUR FRIEND.
I HAD GOOD REASONS...
...AND I'VE BEEN THINKING THEM OVER AGAIN AND AGAIN EVER SINCE...
...BUT I DON'T KNOW IF YOU'VE COME HERE TO--
CRAK
I TOLD CAROL DANVERS SHE COULDN'T STOP ME IF I WANTED TO SMASH YOU LIKE A BUG.

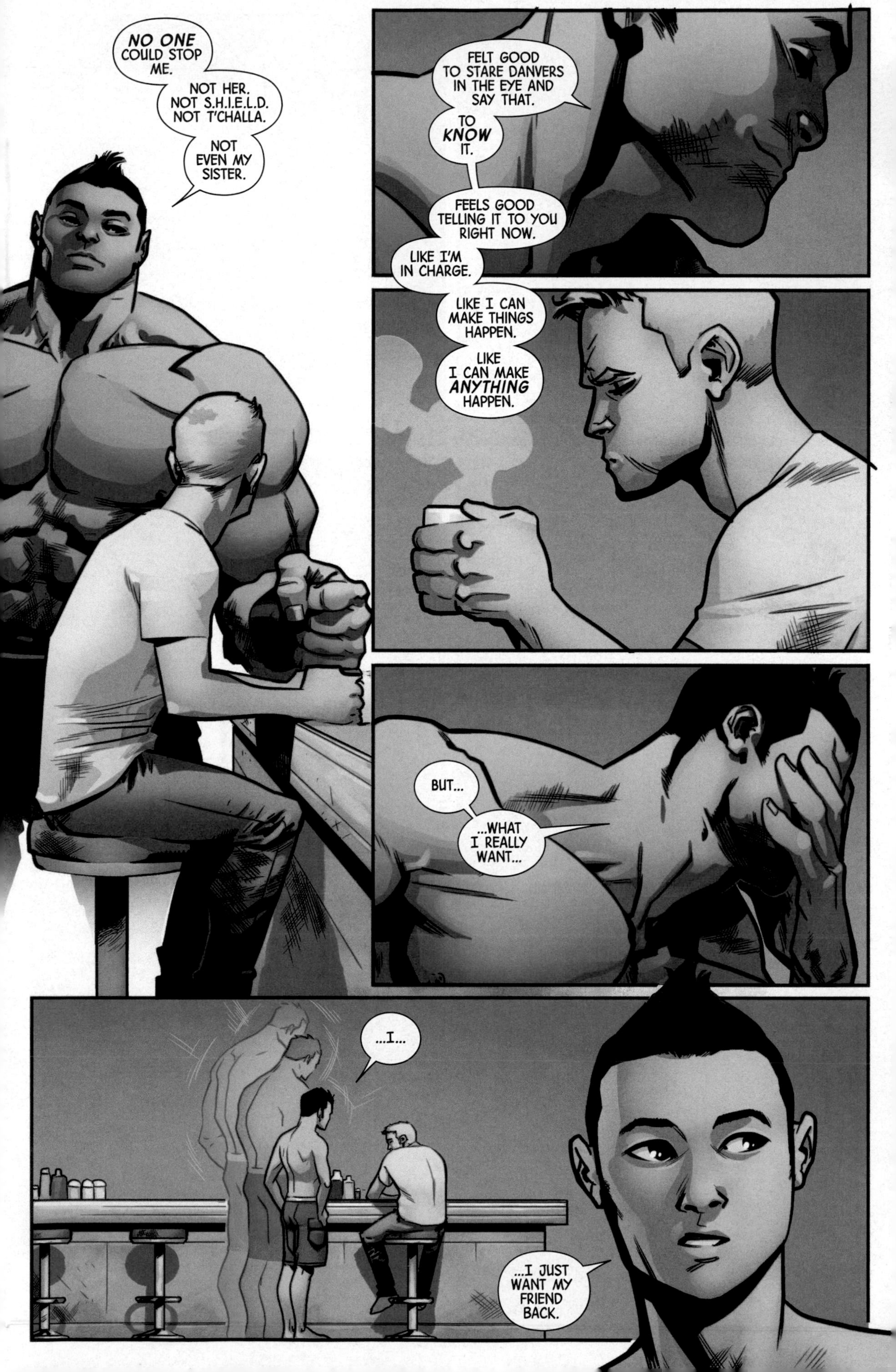
NO ONE COULD STOP ME.
NOT HER. NOT S.H.I.E.L.D. NOT T'CHALLA.
NOT EVEN MY SISTER.
FELT GOOD TO STARE DANVERS IN THE EYE AND SAY THAT.
TO KNOW IT.
FEELS GOOD TELLING IT TO YOU RIGHT NOW.
LIKE I'M IN CHARGE.
LIKE I CAN MAKE THINGS HAPPEN.
LIKE I CAN MAKE ANYTHING HAPPEN.
BUT...
...WHAT I REALLY WANT...
...I...
...I JUST WANT MY FRIEND BACK.

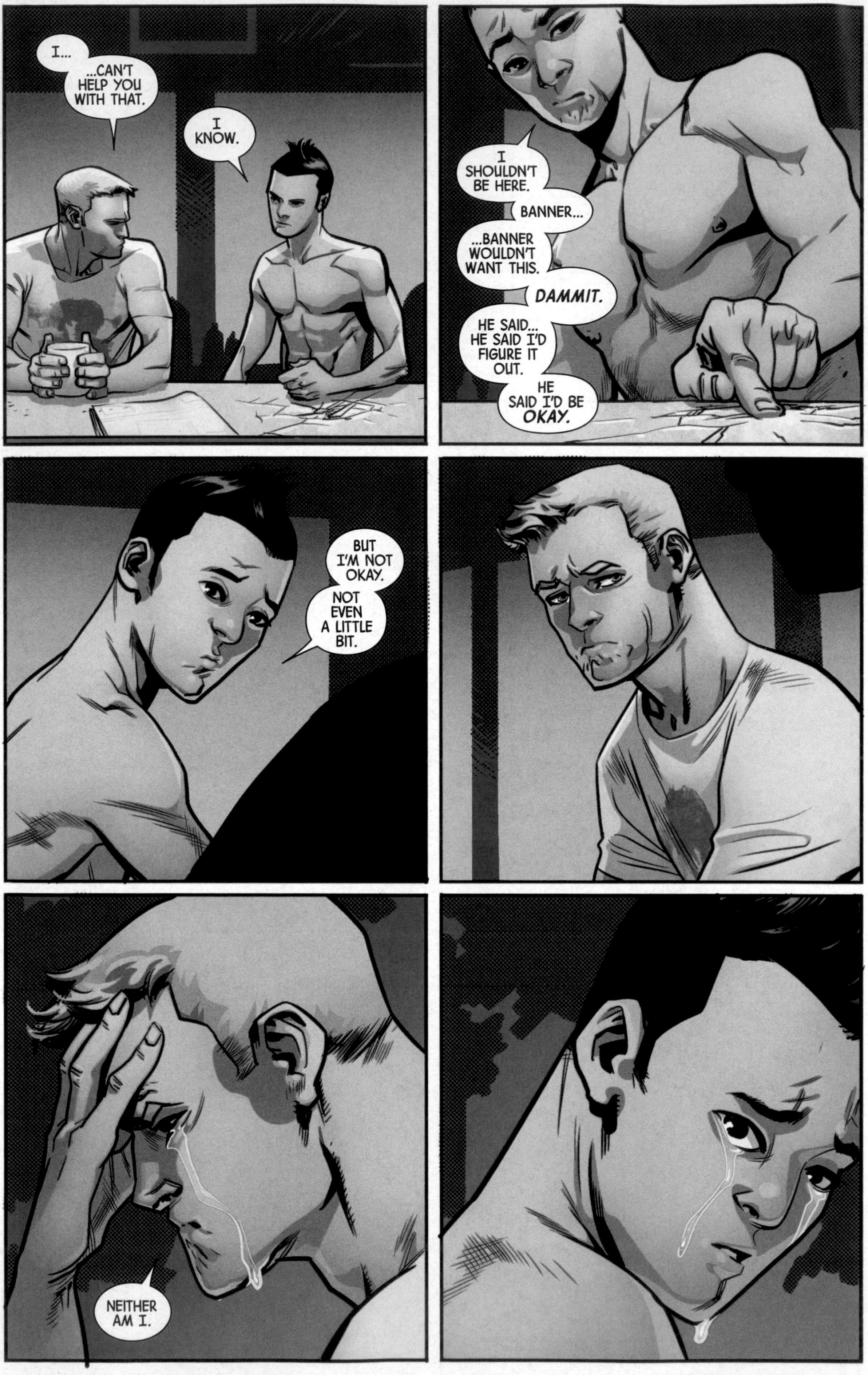
I...
...CAN'T HELP YOU WITH THAT.
I KNOW.
I SHOULDN'T BE HERE.
BANNER...
...BANNER WOULDN'T WANT THIS.
DAMMIT.
HE SAID... HE SAID I'D FIGURE IT OUT.
HE SAID I'D BE OKAY.
BUT I'M NOT OKAY.
NOT EVEN A LITTLE BIT.
NEITHER AM I.

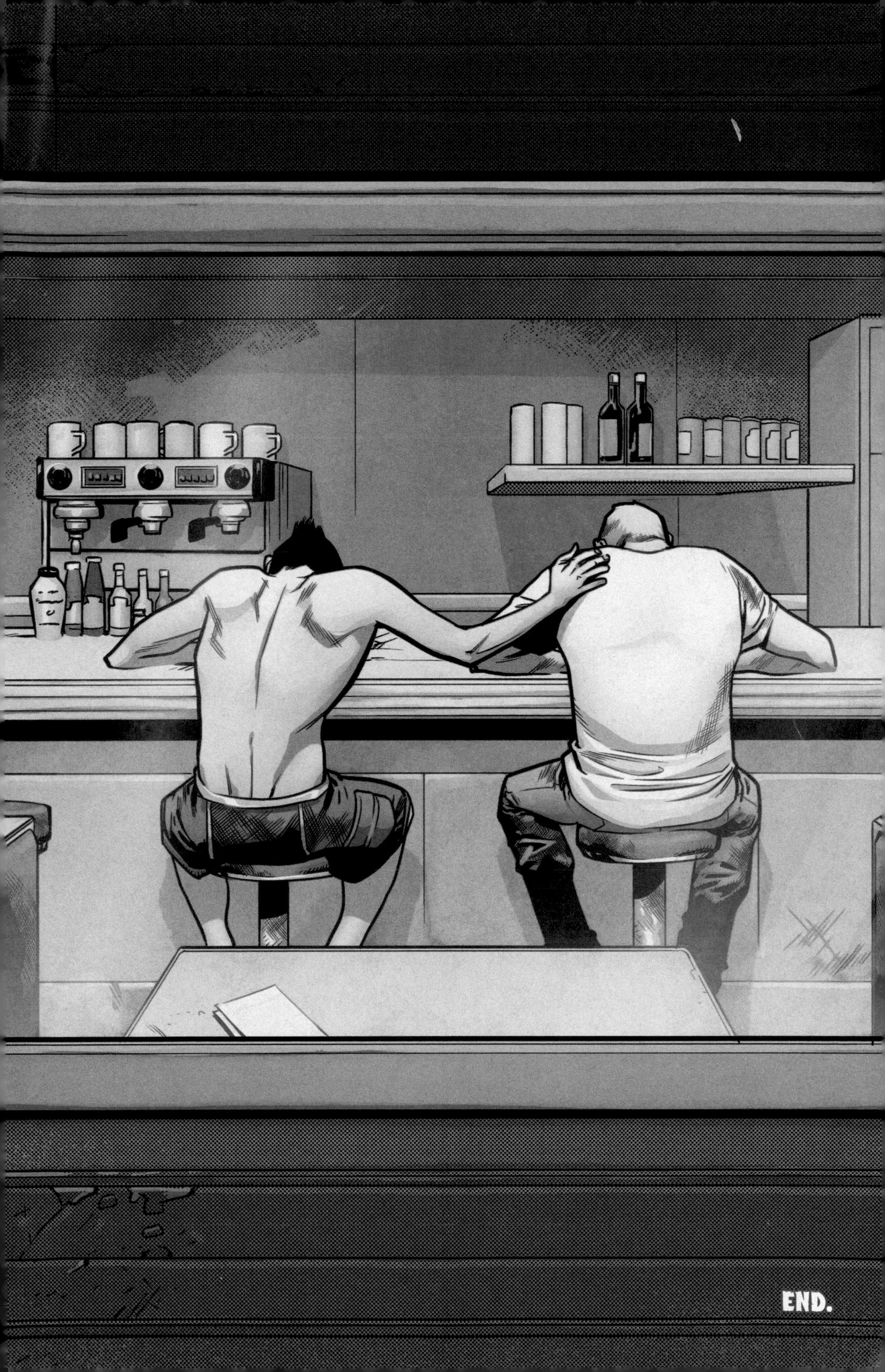
END.

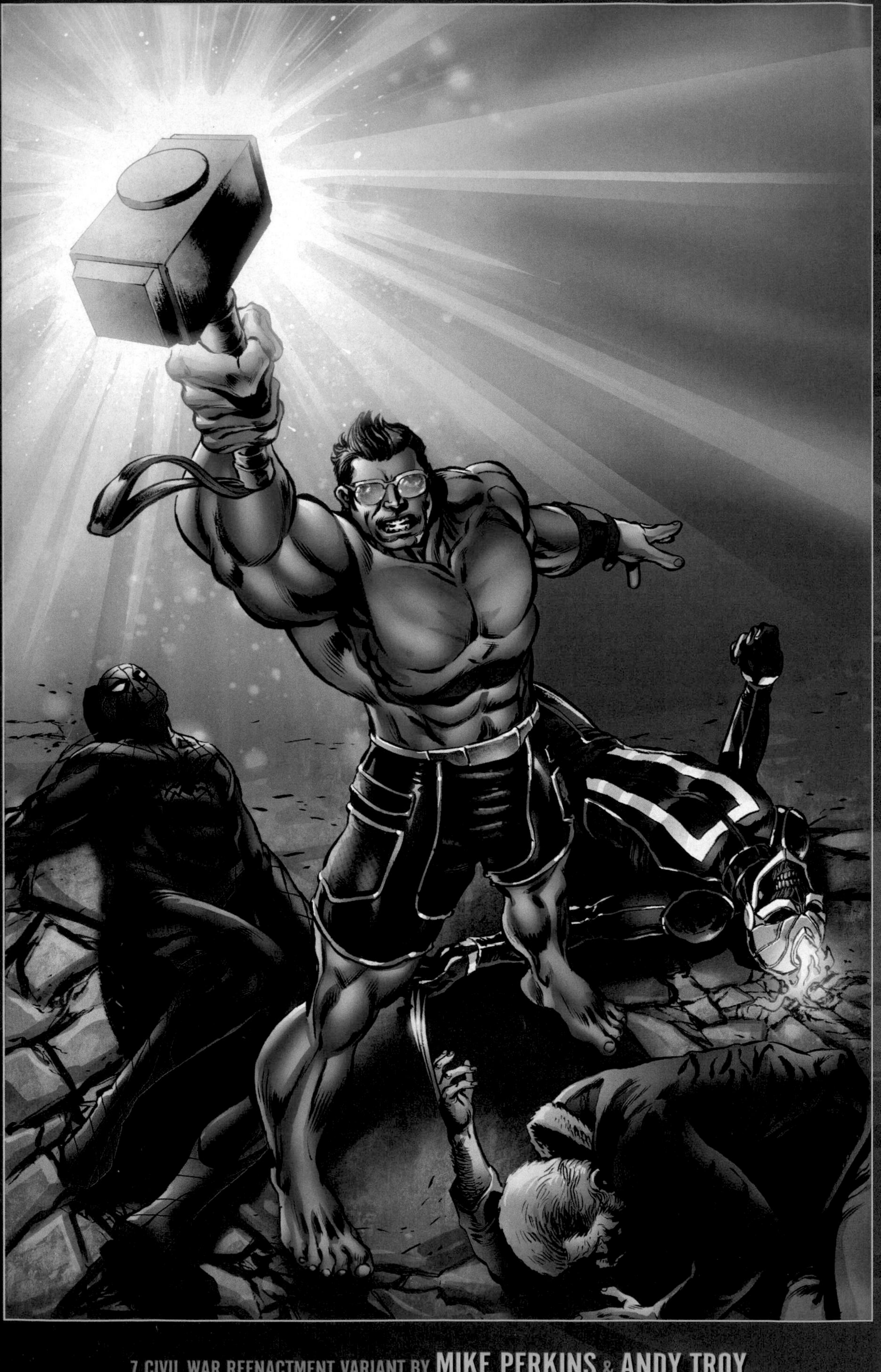

7 CIVIL WAR REENACTMENT VARIANT BY **MIKE PERKINS** & **ANDY TROY**

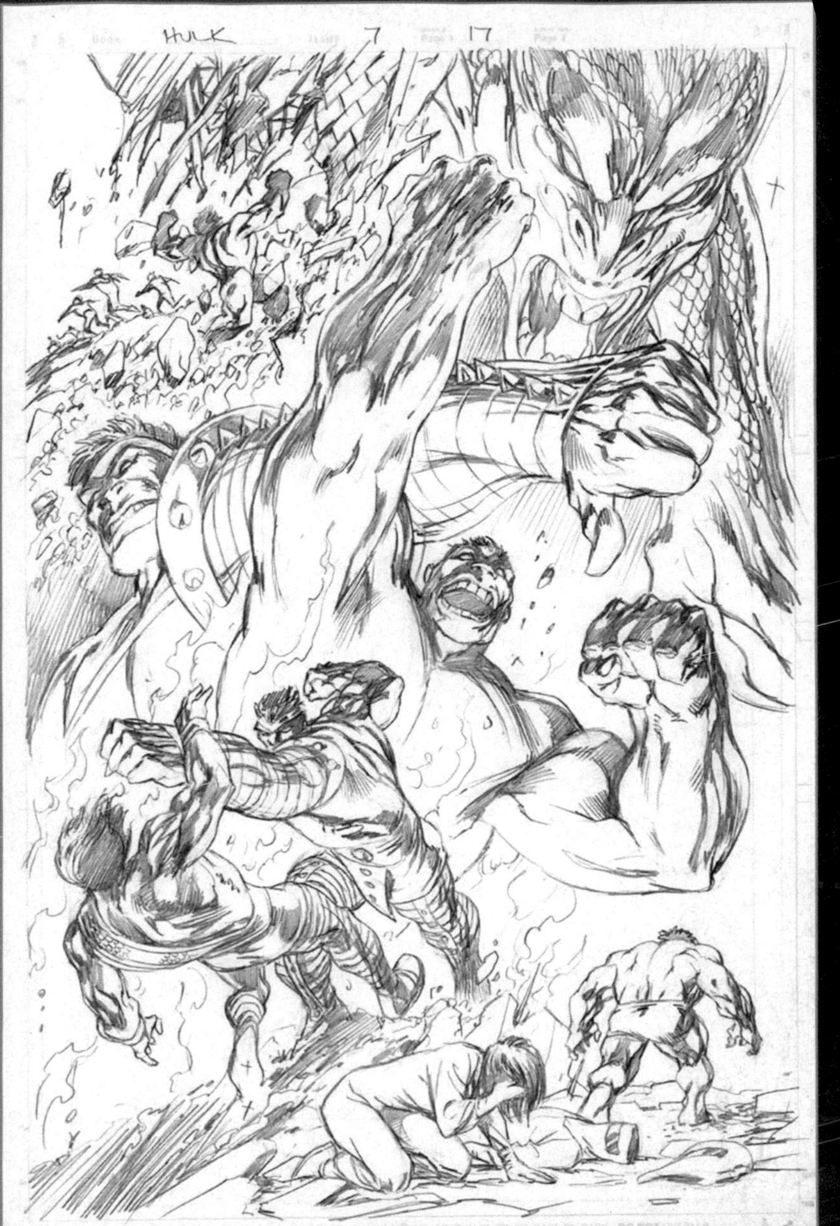
HULK
7
17

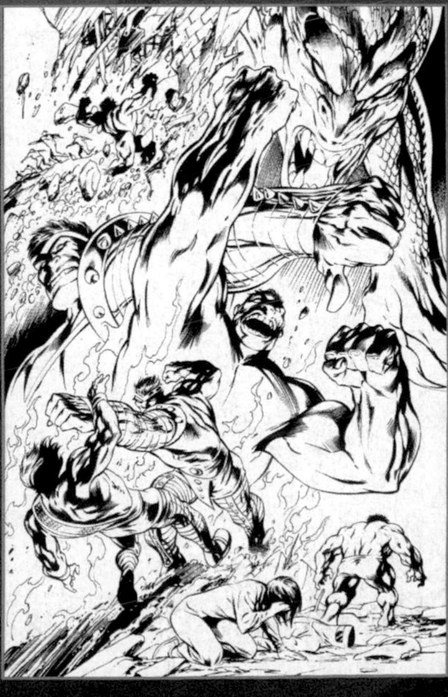

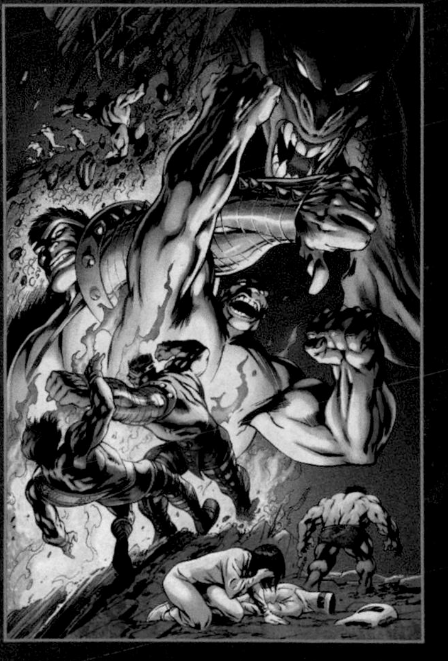

HULK #7, PAGE 17
ART PROCESS BY
ALAN DAVIS,
MARK FARMER &
CHRIS SOTOMAYOR

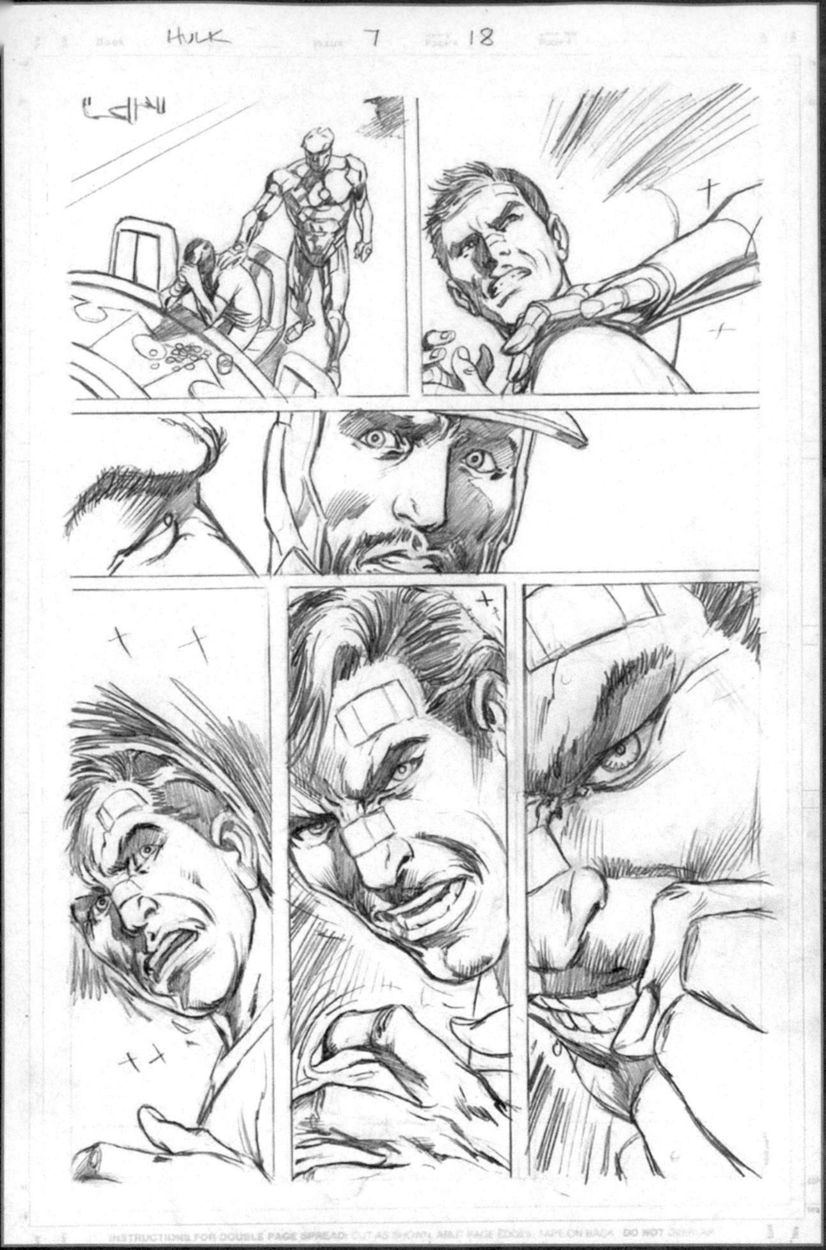
HULK
7
18

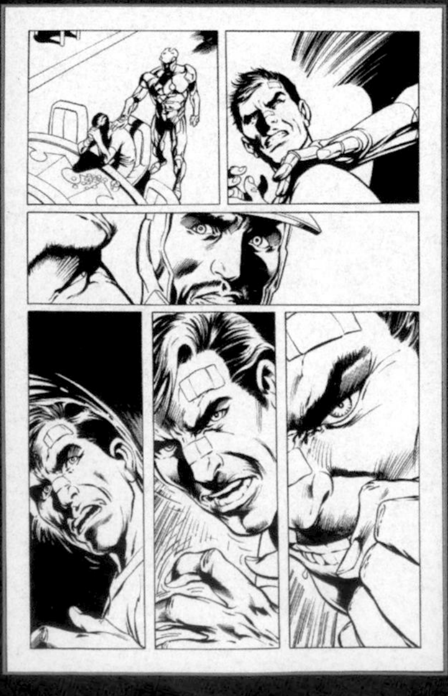

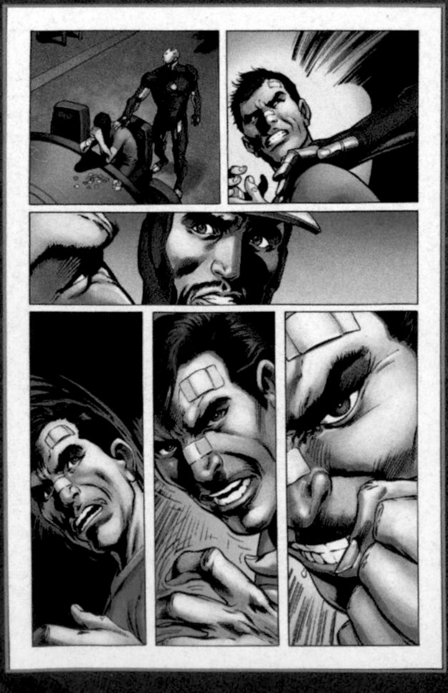

HULK #7, PAGE 18
ART PROCESS BY
ALAN DAVIS, MARK FARMER & CHRIS SOTOMAYOR

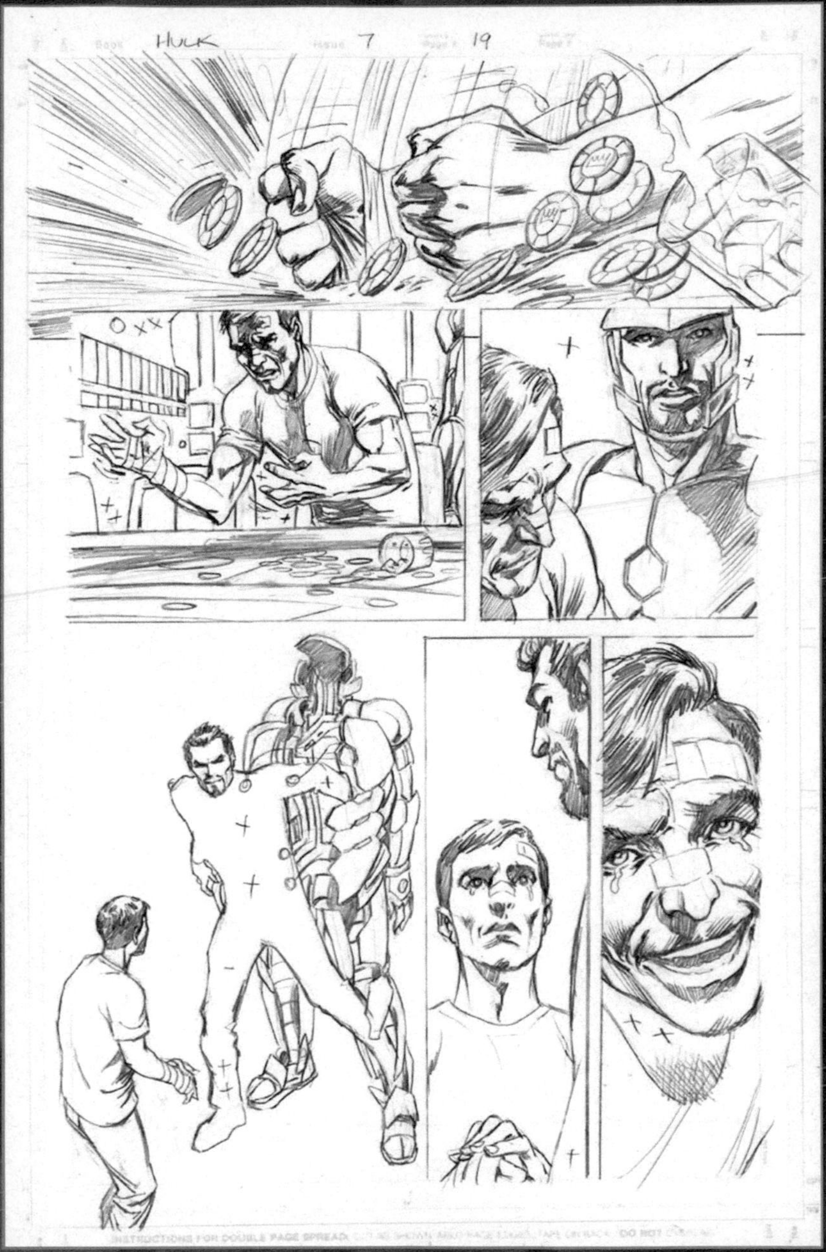
HULK
7
19

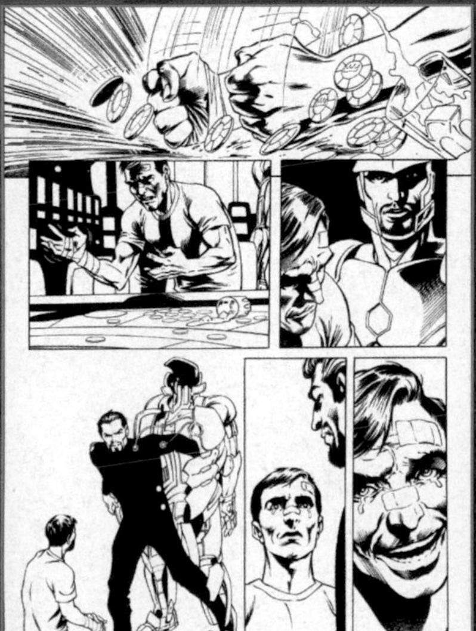

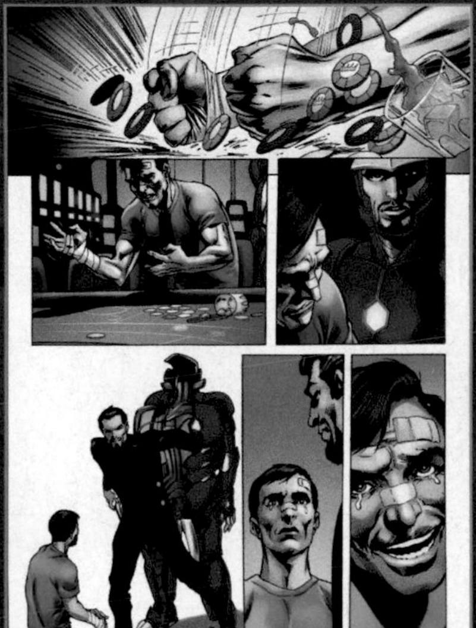

HULK #7, PAGE 19
ART PROCESS BY
ALAN DAVIS, MARK FARMER & CHRIS SOTOMAYOR

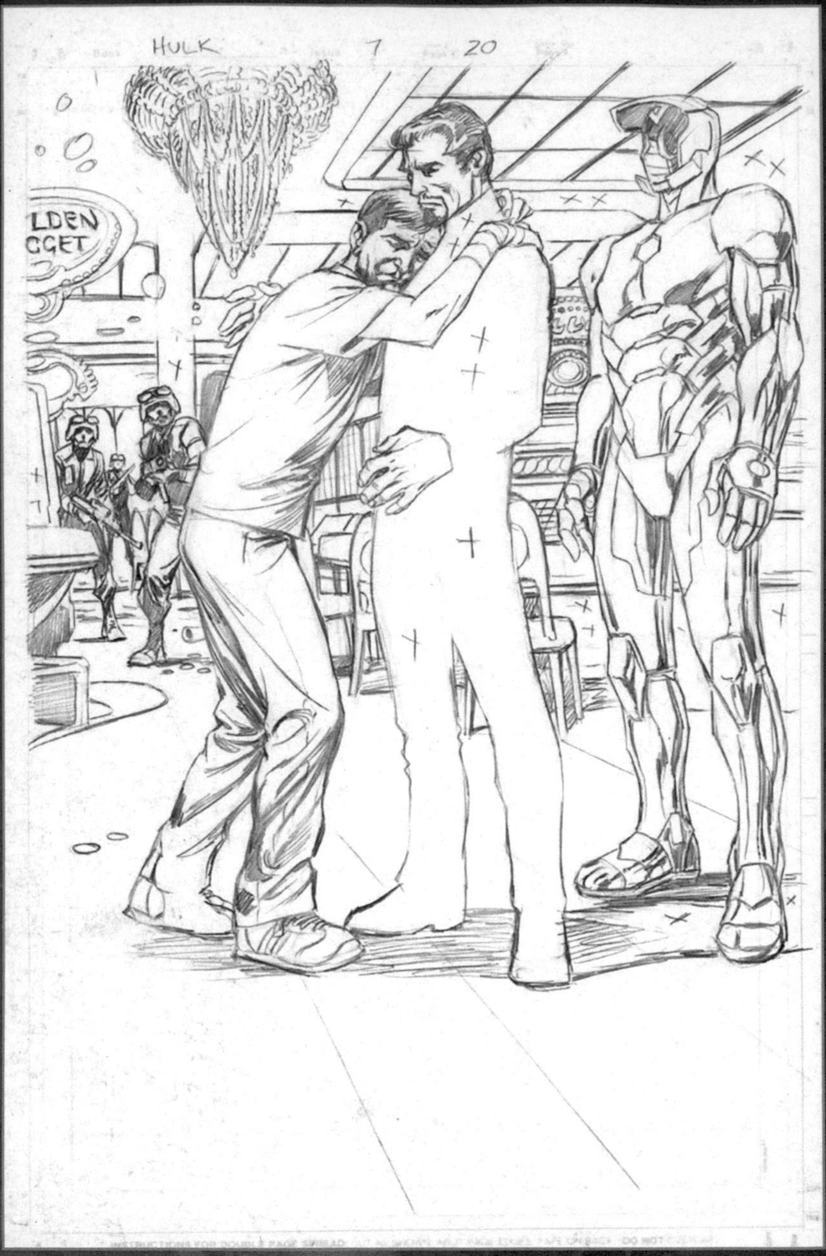

HULK
7
20

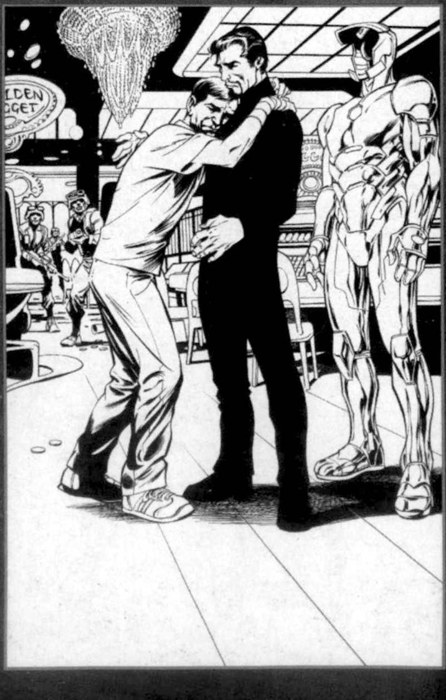

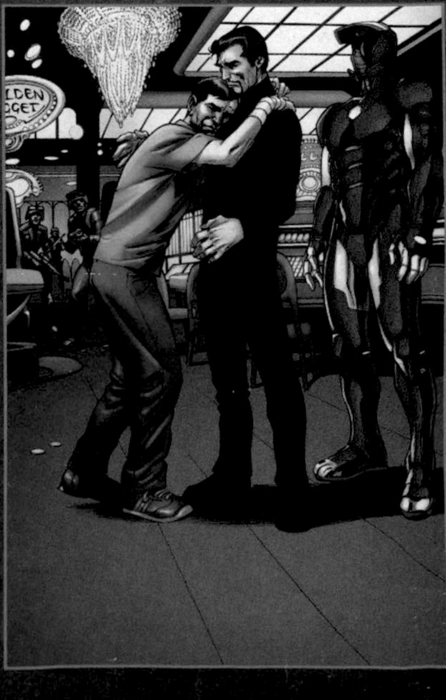

HULK #7, PAGE 18
ART PROCESS BY
ALAN DAVIS, MARK FARMER & CHRIS SOTOMAYOR